W9-ASR-135

Hoover Institution Publications

Heinrich Himmler:
A Nazi in the Making, 1900-1926

HEINRICH HIMMLER:

A NAZI IN THE MAKING, 1900-1926

Bradley F. Smith

Hoover Institution Press
Stanford University
Stanford, California

The Hoover Institution on War, Revolution and Peace, founded at Stanford University in 1919 by the late President Herbert Hoover, is a center for advanced study and research on public and international affairs in the twentieth century. The views expressed in its publications are entirely those of the authors and do not necessarily reflect the views of the Hoover Institution.

Hoover Institution Publications 93

Library of Congress Catalog Card Number: 79-137403
Standard Book Number 8179-1931-7
Printed in the United States of America

To my mother, Edna Barrie Smith
and in memory of my father, Frederick Charnley Smith

Contents

Acknowledgments

Many institutions and individuals generously assisted me in the preparation of this volume. I would like to extend special thanks to the libraries which bore the brunt of my requests—the New York Public Library, the Library of Congress, the Harvard University Library, the University of California Library, Berkeley, and the Hoover Institution, Stanford University. As so often in the past, Mrs. Agnes F. Peterson of the Hoover Institution provided invaluable aid in locating materials. Dr. Alfred Vagts, Professor Harold J. Gordon, and Professor Werner T. Angress helped me to cope with some especially difficult research problems. Despite differences in interpretation, Professor Peter Loewenberg kindly shared his ideas on Himmler with me.

Professor Angress and Mrs. Peterson, as well as Professor George Stein, read the first draft of the manuscript and made many helpful suggestions. Klaus Loewald and Mary J. Smith assisted in the gathering of materials. The editorial personnel of the Hoover Institution, especially Mrs. Carole Norton and Mrs. Catherine Berry, were ever helpful and considerate. To all of them and to my students at Cabrillo College, Aptos, California, and Miles College, Birmingham, Alabama, who tolerantly endured the hazy moments that resulted from the researching and writing of this book, let me add a quiet thank you.

A grant-in-aid by the American Council of Learned Societies during the summer of 1967 was a major help in completing the research.

Of course, despite the generosity of everyone concerned, the responsibility for the final product remains with me.

BFS

Introduction

Heinrich Himmler's name stands today as the symbol of the mass murders committed by the Third Reich. It was Himmler who ran the *SS*, and it was his direct orders which sent millions of people to their graves during the years of Nazi domination. His place in the pantheon of genocide is assured. For those who seek to understand the phenomenon of Nazism, however, Himmler's significance is not confined to his achievements as a mass killer. Historians will be occupied for years to come with the question of his initiative and responsibility for the establishment of the extermination policies and for the creation of the instruments of genocide, the *SS* and the extermination camps. And all who attempt to explain the Nazi system will have to face the central problems of his role as head of the German police and his part in the creation of a mightly *SS* empire, including the formation of the *Waffen SS*.

At nearly every critical juncture in the history of the Third Reich the historian encounters Heinrich Himmler. From the *Machtergreifung* in 1933 until the final debacle in 1945 he was always ready to assume important new tasks and responsibilities. His duties as *Reichsführer SS* and chief of the German police should have overwhelmed any man, especially as his responsibilities involved a cornucopia of horrors. But for twelve years he continued to assume new duties, ranging from the gathering of military intelligence to the production of war material in the concentration camps. In 1945 he even became an army field commander, although he had no military command experience. In this instance his assumption of responsibility led to a complete fiasco. But such disasters were rare. In the vast majority of cases any task that Himmler undertook was carried through with ruthless efficiency. Other officials might falter and lose Hitler's favor, but until the very last days of the regime Himmler carried on, earning the nickname *"Treuer Heinrich,"* Hitler's "loyal Heinrich," the man who got things done.

Himmler will remain a perplexing problem in part because he occupied such important posts in a system which poses the most searching moral challenges to the conscience and confidence of Western society. But Heinrich Himmler is also a formidable riddle in his own right. Try as he might—and he tried very hard—he never looked convincing in his role as dreaded police chief and mass murderer. The swastikas, death's-head insignia, and tailored uniforms could not hide the fact that Himmler was a plump man with a blank visage and balding head, who invariably seemed the most clumsy and awkward figure at Nazi gatherings. His conduct and manner of life make it difficult for us to accept him at face value as a master of genocide. He was a fussy little man, pedantic to the point of caricature, who loved dogs, children, and family life. He railed against the timid middle class but embodied most of the middle-class virtues, especially thrift, sobriety, and a belief in hard work. Yet his devotion to the traditional virtues and his near obsession with sexual morality did not prevent him from keeping his secretary as his mistress and fathering two children by her. His taste in art, music, furniture and clothing remained within cozy bourgeois limits, while his *SS* men in their awesome black uniforms personified the new era of sleek political terror.

Side by side with his scientific and technical enthusiasm Himmler also had a strong leaning to the mystical and occult. Of all the Nazi leaders he most closely approximated the picture of the powerful figure surrounded by astrologers, faddists, quacks, and mystics. Even his self-image appears to have embodied a bewildering array of inconsistencies and contradictions. On the one hand he saw himself as the iron man who performed distasteful, often horrible, tasks in order to create a new racist order. On the other, he was sincerely mystified to learn in 1945 that he was not considered a suitable figure to negotiate with the Allies. His reputation as a bloody murderer seems never to have penetrated his consciousness. He was a remote-control killer who had no stomach for blood and found his deepest pleasure in playing father to his army of *SS* subordinates. Most perplexing of all, he showed little inventive ability and lacked any trace of the creative but murderous genius so evident in Hitler.

These anomalies and paradoxes, hovering as they do between horror and farce, have long interested journalists, political observers, and historians. Most of the early descriptions of Himmler made by non-Germans portrayed him as a bloodthirsty monster. Konrad Heiden, however, used a brief but generally accurate account of Himmler's life, published in 1944, to support his argument that most of the Nazi leaders were mediocrities.[1] And in the memoirs which

Otto Strasser published during World War II Himmler emerged as a nonentity who had risen to power through a stroke of fortune and then turned against his former friends.[2] This picture, embellished by additional and fanciful biographical detail, also appeared in two books by Strasser's English friend, Douglas Reed, which appeared in 1940 and 1953.[3]

In the immediate postwar period a new picture of Himmler emerged as a result of the shock produced by the revelation of Nazi atrocities and the records made public at the Nuremberg trials. Willi Frischauer used the Nuremberg evidence and material gathered from interviewing Heinrich's brother to portray the leader of the *SS* as "the evil genius of the Third Reich."[4] In Frischauer's account most of Himmler's pedestrian characteristics disappeared, leaving the image of a cold and ruthless killer. Lacking evidence to explain how Himmler evolved from a middle-class Bavarian to a professional monster, Frischauer speculated that the family had somehow inculcated in him the doctrines of racial superiority and Germanic mysticism.

Until the late 1950s all efforts to explain Himmler's development were hampered by the dearth of documentary material. Himmler seemed, like the other Nazi leaders, to have carefully destroyed anything which would throw light on his personality or the process by which he had attained power in the Nazi system. Then in 1957 six diaries which Himmler had written in his youth were made public. This discovery permitted Werner T. Angress and myself to reach some tentative conclusions regarding Himmler's background and the main steps in his personal development;[5] but since the diaries only covered brief intervals in Himmler's life between the ages of fourteen and twenty-four, they did not enable us to develop a complete picture of the young Himmler. During the next ten years, as various U.S. agencies released additional Nazi documents, more of Himmler's papers became available. Once these materials were brought together and collated, it was clear that the Himmler papers offered a unique opportunity to appraise the formative phases in the life of a Nazi leader.

Among the Himmler materials now available are seven diaries covering short periods of his life between 1910 and 1922. A few loose diary pages from 1924 constitute a valuable supplement to this collection. Hundreds of items from Himmler's incoming and outgoing correspondence for the years 1918-26 have also been preserved, together with a long annotated list of his readings comprising some 270 entries. Beyond this there are numerous family documents and Heinrich's own collection of official papers and personal mementoes ranging from his military records during World War I to the receipt for a pair of pants he purchased in the early 1920s. All told, the materials directly related to Himmler's childhood and youth number some four to five thousand items.

Much of this material had been carefully filed by his *SS* staff; the rest seems to have been preserved with equal care in his various residences. Apparently the records were scattered during the hectic last days of the regime and the period of Allied occupation which followed. A number of factors seem to have induced the *Reichsführer SS* to assemble his collection of personal documents. The need to establish his own Aryan descent required extensive investigation of family documents, and his father's penchant for maintaining family records provided additional material. Heinrich shared his father's enthusiasm for keeping private papers, so that by the time he achieved prominence he had amassed a substantial document collection of his own. His desire to establish a lasting record of his part in what he believed to be permanent revolutionary changes constituted his final motive for having the scraps of evidence brought together and systematized in the mid-1930s.

Despite its abundance and the bureaucratic efficiency with which it was first assembled, much of this source material is difficult to use. Few of the items were typed, and Himmler compounded the difficulty of reading them by writing in both Roman and German script. In addition, from 1915 on he intermittently used Gabelsberger shorthand in his diaries, notes, and correspondence. Two hundred and fifty entries in his reading list and half of the letters he wrote home in 1918 were in shorthand. The varied forms of writing combined with the low-grade paper available during and after World War I have tended to nullify some of the advantages of massive documentation.[6] With due allowance for these problems, however, and for the fact that gaps in the documentation still remain (for example, Heinrich's diary for the crucial months of 1923 is missing)[7] the materials now at hand constitute an unusually rich collection of sources for the study of a young man's route to professional Nazism.

But the materials will not speak for themselves, and it seems only fair to advise the reader of the way I approach them. This study lays heavy emphasis on the primary documentation, not because it hopes to catch some shadow of Himmler's "real past" or because the writer has a blind faith in the reliability and value of written records, but because it seems best to build on the only direct evidence we have. The stress on the importance of documents is accompanied by a certain skepticism about the validity of any interpretation of a historical topic. No matter how complete the documentation may be, it is always spotty, while the possible inferences are limitless. And the feeling of remoteness from the people and forces involved is almost overwhelming. The importance of time itself and the complexity of the social and personal pressures that bear on an individual when viewed in historical context also tend to make me chary of sweeping generalizations or the discovery of "secret keys" that can explain the whole phenomenon. I have reservations too about the deterministic features of much psychological and Marxian analysis which invite one to infer conclusions without direct evidence of causes, or causes without direct evidence of effects. The intricacies and contingencies involved in any specific historical process give me little faith in explanations that are applicable at all times and in all places.

When applied to the study of the young Himmler's development, these considerations lead me to emphasize the interaction between the process of maturation and the changes in the environment in which he matured. This means a stress on the way he conceptualized his relation to the larger political and social environment as well as his ties to his immediate circle of family members and friends. Himmler's importance lay, not in the intricacies of the formation of his personality but in his later political activities. His route to *Reichsführer SS* was an ideological as well as a personal road. It is the first steps on that double road which this work endeavors to trace.

For easier comprehension of the course of this travel, certain features of Himmler's life and career must be clearly borne in mind. Heinrich Himmler did not begin his career as a killer or a policeman but as a loyal, hardworking Nazi party official. He spent nearly ten years in the party administration prior to the seizure of power, quietly working his way upward and expanding the range of his activities. When the *Machtergreifung* finally came in 1933, he added government offices to his party positions and, especially after the Blood Purge of 1934, advanced rapidly in the party and state hierarchy. Each newly acquired post was added to the interlocking empire that he formed. Apart from Hitler's favor, the only factor that bound the system together was Himmler's success in intertwining all his offices and powers and linking them together by making his important subordinates *SS* members. Until near the end of the regime he pursued the great game of accumulating titles, responsibilities, and bureaucratic trophies.

In addition to its success, Himmler's bureaucratic career had two noteworthy features: a heavy dependence on military and quasi-military activities and an absence of scruple about accepting assignments that others would have considered revolting. But this is to say little except that he was a good Nazi bureaucrat. The system demanded the ability to function in a military setting and the performance of harsh and loathsome tasks. From this vantage point, the first step in dealing with the question of Himmler's success is to investigate his reasons for choosing a career as a professional Nazi and the factors in his personality and upbringing that prepared him to succeed in that career.

This study attempts to answer these two questions. It begins with an examination of the family and social milieu in which he matured, with particular stress on the intertwining of social values and the dominant traits of his personality. A decisive role in this process was played by World War I which radically changed the social environment in which he lived and required him to adjust his values to new conditions. In its final phases the war also cast the young Himmler directly into the events that were revolutionizing society. In the postwar years he was forced to train for a career and at the same time resolve the conflict between the value system he had absorbed in the prewar years and the radically altered set of circumstances that prevailed in postwar Germany. After many false starts and much inner torment, Himmler finally resolved the problem by becoming a party official, first in the *Nationalsozialistische Freiheitsbewegung* and later in the

*NSDAP.** It is important to stress that this decision was not particularly arbitrary or unreasonable; when seen against the background of his development and circumstances it made sense. The fact that he never turned back from this decision suggests that a career as a party official fitted his needs. Furthermore, the skills and attitudes that he brought to his employers proved very useful to them. His steady rise over the subsequent nineteen years indicates that he was a nearly perfect example of the Nazi party career man.

---

*The *NSDAP* (*Nationalsozialistische Deutsche Arbeiterpartei*) was the party which Hitler led from 1920 to 1923 and 1925 to 1945. During 1924, following the abortive Beer Hall *Putsch* Hitler was jailed and the *NSDAP* was outlawed. In that interval the *Nationalsozialistische Freiheitsbewegung* was one of the organizations used by Hitler's supporters to carry on political activity.

Chapter I

The Setting

From 1933 to 1945 Heinrich Himmler kept a large staff of *SS* investigators busy exploring the details of his family genealogy. When the final report on the investigations was prepared, only one individual received more than the customary brief entry listing birth, occupation, marriage, and death. This individual was Heinrich's paternal grandfather, Johann Conrad Clemens Matthäus Himmler. The decision to include more detail about the life of Johann may have arisen from the desire to stress that he had once been a senior police official; but whatever the motive, the extra emphasis accorded him reflects the pivotal role he played in shaping the family environment in which Heinrich grew up. It was the life and career of Johann Himmler, more than any other factor, which established the conditions and set the tone of the two succeeding generations of the Himmler family.

Born in 1809, Johann Himmler came from a family of peasants and petty artisans in the Protestant area of Ansbach in northern Bavaria. He received some training as a weaver but seems to have been hampered by lack of money and an inclination for adventure. At the age of eighteen he enlisted as a private in the First Royal Bavarian Regiment; he reenlisted in 1830, and again in 1833. At the time of his second enlistment he was a member of the Second Military Police Company. His early military service was undistinguished and during his first five and a half years he failed to gain promotion to the rank of noncommissioned officer. Although the military records stress that he was not a drinker, part of his difficulty seems to have been a penchant for brawling and general mischief. He was punished by the military authorities on at least six occasions during these five and a half years, the punishments ranging from three days in jail for a fight in a bar to eight weeks' house arrest for debt. In June 1830 he was sentenced to six weeks' house arrest for what the authorities called "immoral behavior with a low woman."[1]

Thus for the first twenty-five years of his life Johann Himmler was indistinguishable even in his vices from thousands of other young Germans of the early nineteenth century who drifted away from the farm and the shop to try their hands as soldiers. The first break in the pattern came in 1835, when he apparently failed to reenlist. For nearly a decade thereafter the official records are silent about his activities, but according to family tradition his love of soldiering took him further afield and he served in Greece and elsewhere. In September 1844 he reentered the Bavarian service, this time as a member of the Royal Police Company in Munich. Here he stayed for ten years. But his private life indicates that not all the adventurous fires had been quenched for while in Munich he fathered at least one illegitimate child.[2]

Obviously the later family pride in the career of Johann Himmler was not based upon these early adventures, except as they dramatized his later rise, and little sign of them appears in the official account of the *Reichsführer*'s ancestors. It was the events from 1854 on which made Johann Himmler important to the family and the genealogists. On April 1, 1854, he was transferred from the Royal Police Company in Munich to the Police Company of Upper Bavaria with the rank of ordinary policeman. In the next eight years he advanced, first to the position of police station commander and finally to the rank of police sergeant (*Brigadier*). In June 1862 he left the royal police service, with its irregular hours and remote duty stations, to take a position in the district administration of Lindau on the Swiss border. Four months later he married Agathe Rosina Kiene, the daughter of a watchmaker and city official in Bregenz. At the time of the marriage Johann Himmler was fifty-three years old and his bride was twenty-nine. From these fragmentary scraps of information it seems probable that Johann Himmler left the police service in order to acquire a settled occupation that would permit marriage with a young lady who had reasonable prospects of a good dowry.[3]

From the outward signs that appear in official records the marriage seems to have been satisfactory. The couple remained together in Lindau for ten years and produced one child, Gebhard, who was born in 1865, three years after their marriage. Johann remained at his post in the administration of Lindau until he died in 1872 at the age of sixty-three.[4]

In addition to siring Gebhard Himmler, the father-to-be of Heinrich, Johann Himmler was to exert much indirect influence on the grandson whom he never saw. His career was the first great success story of the Himmler family. He had struggled upward from humble origins and established a foundation of respectability and relative financial security which permitted future generations to continue the upward movement. To his family he was the personification of the ambition and pride of acquired status which played so important a role in the middle-class thinking of last century. The fact that he was a Protestant certainly did not dampen his or his family's devotion to competitive advancement.[5] But of even more significance to his son and grandson was the occupational form through which he sought to rise in the world. It was not so much the fact that Johann had been a policeman that was important for the future (although his grandson Heinrich with his romantic inclination to find ancestral parallels was probably pleased about it) as the fact that he had risen through the ranks of the royal administration.

Historians have given considerable attention to the close ties that existed between the educated middle class and the royal administrations in Central Europe during the eighteenth and nineteenth centuries. Equal stress has not however been laid on the fact that the lower echelons of these administrations—both civil and military—offered the lower classes the best available means of improving their social status. In contrast to Western Europe and America where trade and business held out the best prospects of advancement, the peasant or apprentice in Central Europe often found his greatest opportunity in the lower ranks of the royal service. There with diligence and ambition he could reach a position which would afford him a comfortable income and the satisfaction of lower-middle-class status. To be sure, even the most gifted peasant's son had no chance of entering the higher ranks of the bureaucracy, for here members of the educated middle class held on to their prerogatives with as much tenacity as the nobles did to theirs; but there was nothing to prevent the self-made lower official from using his position to provide an education for his children that would permit them to move up and become real bureaucrats.

Despite the success of many families, including the Himmlers, in negotiating this two-generation advance into the bureaucratic middle class, it would be a mistake to minimize the value conflicts and the emotional stresses and strains involved. The family's belief in upward social mobility stemmed from the customary middle-class desire for independence and self-reliance. When applied to the administrative systems of Central Europe, this value system was forced to function in an environment in which class privilege, tradition, and hereditary right were paramount. Successful practitioners of the art of administrative-status-seeking had to walk a thin line between personal competitiveness and the necessity for humble loyalty and social subservience. It was necessary to cast ambition in a mold that would stay within the confines of duty and never appear to challenge the system of hereditary privilege. The ambitious lower-class official had to assimiliate a system of values in which competence balanced the art and outlook of a dutiful courtier.

It was Gebhard Himmler, Johann's son, who was forced to grapple directly with such a situation. Johann was fifty-six at the time of the boy's birth, and the period of his uncertainty about what was important in life was long past. Gebhard had little chance to escape having the paternal values stamped upon him at an early age. However, he did escape the potentially hazardous confrontation over values that often occurs in adolescence, because Johann died when the boy was seven; from then on it was through his mother that he came face to face with his father's achievements and beliefs. Agathe Kiene Himmler was a strong woman who appears to have exerted great influence over her son and his family until her death in 1916. Only the rough outlines of her personality appear in the surviving documents, but she must have been a formidable combination of maternal love and ambition for she instilled in Gebhard the ambitions of his father and at the same time helped him develop the complex personality traits necessary for a leap into full middle-class status. How this was achieved and how the boy reconciled his childhood needs with the role expected of him it is now impossible to establish. Except for the fact that he grew up in Lindau with his mother and was raised a Catholic, we have no documentary evidence until he appears in the official roster of the University of Munich for 1884-85 as a student of philosophy.[6]

A university education was the essential prerequisite for a commoner with serious career ambitions. Apparently Gebhard Himmler began his university career without definite ideas about a major area of study or the form his life's work was to take. In the course of an unusually long ten-year residence at the university he focused his attention on philology, including the German and classical languages, and shorthand, in which he retained a lifelong interest. He seems to have been a highly devoted and successful student, the length of whose residence at Munich was not due to any academic deficiency.[7]

In 1894, at the age of twenty-nine, he left the university and embarked on the two occupational roles which were to dominate his career. He accepted a position as a beginning teacher (*Assistent*) at the *Ludwigs Gymnasium* in Munich and at the same time assumed the responsibility of tutor in the household of Prince Arnulf of Wittelsbach. His decision to enter *Gymnasium* teaching was the most important decision he made, for he was to remain in *Gymnasium* education and administration for the next thirty years. In Germany the humanistic *Gymnasium* was the secondary school most closely tied to classical education and, prior to the full onslaught of a technically oriented society, enjoyed the highest social prestige. Many of Germany's best university-trained teachers made their careers in the *Gymnasium* and achieved a standing in society far higher than that of American teachers in secondary education. A Bavarian who rose through the ranks of teacher and professor to that of *Rektor* attained a status rivaled by few non-nobles.*

If Gebhard Himmler's decision to begin *Gymnasium* teaching opened a door which led to full professional middle-class status, his appointment as princely tutor drew him into the center of the system of royal service and patronage. He was employed by Prince Arnulf of Wittelsbach as tutor for his only son, Heinrich. Prince Heinrich, who was then ten years old, was far removed from the throne, being a nephew of the regent (later King Ludwig III) of Bavaria who had two sons, six daughters, and a brother with prior claims to reign. Although there was little or no chance that his young charge would ever reach the throne, Gebhard Himmler nevertheless had excellent prospects of princely (or, more

---

*In *Gymnasia* in other parts of Germany the titles varied. Only in Bavaria and a few other states was the title of professor used in the *Gymnasium.*

remotely, royal) favor if he proved satisfactory to his patrons. This would be the deciding test of whether he had successfully absorbed the values and personality traits of a royal servant.

For three years Gebhard Himmler simultaneously taught in the *Gymnasium* and tutored Prince Heinrich. In both occupations, especially the latter, he performed exceptionally well. He not only secured the favor of Prince Arnulf and his wife for the whole Himmler family but also earned the respect and affection of the young prince as well. From this point on, he was always able to count on help in time of need from either Prince Heinrich or his mother, and this turned out to be a source of security which was to last beyond the prince's death in 1916 and the end of the monarchy in 1918.[8]

In 1897 Gebhard Himmler's duty as tutor to the prince drew to a close in a manner appropriate for a successful academic courtier. Two years previously he had moved from his temporary position as teacher at the *Ludwigs Gymnasium* to a similar position at the *Wilhelms Gymnasium* in Munich. When his work as tutor ended, he was promoted to a position as permanent teacher on the *Wilhelms Gymnasium* staff. There can be little question that this appointment was made easier by the favor of his royal employers.[9]

With a permanent position and a firm foothold on the professional ladder Gebhard Himmler now had the income and prospects necessary for a successful marriage. On July 22, 1897, he married Anna Maria Heyder in Munich. His bride, the future mother of Heinrich Himmler, was the daughter of a businessman who had come to Munich from the Regensburg area. Born and raised in Munich, she had grown up in a family where age relationships were strikingly similar to those in her husband's family. Her father was fifty-six when she was born and died when she was eight. Like Gebhard Himmler, she was raised by her mother but unlike him she was orphaned at the comparatively early age of twenty-one. At the time of her marriage she was thirty-one, and her husband thirty-two. From indirect references to the relative prosperity of the newly married couple it appears that Anna Heyder Himmler had inherited some money and that the union represented an advantageous combination of hard cash and promising career prospects.[10]

Following the marriage the Himmlers moved into a roomy and comfortable second-floor apartment at Hildegardstrasse 6 in the central section of Munich. Twelve months later, on July 29, 1898, their first child was born, a boy who was given his father's name, Gebhard. Two years later Heinrich, their second son, was born. Little is known about personal relationships within the family during the first years, but certain characteristics of the parents which were clearly manifest later were already present. Anna Himmler was an efficient housekeeper who highly valued a set routine. She was careful with money and enjoyed making the day-to-day economies which allowed the family to live comfortably on the salary of a junior teacher and still maintain the amenities of middle-class life.[11]

In her treatment of the children Frau Himmler displayed the same traits that characterized her as a homemaker. She was deeply concerned about their welfare and took her maternal responsibilities very seriously. She established precise schedules and procedures to insure that the children's physical needs, such as proper diet and well-washed clothes, were always met. The effort to give her offspring good manners and correct middle-class attitudes also took up much of her time and attention. Her daily routine was characterized by diligence and a tendency to worry about possible breaks in the routine or failure to do what was right and proper. One may seriously doubt whether the children received many expressions of spontaneous affection, but they did have the benefit of an unusual amount of personal attention and support.

The character and personality of Gebhard Himmler closely paralleled those of his wife. He was unusually conscientious about his work and tended to occupy himself with school business at all hours of the day and night (worried references to *"Vati"* being overworked abound in the family correspondence). His zeal on the job was matched by the pedantry which influenced all his actions. Both at home and in school each activity had its proper time and place. His handwriting was faultless, and his filing system had a slot for every kind of material. Even his hobbies, the collection of stamps, coins, and writings about the Germanic past, reflected his passion for correct organization.

Despite his professional zeal Gebhard Himmler was a devoted family man with a deep interest in his children's activities. He was no aloof father; within the limits prescribed for a genteel *pater familias* he involved himself directly in his children's rearing and development. Often his interest took the form of setting rules and carefully checking to make certain that the youngsters did what was expected of them. Even before the children went to school he systematically examined their pronunciation and speech patterns and kept detailed records of their verbal peculiarities and cute sayings.[12]

Yet it would be both inaccurate and unfair to leave the impression that Gebhard Himmler and his wife were nothing but pedants who drove their children through a series of dreary routines. They sincerely tried to make life happy for them and gave them an ample supply of the toys, games, and diversions which they wanted. They involved their children in their own love of nature and varied the regular routine with trips and long summer vacations in the country. The study of classical literature, including of course the German classics which the parents loved, became a family affair, and the children received constant encouragement to develop culturally and intellectually. Yet even when the softer aspects of the family's life are taken into consideration, the impression of a rigid hierarchical family remains. This is largely due to the social milieu in which the Himmlers lived and to the efforts the parents made to prepare their children for the world in which they in turn would live. To estimate the social relevance of these efforts it is necessary to examine the tone of Bavaria at that time.

At the turn of the century Bavaria shared in the security and optimism which characterized most of European society before World War I. The social order was stable, future development seemed assured, and the majority of people held a common set of beliefs and loyalties. Foremost among the commitments of the average Bavarian was his identification with the young German Reich and its achievements in power politics, economic expansion, and culture. Despite the Bavarian reluctance to join the Reich in 1870-71, thirty years of unification and dramatic growth had engendered a deep German patriotism in the Bavarian people. Conscious of himself as a German in speech, culture, and historical tradition, the Bavarian largely identified himself with the Germany that Bismarck had created.

But alongside his pride in Germany the average Bavarian continued to nurse his old loyalty to the Kingdom of Bavaria. In this he was not just longing for a romantic past; he was identifying himself with a living reality. For Bavaria was in fact different from Prussia and most of the other German states. It had its own ruling house, and much of the governmental activity which affected people's daily lives originated in Munich rather than Berlin. The social tone was also strikingly different from that which prevailed in the North. Not only were there differences in dialect and *Gemütlichkeit,* but Bavaria remained much closer to preindustrial society than many parts of Germany. Despite increasing urbanization traditional agriculture had not yet been engulfed by a rising industry, and the class structure still reflected the economic and political realities of a large noble landholding class, a numerous peasantry, and a proud ruling house. Intertwined with the economic and political realities of this traditionalist society were the power and the importance of the Catholic church. In spite of the large Protestant population in Northern Bavaria the kingdom of the Wittelsbachs was Catholic in name and fact. The church was a living reality for the great mass of the people and enjoyed unusual power and prestige, in part because the most explosive modern forces had so lightly touched the institutional and economic structure of society.

The predominance of the Catholic church and the old Bavarian way of life made for easy cultural and personal relations with people from similar backgrounds outside the confines of the German Reich. This was especially true for Bavaria's neighbors in Habsburg Austria and parts of Switzerland, where social conditions were similar and a common Catholicism extended further than the immediate borderlands. Bavaria's traditional trans-Alpine connections with Italy were strengthened and intensified by the fact that Italy was the home of the church. Similarly the long history of political understanding between Bavaria and France was reinforced by the common religion of the two areas. This did not mean that Bavaria's religious loyalties would lead her to reverse the actions of 1870-71 and consider independence again; it merely revealed that the average Bavarian had a stronger emotional attachment than Germans in other sections of the Reich to the nations and cultures of his coreligionists.

From the vantage point of the present, it is obvious that these likes and sympathies were not consistent. Pride in the new Germany did not erase resentment of domination by Berlin; grumbling about the "Prussians" was one of the most popular pastimes in the land of the Wittelsbachs. Similarly the rising levels of hatred and diplomatic tension engendered by the alliance blocks conflicted with the traditional cultural and religious loyalties of Bavarians. It was difficult to hate France as the "national enemy" while at the same time valuing French culture and the historic ties to "Catholic France." What kept the inconsistencies from tormenting most Bavarians—aside from a tendency toward political passivity—was the conviction that the social fabric was so strong that they could indulge their conflicting loyalties with little fear that they would ever have to choose between them.

The relative backwardness and conservatism of Bavaria held the most radical forces at bay. Industrialization existed; the Social Democratic party had some support; there was a nucleus of racist, radical nationalists as well as of Munich intellectuals who craved drastic change. But in face of the overwhelming weight of throne, altar, and the established class structure there appeared little danger that any of these groups would seriously upset the prevailing order. A conservative Bavarian such as Gebhard Himmler could cheer the Kaiser, enjoy the French classics, patronize the peasants, favor progress, be proud of Germany's modernity and Bavaria's traditionalism, and still believe that his world was well ordered.

Although no documented account of how the average Bavarian coped with this jumble of beliefs and loyalties can be presented, it is possible to speculate on some of the factors that helped him adjust to them. The overlapping character and partial contradiction of his primary loyalties seem to have kept his resentments and prejudices within reasonably safe bounds. There was hatred or dislike of a large number of groups. Anarchists, republicans, socialists, and Freemasons were the primary objects of suspicion and fear. Prussians, Protestants, Poles, Frenchmen, and Jews also aroused varying degrees of dislike and suspicion. But it was difficult to isolate many of these negative symbols from the Bavarian's amorphous collection of national, local, and religious loyalties. Stereotypes of Poles, Frenchmen, German Protestants, Prussians, and German Jews fitted into his category of likes as well as into his category of hates. Even a Bavarian socialist could produce ambivalence among the solid citizenry if he voiced some devotion to Germanism.

The government and church authorities generally discouraged agitation against ethnic and religious groups, further decreasing the likelihood that many people would develop a clearly defined system of enemies and potential scapegoats. The only groups which the authorities condemned without qualification were anarchists, Freemasons, and radical socialists. In Bavaria these groups either did not exist or were present in only microscopic numbers; the agitation against them merely reflected the amorphous panic that periodically seized the rulers of this backward society when they viewed the rapid changes that were taking place in the outside world. The fear and suspicion surrounding the alleged threat of "radicals" and Freemasons bred few tangible consequences (although the anti-Freemason agitation did serve as a significant bridge to political anti-Semitism during and after World War I). Despite alarming acts perpetrated by anarchists abroad and the widely held belief that Freemasons were involved in an international revolutionary plot, few people in Bavaria believed that these groups or the radical socialists would ever seriously alter the Bavarian way of life. The whole exercise in fear and indignation combined the vicarious thrills of a good adventure story with the opportunity to demonstrate the soundness of one's own views by denouncing mythical dangers.

If this hodgepodge of imaginary fears, qualified prejudices, and overlapping loyalties awakens in us a certain nostalgia for the happy days gone by, it is important to remember that the quaint and charming appearances were largely deceptive. The Great War demonstrated that the apparent stability of the conservative states such as Russia, Austria-Hungary, and Bavaria was an illusion. In the clash of modern forces these societies were the ones most profoundly shaken. Furthermore underneath the peaceful and happy veneer many groups, especially the poorer peasants and new industrial proletariat, were caught in a cycle of voiceless deprivation. In addition the value systems which appear so stable and charmingly naive in retrospect were in fact a confusing labyrinth of contradictory beliefs and prejudices which had to be mastered by every successful member of society. One had to know intuitively when to curse the Prussians and when to praise Berlin; when to scorn Polish nationalism and when to affirm one's kinship with all good Catholics. The nuances of belief and expression could be absorbed by the hereditary ruling classes and the very rich against a background of leisure and invulnerability. But for people attempting to maintain a middle position or to rise through the favor of the traditional ruling groups it was essential to acquire the right opinions, attitudes, and prejudices together with a sure sense of timing in their expression. The day of rigid class divisions was ending and the period of radical social change had not yet arrived; only those who were perfectly programmed could succeed in this era of complex and shadowy values.

Seen against this background, the mores of the Himmler family and the system used in raising the children made perfectly good sense. There was nothing in the parents' experience to indicate that the prevailing hierarchical order would not continue. Everything suggested that their children would have to master the values and behavior patterns which that order prized. The only way they knew to attain this end, since the value system lacked consistency and clear guideposts, was to teach the children what was expected of them and to encourage them to internalize the shadings of proper behavior, opinion and feeling. Only in this way would the youngsters achieve the necessary balance of attitudes and beliefs which would lead them instinctively to do the right thing at the right time. Such was the Himmlers' world. It had little room for childish freedom or joyous abandon in play or thought. But, if he did what was expected of him, the child would receive praise and affection and would have excellent prospects for a life of comfort and social esteem.

Chapter II

The Years of Peace

On June 21, 1900, Gebhard Himmler replied to a letter he had received from his former student, Prince Heinrich. The letter was not as formal as most of his letters to the Prince; it began simply "Dear Prince Heinrich" instead of "Illustrious Prince, Most Gracious Prince and Lord"[1] which was his customary salutation. Though informal in tone Herr Himmler's letter exuded a feeling of humble gratitude for the fulfillment of one of his fondest dreams. The Prince had offered to serve as godfather for the Himmlers' second child. At the end of his letter the writer poured out all of his feelings of family pride and gratitude: "I cannot close, dear Prince Heinrich, without expressing my feelings of gratitude that you or her Royal Highness will act as godparent to the child that the dear Lord will send us in the fall. . . . My dear wife asks me to present [*zum Fuss zu legen*] her most humble thanks to you, and through you to her Royal Highness."[2]

The assurance of a princely godparent for their child raised the Himmlers to the pinnacle of self-satisfaction and apparently allowed them to pass through the last four months of Anna Himmler's second pregnancy with a profound sense of confidence and inner peace. When, on October 7, 1900, the baby boy was born, the father could hardly contain his joy. He wrote to Prince Heinrich the day after the birth:

> After consulting the priest of St. Anna I take the liberty of humbly informing you that the baptism of our little Heinrich will occur on Saturday the thirteenth of this month. . . . After the baptism I would like the honor of being allowed to offer you a glass of champagne. It would perhaps interest you to know, dear Prince Heinrich, that on his second day of existence on this earth, our little offspring weighed seven pounds and 200 grams [8 pounds, 5 ounces] and measured 52 cm. [20½ inches]. Thankfully he is lively and always hungry. . . . In joyful anticipation of the coming day of honor [*Ehrentages*] I am, dear Prince, your thankful and happy Gebh. Himmler.[3]

The object of all of this pride and enthusiasm, little Heinrich Himmler, obviously meant more than just a second son—he was a living certificate of achievement and family status. We may assume that his parents tried to assure that, as such, he received sufficient care and attention. For the first five months after his birth the family remained in the Hildegardstrasse apartment, but in spring 1901 they moved into a larger apartment on the Liebigstrasse which was further north and in the central section of the city. Here the family resided for fourteen months, except for the summer months, during which Frau Himmler and the children vacationed in the Alps at Füssen near Hohenschwangau, and Herr Himmler journeyed back and forth between the vacation spot and the city.[4]

We know little about the day-to-day activities in the Himmler household during this period and even less about the actual care of the new infant. Obviously there was no lack of money. The baby's physical needs were amply cared for by his mother and Thilda Nöbauer, a full-time maid and children's nurse who lived with the family. Both parents doted on their little Heinrich; and his godfather Prince Heinrich frequently inquired about him and sent the customary greetings on his name-day. When in early 1902 he began to speak, his father carefully recorded his first words and his way of pronouncing "mamma, papa, Gebhard," and so on. Duly informed of his godchild's early prowess, Prince Heinrich sent his congratulations.[5]

In summer 1902 Herr Himmler was appointed a professor at the *Gymnasium* at Passau. He had been increasingly dissatisfied with his instructorship in classical languages at the *Wilhelms Gymnasium,* and the transfer was doubly welcome. It is improbable that the move to Passau constituted any very sharp break for the Himmlers who had friends and relatives in Passau to make the move and new adjustment easier. With Professor Himmler's higher income suitable quarters were easily arranged, and the family quickly settled into a residence at Theresienstrasse 39.[6]

Early the following year, however, the contentment and security of the Himmlers' new life suddenly collapsed. Passau had a good record in public health and customarily faced few problems with communicable disease. But in the first months of 1903 it was racked by a wave of respiratory illnesses which resulted in a sharp rise in the infant mortality rate. In

February little Heinrich contracted a serious respiratory infection which seems to have settled in his lungs and produced all the symptoms of tuberculosis. In their concern and fright the Himmlers not only used the medical help available in Passau but also brought Dr. Quenstedt, who had delivered Heinrich and been present at his baptism, all the way from Munich to treat him. The danger from contagious diseases in Passau was so serious that the doctors advised that the child be taken out of the city. In early spring Frau Himmler took the children to the little village of Wolfegg, north of Lindau (the area where Gebhard senior had been raised), where they could have the benefit of pure mountain air. While the baby was being nursed back to health by his mother, the local doctors, and Dr. Quenstedt, his father continued his work in Passau and visited the family whenever possible.[7]

The period of Heinrich's convalescence was a time of extreme tension for the family. During the spring and summer of 1903 letters filled with worried comments passed back and forth between Professor Himmler and Prince Heinrich. The boy made some progress but stopped short of complete recovery. Apparently Prince Heinrich shared the family's concern; at any rate he made at least one trip to visit his namesake while he was ill—a courtesy for which the parents were deeply grateful. Finally in July Dr. Quenstedt was able to report that the worst was over, although spots of infection remained in the upper lungs and exposure to contagious disease would constitute a grave risk.[8] Because of the questionable health conditions prevailing in Passau the family faced yet another perplexing decision. After a month's hesitation and careful investigation of conditions with the health authorities they decided to return home to the Theresienstrasse residence. Once in Passau, they could do little but hope that all would be well. At the end of August Professor Himmler wrote to Prince Heinrich:

> We have, thank God, brought the two children back cheerful and in good shape. The examination made by the district physician here on August 28th confirms the results of Dr. Quenstedt's examination in Wolfegg on July 28th, namely that Heinrich has made very great improvement even though the disease is still present in the uppermost part of the lungs. That may heal, in the opinion of both doctors, if the child is spared childhood diseases, especially

> severe measles next winter. We must now leave that to God. As both doctors have confirmed to us, we have done all that humans can do.[9]

The year 1903-4 was thus a tense time for the Himmlers. Writing to Prince Heinrich during the Christmas season Professor Himmler voiced the now familiar mood of worry and gratitude for small improvements: "Things are going rather normally for us now, thank God. An examination by the district physician yesterday showed that Heini's healthy condition, which has been achieved by so much struggle is holding, with the exception of some spots of remaining infection. May it continue! It has been such a dark shadow."[10] The strain resulting from this constant worry and sense of helplessness tended to mar the enthusiasm and satisfaction that the Himmlers had felt when they moved to Passau. The border city must now have seemed a place of isolated and dangerous exile, for in Munich they could count on a wider circle of sympathetic friends and colleagues as well as excellent medical care. These considerations probably played a major part in Professor Himmler's decision to leave his post in Passau in the spring of 1904 and take up a similar position at the *Ludwigs Gymnasium* in Munich.[11]

The move back to Munich achieved its main objective: Heinrich's condition improved steadily and in the course of 1904-5 returned to normal health. The family now lived in a third-floor apartment at Amalienstrasse 86, behind the university and close to all the modern facilities that the capital offered.[12] Heinrich was thus freed from some of the overprotectiveness which his parents had lavished on him during the previous year. His position as the center of attention was further diminished by the illness and misfortune which overtook his older brother, Gebhard, when he began school in September 1904. The Himmlers had enrolled Gebhard in a special program in the cathedral school rather than in the adjacent Amalien school. From the time of his entrance, however, he contracted one illness after another and in the course of his first year there lost a total of 147 days of school as he passed from flu to bronchitis and back again. In fact, he missed so much classtime that he did not receive a first-grade completion certificate. As soon as school ended his parents hustled him off to a vacation haven at Oberaudorf on the Austrian border near Rosenheim. They spent the summer nursing him back to health and preparing him for the second grade while simultaneously remedying the deficiencies of the previous year so that he might obtain his first-grade certificate. Meantime during the early summer of 1905 it had become clear that Frau Himmler was pregnant again and that the third child was due to be born in December.[13]

The combination of young Gebhard's problems and her own pregnancy left Frau Himmler little time or energy for Heinrich's recent illness. With the arrival of her third child, Ernst, just before Christmas, she had additional demands on her attention. Professor Himmler also was much occupied throughout this period, for he had to master his new duties at the *Ludwigs Gymnasium.* At home his attention was first claimed by his wife's pregnancy and later by his new son and the continuing problem of keeping Gebhard well and helping him master his school problems. The professor's professional interests made the latter task close to his heart, and he carefully recorded Gebhard's difficulties and the steps taken to overcome them. With deep parental and pedagogical pride he noted in January 1906 that Gebhard had not merely made up his first-grade deficiencies, he had made the highest grade of any child in the school. The father's pride in this achievement was confirmed in the spring, when Gebhard ranked near the top of his second-grade class.[14]

Meanwhile, although concern for Heinrich's health remained and Frau Himmler never lost her apprehension and fussiness about him, the boy enjoyed a fair measure of freedom and self-reliance during the years 1904-5. This brief phase of independence culminated in the summer of 1906 in another family vacation near Füssen. For Heinrich this was a last happy lull before the storm; in September it was his turn to experience an initial taste of school similar to that which had nearly felled his brother. He too was enrolled in the cathedral school rather than the Amalien school and, like his brother, he was ill most of the school year. He had the usual attacks of colds and flu and in addition mumps, measles, and a recurrence of lung infection. With the help of a special tutor whom the family hired for him, he managed with great effort to complete the year. He achieved high marks in the final examinations, though he did not do as well as his brother (his score was 15 as opposed to Gebhard's 16½ and 16 in his first two years). Following another summer of recuperation in the Alps, he was able to move through the second year of school with a minimum of academic or medical difficulty.[15]

The two boys' success in recovering from their rather traumatic first years of school should not obscure the fact that they were exposed to unusually severe pressures and controls during these years. The precautions and restrictions imposed by their poor health were reinforced by Professor Himmler's rigid supervision of their education. The father took every precaution to ensure that their schooling embodied the social tone appropriate to the family's status and ambition. He recorded his assessment of the qualities and activities of the boys' teachers. He also compiled a complete list of all the students in each class, and beside each name he noted the occupation of the child's father, as if considering how to protect the family from any association which might endanger its social position.[16] No matter what their fears concerning the children's physical condition, the parents never lost sight of their main goal: to prepare their offspring for careers as professional men with close connections with the court.

In fall 1908 young Gebhard was enrolled in the *Wilhelms Gymnasium* where six years earlier his father had taught. At the same time Heinrich was transferred from the cathedral school to the Amalien school for "family reasons," as his father's notes termed them; apparently Professor Himmler had changed his mind about the relative academic and social standing of the two schools. Thus it was in the Amalien school that Heinrich completed his last two years of primary education. There he did well and enjoyed some pleasant boyhood friendships with his classmates.[17]

In summer 1910, following Heinrich's completion of elementary school, the family vacationed at Lengries, a village in the foothills of the Alps and ten kilometers south of Tölz. During these summer months, to underscore the fact that his early childhood was over and the serious business of the *Gymnasium* awaited him, his father had him keep a diary. To show what was required and set the proper tone, Professor Himmler wrote the heading on the diary and made the first entry:

July *13. VII* Departed at 11:50 and arrived safely on the bus in L[engries] at 2:00. We have a very pretty house. In the afternoon we drank coffee at the coffee house.[18]

With this model before him young Heinrich carefully listed each day's events, no matter how trivial. "Unpacked in the morning," he wrote the next day. "There was heavy rain. In the afternoon father and Gebhard left." Some of his entries included a few sentences of detail; the entry for July 28, for example, reads: "We two, Mommy and I, travel to Tölz on the bus. Daddy and Gebhard go by foot over the Mackersberg to Tölz. We remain in Tölz until evening and met Mr. Schnell, a teacher and his children." Most of the entries however consisted of such brief statements as: "*31 VII.* Gebhard has a bad toothache," or "*8 VIII.* Walk in the park."[19]

The diary throughout followed the pattern set by the father: each event was listed, and each day was carefully marked in arabic numerals, each month in roman. The father went over the diary, making corrections or additions to some entries. For July 22 Heinrich had begun by writing "13th wedding anniversary of my dear parents"; above the line his father added "first swim." On August 10 Heinrich wrote "bad weather" and his father added "and the *bad** writing?!"[20]

The unemotional chronicle makes it easy to forget that the writer was a ten-year-old boy. Only occasionally was a hint of childish enthusiasm allowed to show through. On July 15 he wrote: "Morning in the garden. In the afternoon over the Mühlbach to the park. Here we ran into three very young bears of the Grand Duke of Luxemburg. We were very frightened. Before he ran away one of the bears sat up and begged." But even here the words "very young" and "of the Grand Duke of Luxemburg" were insertions by the father to show that pedantic accuracy and awareness of status were the important things in life.[21]

If Heinrich was allowed to play with children other than members of the family, no mention of them appears in the diary. A number of adults, however, were mentioned with their full titles. The high point of the summer's activities was recorded in an entry for August 5: "At 5:45, Princess Arnulf, Prince Heinrich, and family returned from Vienna. We were photographed by Prince Heinrich."[22] Such stress on social

*Underlined in the original.

events, however, did not mean that during the summer he was liberated from his academic duties. On August 1, after two weeks away from his lessons, he began a daily routine of study which continued until he returned to school.[23]

Apart from an occasional chance incident, such as the appearance one morning of a tightrope walker in the village, the child had virtually no escape from this routine. Even his sole quiet diversion, stamp collecting, was a hobby that his father had pursued for years, and we may assume that Heinrich was required to follow it with at least as much meticulosity and supervision as he had his diary writing. Professor Himmler was an enthusiastic collector of books, stamps, and all manner of historical and family memorabilia, and as the boys attained the proper degree of romantic enthusiasm and habitual precision they were allowed to share in this collecting.[24]

In September 1910 Heinrich entered the *Wilhelms Gymnasium,* where he remained for three years. Not surprisingly in view of his year-round routine of study and paternal supervision, he showed himself an excellent student, consistently ranking first or second in his class.[25] His only difficulty was with gymnastics, where he lagged behind his classmates and frequently received cavalier treatment from his instructor or was the butt of his jokes.[26] He was an awkward little boy whose poor eyesight made it necessary for him always to wear glasses or a pince-nez, and this combined with his reputation as a model student to make him fair game. His standing with his peers was hardly improved by the fact that his father had been a professor at the *Wilhelms Gymnasium* and still had close relations with many of its faculty. Despite these handicaps, however, he was on quite good terms with his fellow students because his competitive spirit made him work grimly to hold his own in boyhood games and sports. Through all the jokes about his weakness and clumsiness he persevered, never lost his temper, and seldom relinquished the faint smile which became his trademark.[27]

Heinrich's success in maintaining good relations with his classmates was partly due to the social and class makeup of his schoolfellows in the *Gymnasium.* Most lower-class children ended their education at the primary level or went to the more technically oriented secondary schools. The sons of the higher nobility, on the other hand, were trained in special academies for careers in the royal army and only entered the *Gymnasium* on a part time basis in their last years of schooling. Thus the vast majority of Heinrich's fellow students came from professional and wealthy business families similar to his own. The social activities which people of this class considered suitable for preadolescent boys were hikes, gymnastics, garden parties, and respectable hobbies such as chess or stamp collecting. In some of these Heinrich was able to excel and in the others he managed to hold his own. Throughout these years he had close friends with whom he played constantly and was never left in the position of the good student who is the perennial outsider.

Heinrich did, however, enjoy a special relationship with most of his professors and was something of a teacher's pet. This special relationship sprang from his father's past work at the school and especially during vacations was kept alive by social visits. Perhaps under paternal prompting, Heinrich was always careful to write to those of his teachers whom he did not see during his summer outings.[28] The family worked assiduously to cultivate important people and to avoid any relationship that might cast a shadow on its social standing. While on vacation the boys might occasionally play with some of the neighborhood children, but Heinrich never mentions any of them by name in his diary, merely noting that on this or that activity they were accompanied by, for example, "the landlord's children."[29] Not until 1913 do the names of any other children appear, and then they are those of Edi and Luisa Hager who accompanied their parents on a joint vacation with the Himmlers in Brixlegg, Austria. Generalkonservator Hager, a high government official in charge of museums and monuments for the state of Bavaria, was a man well worth cultivating.[30]

Despite the importance of suitable day-to-day contacts with significant men in the academic or bureaucratic ranks, the major focus of the family's social awareness continued to be the nobility. Although Professor Himmler does not seem to have had frequent contact with Prince Heinrich and the court during this period, the connection was not severed, and one member of the Patin branch of the family (cousins of Frau Himmler) continued to serve at court.[31] The Himmler boys were led to believe that contacts, no matter how remote, with persons of noble birth were events of real significance. For example, Heinrich is careful to note in his diary that, when they attended a forest festival near Lengries during the summer of 1911, "the Grand Duchess of Baden and Princess of Hohenburg were also among the observers."[32] And only one item in his diary during the family vacation in Austria in 1913 warranted underlining in red pencil—the phrase "Austrian Emperor's Day" at the end of the entry for August 18.[33]

A note of envy and bitterness may, as George Hallgarten has stressed, have crept into the boy's worship of the nobility.[34] Certainly, the signs of waste and unearned privilege were clear for all to see. But the direct evidence shows only Heinrich's unswerving devotion and awe for royal rule and noble privilege. Even if he gave up his early dream of military glory and settled for a fancied career as an officer in the imperial navy,[35] because that was the service in which a commoner had the best opportunity of becoming a professional officer, there is no indication that he found this unjust or that he had ever really dared aspire to an army officer's career.

Family values and relationships remained the most important features of his life. In 1911 Ernsti, the third and last of the Himmler children, entered school, and from that time on all members of the family were directly involved in the scramble for academic success. Frau Himmler's importance gradually declined as the children moved into the father's special preserve of academic competition. But assisted by the nurse, Thilda, and by Professor Himmler's mother who resided with the family from time to time, she continued to play her part in instilling proper modes of behavior and in protecting the children from real or imagined perils. Both the Himmler and Heyder families were large, and Heinrich's parents maintained close connections with a great number of their more successful relations. Consequently the boys' social life embraced not only their social peers but numerous cousins and uncles who embodied the virtues and achievements that their parents prized.[36]

The continuity between social ideals and family life also manifested itself in the family's religion. Although his father was a Protestant, Professor Himmler was raised a Catholic, and his wife came from a very devout Catholic family whose Patin branch included a large number of priests. Both parents made every effort to instill religious devotion into their youngsters. Professor Himmler was decidedly not one of those liberal professors who ignored the church themselves while encouraging others to attend it. The whole family not only went regularly to mass but often attended special prayer services. During the summer vacations hardly a day went by without the family going either to church or on a sightseeing trip to some of the religious institutions in the surrounding countryside. On a number of Sundays they attended one or two church services in the morning and spent the rest of the day touring neighboring monastic institutions.[37]

The diary that Heinrich kept during the summers of 1911 to 1913 shows clearly that despite the overpowering demand for conformity he was growing up and widening his interests and abilities. He spent most of his leisure swimming, hiking, or strolling through the countryside and in the adjacent villages. Now that the boys were older, the family made more day excursions such as short train trips or cruises on the steamers that plied the larger Alpine lakes. Often Professor Himmler and the two older boys would hike a few miles across country to a point of interest where they would be joined by Frau Himmler and Ernsti who had come by train or bus. During summer 1912, when the family vacationed near Lindau, the boys had the use of a kayak, and Heinrich spent many hours paddling around the lakes.

By now the diary entries had become longer, more detailed, and better expressed than those made during Heinrich's primary-school period. A typical entry is that for July 26, which begins: "Name-day of my dear mother. In the morning to church. In the late morning a stroll to the interesting little St. Anna Church near Bonderis. In the afternoon to the *Feldkirche.* There we looked at the large establishment and collections of the Jesuits." Here and there some feeling about what he is seeing and doing peeps through. Describing the trip to Lindau in August 1912, he begins with his usual fussy precision, "11:37 departed for Lindau," but near the end of the entry he notes that "the lake is splendid and rather wild."[38] Yet all too often even his emotional responses seem merely to parrot those of his parents. His account of the family's journey to Lindau a month earlier begins: "At 10:20 dear Mommy and we three boys left for Lindau. After a four-hour trip we reached the splendid Bodensee whose beauty and size charmed us completely."[39]

Professor Himmler still checked over the diary and made

corrections and additions. But Heinrich himself was by this time sufficiently imbued with the pedantic spirit to systematize every aspect of his activities. In 1911 every time he took a dip in the water he not only mentioned it in his diary, but listed it in order—"First swim," "Second swim," and so on. The grand total for the summer reached thirty-seven.[40]

Yet with all his father's and his own prodding, Heinrich could not completely overcome the fact that he was somewhat careless and untidy. He often forgot to write up his diary and then had to go back to it later and sort it out as best he could, garbling details and occasionally spreading the same event over two or three days. When he could not remember a point, such as the exact minute someone left, he would leave the spot blank as if to show his good intentions: "8:25 Gebhard and I picked up Thilda [the family's nurse] at the train station. . . . Stroll to the castle. At ——— o'clock, Thilda went back to Fischbach."[41] But these occasional lapses did not seriously affect his willing acceptance of and participation in the established program. Every summer, after a break of two or three weeks, he returned to his studies and put in a half day's work until regular classes began in the fall. In summer 1911 his father also put him through a course in Gabelsberger shorthand in addition to his regular studies.

Heinrich's period of intensive study and training at the *Wilhelms Gymnasium* came to a close in the fall of 1913, when Professor Himmler accepted the post of *Konrektor* (deputy principal) at the *Gymnasium* at Landshut, 70 kilometers northeast of Munich.[42] This position permitted him to continue some teaching and at the same time to gain the experience which would qualify him for a post as a full *Gymnasialrektor* in the not-too-distant future. Landshut was situated close enough to Munich to allow the new *Konrektor* to keep in touch with the important educational activities and maneuverings for promotion that took place in the capital. But for the boys the move was a disruptive break with the pattern of life they had enjoyed at school and with their boyhood friends, and Heinrich dallied in Munich as long as he could, apparently staying with friends or relatives after his parents and brothers had moved into the new home at Altstadt 1½.[43]

If Heinrich's departure from Munich was not altogether happy, his brother Gebhard's experience was worse. In the midst of the preparations to leave he again became gravely ill and shortly after arriving in Landshut he was hospitalized with pleurisy. He remained in serious condition throughout the last months of 1913 and the early months of 1914 and did not completely recover until near the end of the school year.[44] This probably cast a gloomy shadow over the family's efforts to adjust to a new life. The boys in particular had to find their way in a new school and faced the delicate task of forming the correct friendships and acquaintances to match the family's enhanced social position.

All these problems however were shortly eased by a stroke of unusually good fortune. Wolfgang Falk Zipperer, who was one of Heinrich's closest school friends in Munich, and had recently lost his father, moved with his family to Landshut. His mother had married again and his stepfather had taken a post in Landshut. For Heinrich this meant the continuation of an old friendship which was to develop into a close bond that would last through youth and adulthood.* Throughout the next few years Heini and Falk attended school together, often played together after school hours, and carried on a steady correspondence during summer vacations. For the Himmler family also Falk's arrival in Landshut was a godsend. His stepfather was His Excellency Ferdinand von Pracher, whose former position had been that of first minister in the State Ministry for Churches and Schools, which meant that he exercised supervision over the whole school system, including of course the *Gymnasia.* Von Pracher's new position in Landshut was that of president of the Regional Government of Lower Bavaria, one of the eight provincial governments of the kingdom. He was in fact one of the most powerful administrators in the royal service and through his extensive connections at court and in the educational system wielded significant influence. Thus after a shaky beginning the move to Landshut brought to Heinrich the renewal of a happy childhood friendship and to his parents the prospect of a bonanza in the game of influence and patronage.[45]

*Falk Zipperer seems to have been the only boyhood friend with whom Heinrich remained on close terms into the Third Reich. In 1937 Zipperer was an *SS Hauptsturmführer* (captain). Zipperer's book *Das Haberfeld Treiben, Seine Geschichte und seine Deutung* (Weimar, 1938) was dedicated to "Heinrich Himmler, dem Jugendfreund und Mannesgefährten." Zipperer also contributed an article to *Festgabe für Heinrich Himmler* (Darmstadt, 1941) which commemorated the *Reichsführer*'s 40th birthday. The notorious *SS* medical experimenter, Dr. Karl Gebhardt, knew Heinrich when the Himmlers lived in Landshut, but he was a classmate of Gebhard Jr. rather than Heinrich, and his boyhood relations with the younger Himmler were not as close as he later implied.

The family's summer vacation in 1914 reflected the happiness and satisfaction of their new life in Landshut. The place chosen this year was Tittmoning, east of Munich and adjacent to the Austrian frontier. The Lindners, old friends of the family who lived in Tittmoning, arranged for the Himmlers to have a pleasant house there. Heinrich's first diary entry typifies the contentment felt by the family at this time: "15.VII. Left Landshut at 10:31. After a hot trip arrived in Tittmoning at 1:45. A charming house with a splendid garden. Unpacked. Then Gebhard and I went to the Ponlach valley. I received lots of nice things for my name-day which pleased me. In the evening we were in the garden with Agnes and Julie [Lindner]."[46]

The initial impression of happiness and good fun was confirmed by the experiences of the succeeding weeks. The Himmlers set out on their customary round of hikes, strolls, sightseeing visits to churches, and occasional boat and train trips. The weather remained consistently good, and the boys were able to spend pleasant evenings in their garden playing with the Lindner children. Heinrich practiced the piano in his spare time and played an occasional game of chess with his older brother. Together with the Lindners they set up a theater and produced a play for their families and friends. Apparently the run lasted only two performances, one of which grossed 1 mark 50 pfennig and the other 80 pfennig.[47]

In the course of the summer the Himmlers took a number of short trips to visit friends and relatives. Heinrich had a tendency to exaggerate the warmth of their reception, using the stock phrase, which he was to continue to employ in later years, "They were very happy to see us [*sie eine grosse Freude hatten*]."[48] But the Himmlers obviously had many friends who welcomed their visits and seem to have enjoyed returning them. In late July the Himmlers had social gatherings in their garden in Tittmoning complete with lanterns and fireworks.[49]

Heinrich's diary entries for most of July 1914 mirror the calmness and security of this vacation life. Then in the entry for July 29 the world crashes in! "Gebhard's birthday. *Beginning of war between Austria and Serbia.* * Outing to the

*Words in italics are underlined in the original.

Waginger See. Agnes and Julie go with us. . . . En route we become very sick. I go right to bed. During the night Mommy became very sick."[50] As if to resist the terrible words he had underlined in red, Heinrich made his customary entry on family activities the next day and tried to do so again on July 31. But he went back and erased both entries, leaving only the words "Played" at the start of one entry and "Went to Ponlach" at the end of the other. In the middle, written over the erased notes, are the words, again underlined in red: "*Announcement of a state of war*† *in Germany.* [*Verkundigung des Kriegszustands*]."*[51] With that the happy scene in Tittmoning rapidly dissolved. The family's day-to-day activities were pushed aside, and Heinrich's diary begins to chronicle the events of the era now starting:

> 1. VIII. *Mobilization in Germany.** Two Army Corps. Even the Landst[urm].
>
> 2. VIII. Played in the garden in the morning. Likewise in the afternoon. 7:30. *Germany declares war on Russia.**
>
> 3. VIII. *French and Russian attacks on the borders. Planes and spies.** We quickly pack.
>
> (No entry for August 4th)
>
> 5. VIII. *England has declared war.** Italy remains neutral.
>
> 6. VIII. We leave Tittmoning at 4 a.m. and after a long delay in Mühldorf and Neumarkt arrive in Landshut with the luggage around 1:30. We ate in the train station and then took the street car to our *home.* *[52]

This hasty flight from Tittmoning marked the end of an era in the lives of the Himmlers as of most other Europeans. In one week their summer vacation, with its happy outings and parties in their pretty garden, had been ruined. The four years to come were to prove that along with it had perished much of their way of life.

---

†A "state of war" meant a condition of readiness prior to a declaration of war.

*Words in italics are underlined in the original.

Chapter III

A Boy's War, 1914-16

The family's return to Landshut in early August 1914, nearly a month before school began, gave Heinrich time in which to immerse himself in the novelty and excitement of the first weeks of war. He was so captivated by the news from the front that he resumed his diary, writing long entries filled with battle reports, observations on the war, and his daily round of activities. A typical entry is that for August 23:

> 23 Sunday August. Around 10:00 in the *Martinskirche*. Met lots of people. Then in the garden with Ernsti. Victory of the German Crown Prince north of Metz [Longeville?]. Prince Heinrich wrote to daddy. . . . Wonderful German answer to Japan's ultimatum. The Germans in Gent. Played piano. After coffee we visited Nachtigalls . . . .Thilde told me of a heavenly sign that she may have seen. The Bavarian troops were very brave in the rough battle. Especially our 16th. . . . The whole city is bedecked with flags. The French and Belgians scarcely thought they would be chopped up so fast.[1]

The boy's enthusiasm and patriotism knew no bounds, and a single entry often covered two or three of the small diary pages. When there was so much news that he could not include it all, he inserted references indicating where more information could be found: "Victorious march of the German army in Belgium," he writes on August 28. "For details see Telegram of the *Muenchner Neusten Nachrichten*, No. 17."[2] The diary blended together records of family activities and reports of bloody victories:

> 26 August. Played in the garden with Falk. 1,000 Russians captured by our troops east of the Weichsel. Advance of the Austrians. In the afternoon worked in the garden. Played piano. After coffee we visited the Kissenbarths. We were allowed to pick plums from the tree there. So frightfully many have fallen. We now have 42 cm. Cannons.[3]

Whether the writer was concerned about the number of plums which had fallen or the number of men who had died remains obscure.

As the weeks of combat dragged on without any decisive results, the boy's interest began to wane, and the diary entries became shorter; often they were omitted for weeks at a time. After school started he was too busy to devote much time to his military chronicle, yet he made enough notes to allow the reader to form a fairly reliable picture of his attitude towards the war. Above all, of course, he was carried away by the glory and excitement of military action. He identified completely with Germany's cause and never doubted the justice of her position or the inevitability of her ultimate victory. Like most boys of his age, he dreamed of being able to join the heroic legions. "Falk and I," he writes on August 28, "would like, best of all, to be in the middle of it."[4] A year later, when his brother Gebhard has reached the age of seventeen and entered the *Landsturm,** he cannot contain his envy: "Oh if I were only as old I would have been out there long ago."[5]

Heinrich's eagerness to take part extended even to the prosaic activities occurring in Landshut. When Gebhard was allowed to accompany his parents on a visit to wounded soldiers, and Heinrich had to stay home, the younger boy fairly sighs, "I envy him very much."[6] Some of his elders were somewhat apprehensive about this eagerness for military service. During the first phase of the war R. Hornburger, a friend of the family, sent him a picture postcard of German troops in action. On the card he wrote: "As well as I know you, my dear Heinrich, I'm sure you are enthusiastic and would like, as shown in the picture, to drive the enemy into flight. However, I thank God that you are not old enough and hope that you will always be kept safe and sound."[7]

Heinrich's youthful ardor should not be attributed to blind bellicosity or an innate military spirit. He was a young boy just entering adolescence who knew that there was no immediate prospect that he would have to go; his eager fervor reflected little more than his desire to grow up and be part of the great world beyond his sleepy town, a world that was in process of exploding. Militarism and mayhem had become the norm, and a young boy could hardly avoid the siren's call. Heinrich's enthusiasm was normal. What is surprising is

*A branch of the German army's reserve system.

the note of detachment and skepticism which appears in the diary entries. Despite his eagerness to get news from the front, at least once (September 1914) he notes that the reports have been tampered with: "On the telegram sheet a small word had been tucked in that made the situation seem more serious, and it was *not** in the newspaper extra."[8] Although he absorbed much propaganda intended to foster hatred of the enemy and kept newspaper clippings such as a poem entitled "Hate England,"[9] he was able to see enemy soldiers as human beings. When a trainload of wounded French soldiers stopped in Landshut at the end of August 1914, he felt sorry for them and was genuinely indignant about the unpleasant and insulting behavior of the civilians toward them. This may have been partly due to his low opinion of the civilian attitude to the war, for his diary abounds with references to the Landshut population's fears and lack of war enthusiasm.[10]

In part, this more balanced attitude toward wartime events reflected that of his family and of many other members of the professional middle class. With their sincere devotion to the German cause and their personal commitment to contribute to it in any way they could went an undertone of sadness and a desire to hold as tightly as possible to their own less partisan and more cosmopolitan way of life. As Heinrich describes the family's visit to church, buying of flowers and so forth on the occasion of his father's and brother's name-day in 1914, he adds that the temper of the times "is definitely not the right spirit for a name-day."[11] On other occasions he shows that even in the midst of the bloody struggles with France he knows that in saying goodbye, the proper word to use is still "*Adieu.*"[12]

The family's attempt to hold on to the old ways gradually gave place to its absorption into the activities of the homefront. Frau Himmler sewed and knitted for the troops and visited the wounded. Professor Himmler had to grapple with a host of administrative problems as the demand for men cut into *Gymnasium* enrollments and it became increasingly difficult to continue programs in the higher grades. Young Gebhard, whose artistic nature was inclined to painting and music, found himself nonetheless engaged in

*Underlined in the original.

military training programs, starting with the *Jugendwehr** and going on to membership in the *Landsturm* in 1915.[13]

During the first months of the war Heinrich's role was restricted to watching, cheering, and playing war games with his friend Falk. So eager were these games that in Heinrich's diary it is often difficult to separate them from battle reports: "29 [August 1914] Saturday. Studied until 10:00. Played shield and sword with Falk. This time with 40 Army Corps and Russia, France, and Belgium against Germany and Austria. The play is very interesting. Victory over the Russians in East Prussia."[14] The young diarist was delighted with wartime innovations such as the daylight-saving time introduced in 1916 which enabled him to sit in the garden in the evening and write his entries.[15]

In early 1915 it was Heinrich's turn to begin military training by enrollment in the *Jugendwehr.* The boys were issued weapons and received close-order drill in addition to lectures on military organization, fortification, and tactics. Occasionally they participated in small-scale field exercises under the direction of regular officers, and they frequently appeared at patriotic ceremonies held by the *Gymnasium.* Heinrich was somewhat ambivalent about these *Jugendwehr* activities. The lectures and field exercises he usually found interesting, and sometimes he thought the unit performed well; but the amateurish tone of the organization offended him. In 1916 he describes it as "something of a joke."[16]

Heinrich's involvement in the *Jugendwehr* and his dreams of one day entering the war led him to pay more attention to his physique and the need to build up his strength. Although of normal height, he was already self-conscious about his soft, pudgy appearance and general lack of stamina. At one point he decided on a program of exercises, but apparently his resolve did not last long.[17] He was often ill with colds or flu which forced him to be absent from school and did nothing to lessen his mother's protectiveness. In 1915 he complained of stomach trouble, a problem that was to plague him for the rest of his life. His attitude toward his illnesses alternated between self-pity and a resentment against a weak constitution which might limit participation in the military. "In the afternoon to training," he writes on September 25,

*A program which had been started in the 1890s to give secondary school students some preparatory training for the army.

1915. "The exercise was pretty poor. I lay in a rather wet field for a quarter of an hour; however, it didn't hurt me at all."[18]

This sensitivity about his health and unsoldierly appearance was evidence of the fact that Heinrich was still a young boy. His military dreams were only an aspect of the overall process of growing up, and, despite his fascination with the war and his military training, he had to progress gradually into maturity in a conservative and protected environment dominated by his parents, his teachers, and his middle-class peers. Professor Himmler and his wife were not about to relax their system of training because of the war. The boy was kept as much as possible within the narrow confines of his class and the activities appropriate to it. The family continued the long walks it had always taken, and the boys sometimes accompanied their parents on social calls to such people as the *Rektor* of the *Gymnasium* or a local baron. From time to time Heinrich was invited to participate in polite amusements, including magic-lantern shows with groups of children from the professional middle class and the nobility. His diary continues to include the correct titles of important persons and to make careful note of friendly receptions by such people as Falk's mother. "Gebhard, Ernsti, and I were invited over by Falk and Ina [Ina Pracher, Falk's half-sister]," he writes on August 24, 1914. "We played with a steam engine. Then drank tea with Frau *Präsident,* who was very nice [*sehr liebenswürdig*]."[19]

At home Heinrich followed a quiet routine, practicing the piano, arranging his stamp collection, and playing with toy soldiers. Occasionally he played chess with his brother Gebhard or joined him in a four-hand piano concert for the family. Once his parents took him to a concert, which he found "very long, but also very beautiful."[20] His diary makes no mention of any rough-and-tumble games with other boys. His only strenuous play was at school, in the organized program of the *Jugendwehr* or the gymnastic club which he joined in early 1917. After his parents had given him a bicycle early in 1916 his brother Gebhard took him along on bicycle outings. These, however, were not an overwhelming success, because Heinrich had a penchant for falling off his machine, tearing his clothes, and suffering other mishaps.[21]

Family and church ties remained strong. Heinrich was sincerely devoted to his parents and brothers, and carefully recorded descriptions of their minor illnesses. When his paternal grandmother died in 1916, he seems to have been deeply affected and noted the exact time of her death. As he grew older his devotion to the church did not diminish; if anything, it grew stronger. Perhaps under the impact of the war, the family's church attendance became even more frequent, and the boy often accompanied his parents and brothers to service three or four times a week. His diary makes careful note of events of importance to the church—for example, the selection of a new Pope. During the summer of 1915 the family went on an extended pilgrimage of local churches in fulfillment of a vow made two years earlier when Gebhard was seriously ill.[22]

Heinrich had a number of friends his own age, but his closest companion continued to be Falk Zipperer. Both collected stamps, liked war games, and, as the years passed, became increasingly interested in writing. In addition to keeping his diary, Heinrich also tried his hand at stories and poems. Falk was even more deeply concerned with writing and was often called upon to compose and present poems at school. The boys spent many hours examining each other's work and exchanging opinions. In writing, Heinrich was the junior partner. But when it came to collecting, his achievements stood out, and Falk served as audience. In addition to stamps and perhaps picture postcards, Heinrich collected coins, and pressed wildflowers, a hobby he had learned from his mother. From his father he had acquired an interest in stones and artifacts from the Middle Ages and especially during the summer vacations he endeavored to uncover traces of the Germanic past. The romantic, often ludicrous, enthusiasm for medieval Germany which he was to manifest in later years probably stemmed from these early efforts.[23]

Although the mode of his life remained within the limits set by his parents, he showed signs of developing some independent judgement. The diary entries not only give free rein to his scorn for the timidity and narrowness of the local petty bourgeoisie but sometimes also record the fact that he was unimpressed by people whom his parents esteemed. He was particularly hard on the wife of the *Rektor,* an exhibition of *lèse-majesté* which would have been unthinkable for him a few years earlier. His status as a "mere child" irritated him, and he was deeply offended when he discovered in the summer of 1915 that at his age he was considered so unimportant that he could enter Austria without a passport. Among his peers also he was anxious to be taken seriously; when one of his sick classmates was not sufficiently appreciative of a visit from him, Heinrich refused to see him again.[24]

The *Gymnasium* continued to be the central focus of his life. Curriculum requirements grew more taxing, and in order to maintain his high ranking in the class he had to spend much of his time studying. He apparently succeeded in remaining consistently second in his class. His father continued to supervise his studies and drill him in his lessons, especially those for his language classes. At the same time, however, the boy's enthusiasm for school was somewhat dampened, and certain subjects, mathematics in particular, became sheer drudgery. He had difficulty in algebra and some other subjects, and noted early in 1915 that a special examination had "not gone especially well."[25] His ability to please and maintain close relations with his teachers also fell off. In September 1914 he was deeply troubled by what he termed a "misunderstanding" with one of his professors; he tried to resolve the problem by a personal visit but he was unable to convince the professor of his innocence. Apparently Heinrich had been somewhat obstructive while making classroom reports and answering questions. A few days later he noted lamely in his diary that some of his other teachers had also complained of his conduct. A year later when it seemed likely that he would again be assigned to this professor, he was deeply concerned; though conceding that on this occasion the professor was "very nice" to him, he heaved a sigh of relief on learning that he had been assigned to another class. As his ability to charm his teachers diminished, he became critical of other students who tried to improve their positions by using schoolboy blandishments. On one occasion he even tried to dissuade Falk from trying to curry favor with a teacher.[26]

Part of Heinrich's difficulty in maintaining his position near the top of the class arose from his carelessness. This, together with his lapses in responsibility both in and out of school, bothered him. When, as often happened, he fell behind in writing his diary, he would reproach himself. "I must admit that I was really very bad," he writes in late September, "because I neglected my diary the whole time [two and a half weeks]."[27] Actually, compared with most boys of his age he was a model of conscientiousness and responsibility; but his family's rigid system and his own sense of duty made every failing seem heinous.

The tasks ahead of him and his remorse about his failings made the family's annual vacations especially important for young Heinrich. Though these trips offered no escape from close parental supervision, they did at any rate give him a change and a chance to unwind. The vacations, whether at Burghausen near Tittmoning (in 1915) or at Kellberg north of Passau (in 1916) provided a round of activities that varied little from year to year. Interspersed among the countless strolls in the countryside were family trips, opportunities for swimming, and visits to the churches in the area. When left to his own devices, Heinrich read, paddled a canoe, and now and then played croquet or some other quiet game with other children vacationing in the area.

On the surface the amusements and way of living might seem unchanged from earlier summers, but even here the changes brought by the war were felt. Describing the trip to Burghausen in 1915 Heinrich wrote: "I remember clearly last summer when we stood on the train platform and exercised at approximately this time. It was then the 6th of August as we came home from Tittmoning. A few days later they all went off to war cheerful and happy. How many are alive today? "[28] The war colored the happy diversions of the vacation time. In August 1915 the Himmlers held a fireworks display as they had done in earlier years, but this time it was to celebrate the fall of Warsaw to German troops.[29] By 1916 good food was becoming more difficult to obtain and was more readily available in the country districts than at home in Landshut, although the wartime controls on consumption and purchasing were supposed to apply everywhere. Heinrich carefully kept a clipping from the *Passauer Zeitung* of August 1916 which denounced a "blonde Saxon lady" who while visiting near Passau had hoarded food and sent it home. On the side of the clipping Heinrich noted: "Bad Kellberg near Passau. These blonde Saxons are Frau Fabrikdirektor [factory manager] Weitzer and her daughter. . . . They sent food home almost every day. They told us how badly it went with them. A half pound of frozen meat for each person since May 1915. Milk only with a doctor's certificate. Potatoes are the chief food, and sometimes they are wanting." This comment reflects the increasingly serious impact of the war on daily life; it also suggests the possibility that the Himmlers—perhaps Heinrich himself—were directly involved in the denunciation of the hoarders. The boy's wealth of information on the incident certainly suggests that he played some part in its exposure.[30]

Whether or not Heinrich took any initiative in this incident, it is clear that during these years he was becoming more self-assertive and more conscious of approaching adulthood. His attitude toward sex during puberty and early adolescence has a certain significance. The prudery and shyness which he later manifested were probably already there during this period, and this, combined with the fact that everything he wrote was subject to parental scrutiny, made him conceal his sexual awareness under a cloak of secrecy. His diaries do not include a single reference to sex, and there is no hint of any typically adolescent humor or curiosity. They do however show him taking a new interest in Luisa Hager, the one girl of his own age whom he had known well since early childhood. He wrote to her from time to time, and when the Hagers came to visit, Gebhard and the Hagers' son Edi paired together, while Luisa and Heinrich shared each other's company. The Himmler parents of course did nothing to discourage a closer friendship with the daughter of a senior government official, and by early 1916 the boy was becoming more interested in his rediscovered friend. He notes that although Edi had grown very much taller, he himself is the same height as Luisa. As the two of them wander through Landshut, she confides to him that he has changed a good deal. In early May, when the Hagers have returned home after one of their short visits to Landshut, Heinrich wonders if Luisa will write to him "as she promised to do." When on the next day he receives a card from her, it pleases him "very, very much."[31]

In normal times Heinrich's interest in Luisa would probably have evolved into one of those long, platonic courtships common among the well-to-do classes in prewar Germany. But the year 1916 was far from normal, and Heinrich's first stirrings of interest in the opposite sex were submerged in the rising tempo of the war. It was in 1916 that the forces of total warfare which had been gradually accelerating since the opening of hostilities reached their climax. During this year the great battles of Verdun and the

Somme poured out the human and material resources accumulated over the preceding two years. But these indecisive battles served only to strengthen the belligerents' resolve to continue the struggle. Determined to fight, yet deprived of the reserves which had been burned up in the Western campaigns, Germany was forced to tighten the screw in order to acquire the necessary manpower and equipment. The government extended its control over the civilian economy, intensified rationing, and by the end of the year had instituted a system of national service which made all able-bodied males above the age of seventeen subject to service in the armed forces or in jobs important for the prosecution of the war. All this brought the war closer to Heinrich. At the same time he was growing up, becoming more capable, and steadily approaching the point at which he would meet the requirements of war.

The deadly serious character of the war as it moved into its third year meant that it interfered more directly in the lives of the people around the Himmlers. The happy veneer of middle-class life in Landshut was being stripped away. First it was the turn of Gebhard's friends and classmates—most of whom were now eighteen years old—to face the choice of trying to stay in school, attempting to get a commission, or accepting the seemingly inevitable and going into the ranks. Sprinkled through Heinrich's diary and the family correspondence in 1916 are references to friends of Gebhard who have decided to join up or to enter officer training. With his class scheduled to be called up in September, Gebhard himself seems to have been troubled about what to do. As early as January 2, 1916, he discussed the issue with Heinrich as they took one of their evening strolls. In the late summer of 1916 he finally decided to enter officer training.[32]

Meanwhile the ever-increasing demands of the war began to move in on Heinrich's peers. In May Luisa Hager obtained her parents' permission to leave school and take up war work. Heinrich himself was increasingly anxious to escape from his sideline position in the *Jugendwehr* and become involved in the real war. On May 3, 1916, his unit participated in a memorial service for a lieutenant who had been killed in action just four weeks after making an inspection tour of the *Jugendwehr* in Landshut. Heinrich had been impressed by him as a "truly fine officer and a splendid man" and was sincerely grieved to discover that at the time of his death his baby was only four weeks old.[33]

In November 1916 word reached the Himmlers of another tragedy which went far beyond anything they had so far experienced in bringing the horror of the war into their family circle. Prince Heinrich had been slightly wounded early in the conflict and had later served at Verdun. In 1916 he was transferred to Romania where he immediately established himself as a heroic and competent officer. After a very short period of service there, however, he died of wounds. Only thirty-two years old at the time of his death, he had been a dashing commander, repeatedly decorated for bravery under fire. The only member of the House of Wittelsbach to be killed in action, he was deeply and sincerely mourned throughout Bavaria.[34] But it may well be imagined that nowhere, not even among his own family, was the prince's death felt more keenly than in the Himmler household. Despite the family's acute sense of status, it was not the loss of their chief patron that mattered most to them in 1916. Professor Himmler had been very fond of his former student and had sincerely lived the conservative ideal of love and devotion to his "Prince and Lord." Even so, the impact of Prince Heinrich's death went yet deeper than the personal loss. To the Himmlers he had been the symbol of the very best in the old tradition and had embodied in his person those vistas of "bright sunlit uplands" which they hoped would come again after the war. His death brought home to them the horror of the war with all its waste and suffering and showed clearly that their way of life would never again be the same. In extending his condolences to Professor Himmler on Prince Heinrich's death, one old friend of the family, Professor Dicknether, wrote, "How much bitter sorrow has been brought by this war! When will it ever end!"[35]

For young Heinrich Himmler the prince's death had a special significance. Prince Heinrich had not only given his godchild a unique status within the Himmler family; he had also symbolized for him the security and prospects which he would enjoy as a favored member of the established order. His death, coming on the eve of his godchild's attainment of eligibility for war service, eased the transfer of young Himmler's hopes and aspirations from the old order to the new. Even though the traditional values and mores had been firmly stamped upon him, many of his boyish dreams came increasingly to focus on the new world of war. As the year 1917 approached, the war was about to take charge of his life, and each time a connection with the old regime was severed, it became easier for him to welcome the war as his world and his future.

Chapter IV

A Young Man's War

In the first months of 1917 the pressure that the departure of more and more young people headed for war exerted on Heinrich continued to mount. From Gebhard, who was undergoing training with the Sixteenth Bavarian Infantry Regiment in Passau, the family received a steady stream of letters reflecting the excitement and adventure of a soldier's life. The fact that the family's attention focused on Gebhard, though chiefly due to parental apprehension, did nothing to lessen Heinrich's impatience with his role as the small boy on the sidelines. Then in April, Falk Zipperer dropped out of *Gymnasium* and entered the officer-training program of the Second Bavarian Infantry Regiment whose training camp was in the Oberpfalz. Thus the two young men closest to him were now in military service. The boy pleaded with his parents to be allowed to quit school and join too.[1]

In early June Heinrich's father finally yielded to his badgering and agreed to initiate the process of application for his acceptance as an officer candidate. Professor Himmler knew that, even though the war had gnawed away at the traditional system, the selection of officer candidates still rested on the old foundations of privilege and influence. Although the requirements for an officer candidate had been relaxed to meet the demands of war, the successful middle-class aspirant still needed substantial help from persons of privilege. On June 7 Herr Himmler wrote Princess Arnulf's chamberlain requesting assistance in preregistering Heinrich as an officer candidate in the First or Second Infantry Regiment. He stressed the fact that without the "favorable assistance" of the princess he "would never succeed" in this endeavor. His letter shows clearly that he was not altogether enthusiastic about his son's military plans. He emphasized that he did not wish him to enter training before his seventeenth birthday (October 7, 1917); if by chance the war had ended by then, he did not wish him to enter the service until he had completed *Gymnasium.*[2]

Despite this somewhat qualified petition, the princess' response was generous. On June 11 her chamberlain replied that he had written the commander of the First Regiment urging Heinrich's preregistration as an officer candidate and was sending Heinrich 1,000 marks in German war bonds to pay the acceptance fee, as a gift "of his late godparent, his Royal Highness Prince Heinrich of Bavaria."[3] A few days later he wrote again to make certain that the First Regiment was acceptable to the Himmler family, a rather ironic question as it was a crack regiment and a coveted assignment for officer candidates. Professor Himmler replied that the First Regiment would be fine because "many students from our *Gymnasium* are already in it."[4] On June 23 the application blank arrived, and the professor filled it out in a manner that balanced his own reservations with Heinrich's eagerness to join. He again stressed that he would rather see the boy finish *Gymnasium* first, but, if that was impossible, he wished him to enter training as an officer candidate after he had reached the age of seventeen. He appended an impressive list of references, including a minister of state, Princess Arnulf's chamberlain, and Generalarzt Patin, who was Frau Himmler's uncle. In answer to the last question, which asked if the applicant "had chosen an officer's career as a *life's work,*"* he acceded to the boy's hopes, and replied, "My son Heinrich has the urgent desire to be an infantry officer for *life.*"*[5]

By all the established rules of influence and patronage Professor Himmler's application should have done the trick. But in fact it did not. Heinrich's preregistration for the First Regiment was turned down because the regiment already had a long back list of similar applicants possessing the same kind of support from on high. What the army needed in 1917 was men in the ranks, not lists of potential officer candidates. The rebuff was hard on the boy, for it came at a time when he had finished his seventh year of *Gymnasium* and was drifting through another summer vacation in Bad Tölz. He had been sick again, and since he had not yet had an army physical this was especially disturbing; it raised the possibility that, even if he found a regiment that would accept his application, he might be rejected on health grounds. Through it all the letters he was receiving from Gebhard and Falk exuded excitement and enthusiasm about life in the army and must have compounded his sense of frustration.[6]

Perhaps because his abilities as a courtier had been brought

*Words in italics are underlined in the original.

into question, Professor Himmler rallied to the occasion, and mapped out a campaign to get the boy accepted by some unit. He drew up a list of the twenty-three regiments of the Bavarian army, showing the names of the top officers, the cities which served as their home bases, and the names of important people he knew who had connections with the regimental commanders. This done, he appears to have simply gone down the list, writing to his contacts on his son's behalf. Once again, however, the result was discouraging. On September 2 he heard from his contact with the Second Regiment that there was no room there and that the same was true of all the other Bavarian regiments. Worse still, his correspondent added that even if Heinrich were accepted as a candidate there were so many ahead of him that he would have virtually no chance of obtaining a commission during the war. Professor Himmler was still not ready to admit defeat; five days later he applied to the Eleventh Infantry Regiment.[7]

While his father was still fighting the battle of the applications, Heinrich temporarily lost hope and seems to have believed that he might be taken into the service as a common soldier. A few weeks after the term began he decided to quit *Gymnasium* and applied to the city of Landshut for service in the *Hilfsdienst.** On October 6, 1917, the day before his seventeenth birthday, he was notified that he had been accepted, on the basis of the "recommendation of the [*Gymnasium*] *Rektor*"—at this level Professor Himmler's influence worked well—and had been assigned to work in the *Kriegsfürsorgebüro,* a social welfare organization concerned with orphans, widows, and so forth.[8]

For six weeks Heinrich worked at his *Hilfsdienst* assignment. Then the Bavarian School Ministry issued a special order that showed that he was in no danger of being drafted and that his panicky decision to leave school had been unnecessary. On November 19, still without any solid prospects of acceptance into officer training, he reentered the *Gymnasium.*[9] One month later (December 23) without any prior warning he was notified that he had been accepted as an officer candidate in the Eleventh Infantry Regiment. Ordered to report to Regensburg on January 1, he spent his last week as a civilian gaily getting his gear together and writing

*The program of war work for those who had not been called into the army.

countless letters to friends and relatives announcing that at last he was a soldier.[10]

The officer-training program normally extended over one or two years and was conducted at a series of special schools. The candidate's initial title was that of *Fahnenjunker* (cadet). After three to five months of training he was designated a noncommissioned officer with the rank of corporal. In peacetime he would normally receive a further one to three months' training and then be sent to war school for eight to nine months. After completing war school he would be designated a *Fähnrich* (a rank similar to that of warrant officer) and be assigned to a unit to perform the normal duties of a noncommissioned officer. After satisfactory performance in this rank he would receive his commission. In 1918, however, owing to the demands of war this system had been speeded up. After the initial period of training and his designation as a corporal the *Fahnenjunker* was usually put through a specialized training program in heavy weapons, machine gunnery, or tanks, and then assigned to a unit as a *Fähnrich.* If his regiment escaped heavy losses among its lower officers, he would remain a *Fähnrich* throughout the war; if, however, the casualty rate was high, he might be sent back for accelerated training leading to a commission. In rare cases a *Fähnrich* might be given a battlefield commission, but even then he usually had to complete the modified war school program at the first opportunity.[11]

Arriving at the 11th Regiment's training camp near Regensburg in the first days of January, Heinrich had little time to worry about the tortuous route ahead of him. He was completely caught up in the adventure of being a soldier and the problems of his first stay away from home. He was thrilled by the rituals of military life–the uniform, the oath (which he described as "very fine"), and his first inspection–which were all proudly recounted to his parents and younger brother. With the pride and status-consciousness of a seventeen-year-old who had just left the classical *Gymnasium* he signed his third letter to his parents with a Latin flourish, "miles Heinrich" (soldier Heinrich).[12]

Despite his pride in soldiering Heinrich had a hard time adjusting to the comparatively Spartan conditions and to the separation from home and family. The long years of tight control had made it difficult for him to be on his own, and he suffered from acute homesickness. In his first month at

Regensburg he wrote twenty-three letters home, and though he received ten or twelve in reply, he continually complained that the family did not write enough. The first sentence of his letter on January 24 is typical: "Dear Mommy, Many thanks for your dear letter. Finally I received something from you." Two days later, having received another note from home, he starts off in the same vein and adds, "I have waited a painfully long time for it." And two letters in three days do not stop him from lamenting on the 29th, "Again today I got nothing from you."[13]

His early letters combined pleas for mail with complaints about his living conditions: his room was barren and cold, and he suffered from the attentions of bedbugs; he found the food sparse and uninviting and pleaded for packages of food and enough money to allow him to eat at the canteen or the beer-hall restaurants in town. Trivial mishaps, such as the inadvertent picking up of the wrong clothes at the bath, assumed the dimensions of minor tragedies and were reported in detail to the family. In part these complaints and lamentations were appeals for help from Frau Himmler. In response, she dispatched a succession of money orders and of parcels containing food, extra bedding, insect powder, and clean laundry. Apparently much advice and many expressions of worry accompanied the provisions that arrived from Landshut. Under the impact of these messages Heinrich, aware that he must maintain his stance as a brave soldier, would sometimes try to retract the complaint that had set the whole operation in motion. But he always waited until he received the package before changing his tune, and his reserve never lasted long. In the matter of food he was completely unashamed and his letters are filled with appreciative remarks about his mother's cooking ("the *Apfelstrudel* which I ate after the training session was marvelous") and with requests for snacks such as apples and cookies.[14] These requests were sometimes accompanied by the argument that the package would enable him to snack in the barracks and thus lessen the money the family would have to send him for support. Judging from his exuberant descriptions of his eating habits, there was probably some merit in this argument. "This evening I ate *Schweinebraten* in the Bischofshof" (a beer-hall restaurant), he wrote on January 21, "and even though it was excellent it wasn't as good as yesterday. It was still fine." Then as if to underscore the link between his appetite and his devotion to duty he added, "I am, however, today again a soldier, body and soul."[15]

In his loneliness he pinned his hopes on getting a pass to go home, but for the first six weeks of training he failed to obtain one. A visit from his brother Gebhard, who came over on a pass from his duty station at Bamberg, helped to tide him over. He also made many calls on family friends and relatives in the Regensburg area (one of the first things he asked to have sent from Landshut was a pack of visiting cards) and enjoyed the warm reception he received and the opportunity to share the comforts of their civilian life. As much as possible he clung to the routine of home and frequently attended church. Nevertheless for much of the time he was unhappy and upset. Vague hints of poor health and complaints of depression because he had "nothing to do and froze the greater part of the day" threw his parents, especially his mother, into panic.[16]

At the end of the first week, with even more than the proverbial gullibility of a new recruit he picked up a story that he was not going to be kept in officer training but was scheduled for immediate shipment to the front. This tale reduced him to greater depths of gloom and washed away his ardor for combat. To his parents, however, he explained that it only upset him because it would mean the end of his aspirations to become an officer. In desperation he asked them to get in touch with Lieutenant Zahler (apparently Ludwig Zahler, his second cousin who was in the Eleventh Infantry Regiment) and request his help in the matter. The prospect of his assignment to the front terrified his mother as much as it did the boy himself, and their fears were not completely allayed by the authorities' firm assurances that he would remain in officer training. A month later Lieutenant Zahler was still assuring Heinrich that he was not going to be shipped out and urging him to calm down and go through the program.[17]

Although the threat of combat kept cropping up every few weeks, by the middle of January Heinrich had settled into a more satisfactory routine. Many of his letters included the phrase "things are going fine with me,"[18] and the number of complaints and scare stories decreased. He enjoyed the training exercises, particularly the field maneuvers, and found his superior officers and the NCOs who conducted the course uniformly "very nice." His effort to be a big boy and play the part of a soldier became more successful. He had himself photographed in uniform and sent copies to friends of the family. Toward his twelve-year-old brother he adopted a tone of big-brother camaraderie spiced with a note of superiority and periodic jabs at the failings of "little Ernsti."[19]

Perhaps the most convincing indication of his improved adjustment and of his desire to appear more mature was the fact that he was smoking, although he had to beg the tobacco from his father. He also indulged in occasional pronouncements about the general course of the war. Thus on one occasion the way in which the press handled an erroneous report of Ludendorff's resignation "didn't please" him; on another he reported with enthusiasm that the garrison in Regensburg was being held in readiness for possible use against a strike in Nuremberg and added sarcastically, "One notes, however, once again, the splendid German unity."[20]

His letters home, though seldom falling below three a week, grew less frequent. Yet his requests for mail were as insistent as ever, and from time to time he became quite unpleasant about the dearth of replies: "Dear Mother," he began a letter on March 23, "Many thanks for your nice news (which I didn't get). It is really mean of you not to have written."[21] He was still capable of falling into panic over the possibility of being sent to the front and could still feel it necessary to buy war bonds to keep in the good graces of his commander. Even in his good moods he appears to have needed continuous expression of his mother's devotion and concern. Repeated scare stories, especially about his health, were apparently unconscious efforts to elicit demonstrations of affection. Often after an incident had passed he would comfort her with such phrases as "dry your tears," as if seeking to induce additional expressions of her love.[22]

The main cause of his increased ability to keep the pressures and feelings of inadequacy under control was the resumption of direct contact with his family. In early February his father came to Regensburg for a weekend with him. Shortly thereafter Heinrich began to get the long-sought passes for weekends home; between February and June he received at least fourteen passes or short leaves, which meant that he went home three weekends in four. Even for a seventeen-year-old this was a comparatively pleasant form of military service.[23]

He seems to have been comforted and strengthened by the renewal of direct parental supervision. As in earlier days, parental concern in the Himmler household meant rigid record-keeping and accounting—every letter, package, and money order was duly noted down by Heinrich and his mother. It also meant the maintenance of proper social forms and the performance of small social duties, such as sending a postcard home whenever he visited relatives or family friends. A letter to his mother on March 11 expresses his embarrassment at having failed to write her while he was on a weekend visit to Gebhard who had been transferred to Passau. It also meant a revival of his parents' interest in proper thoughts and values as well as correct behavior. On March 1 Heinrich gravely assures his mother that his father need not worry, he is not reading Zola. The danger of corruption by a realistic socialist writer was apparently more threatening than the risks of war![24]

He cultivated no close friendships with his fellow trainees but worked hard to excel and to impress his superiors. When near the end of February his commander praised his work in the course, he was very gratified. More at peace with himself and his position, he resumed many of the interests that he had enjoyed before entering the service. After one weekend at home he took his bicycle back to Regensburg and began making tours of the neighborhood in the late afternoons and evenings. Frequently these outings brought him to the home of the Wills, who were old friends of the family, or of his second cousins, the Patins. He prized these quiet evenings and often reported to his parents the special pleasures, such as an occasional large piece of cake, he got from them.[25]

Amidst all of his other activities he maintained a steady correspondence with such "right" people as former teachers, well-placed relatives, and influential family friends. A frequent recipient of his letters was Frau Hager. He was still interested in Luisa and badgered his parents for news about her when they went to Munich. Somewhat on guard against writing her too frequently, he usually alternated his letters between mother and daughter. Not all the attention to Frau Hager, however, was due to his interest in Luisa; sometimes he received a package and sometimes some of the free opera and theater tickets to which Herr Hager was entitled by virtue of his official position.[26]

In Regensburg Heinrich revealed a touch for manipulating

and arranging things that in the American army would have earned him the title of "operator." In April, when his brother Gebhard's unit passed through the city on its way to the front, he had a field day, arranging special housing, acquiring food, and taking care of odds and ends. From then on he acted as self-appointed middleman for the packages that went back and forth between Landshut and Gebhard's unit in Lorraine as well as for the lesser traffic between the Himmlers and their friends in Regensburg and Munich. Throughout these transactions he kept a careful record of every penny he expended, including the 1 mark and 50 pfennigs for cookies and 20 pfennigs for postage that he spent on April 26 for a package to Gebhard. With the same sure touch for his own interest he followed up any lead that might turn out to his advantage. When he learned from his uncle that some soldiers had been allowed to take their *Gymnasial* midyear examinations while in the service, he immediately passed the news on to his father with the request that he be allowed to do the same. Professor Himmler duly petitioned the ministry and included the details of the other cases without any misgiving that he might be compromising the people involved. It led nowhere, however, for the regulations had been changed and inservice promotions of former students were no longer allowed.[27]

Periodically Heinrich was gripped by panic about his position and the army's plans for his future. Perhaps his parents' pedantic control of all the petty details of his life made it harder for him to endure the capriciousness of the army. In any event, the slightest alteration in the routine set him off on a round of worry and speculation. When in late May the first phase of the *Fahnenjunker* course was drawing to a close, he became very anxious about whether he would be advanced to the next phase of the course. His apprehension remained even after his official designation as a corporal in the middle of May and was not finally overcome until early June, when he received orders to report to the qualifying course at Freising on June 15, following a few days of extra leave at home.[28]

The assignment to Freising which was only thirty-five kilometers from Landshut, brought Heinrich even closer to his family. During his three months there he had nine passes and short leaves and thus went home as often as he had during the latter part of his time at Regensburg. In addition two of his former classmates in Landshut, Robert Kistler and Martin (Kraus?), were also in the Freising course, which meant that for the first time since joining the army he had real comrades. The training program in the qualification course was however more rigorous than that at Regensburg. He enjoyed it, especially the maneuvers, but he was forced to spend more time in study and often complained about his lack of leisure.[29]

The pattern of his leisure-time activities continued to be much the same as at Regensburg except that, as there were fewer family friends in Freising, he did not make many evening social calls. Now and then he did some personal reading, usually classical *Novellen* such as Paul Heyse's *Vetter Gabriel,* which his father had given him to read on the train. He was perfectly happy with the approved material and showed no hankering for forbidden fruit such as Zola.

His personal idiosyncrasies, including his love of a good meal, remained the same. On July 2 he was so busy that he could only write a short card to his father and had to resort to shorthand in order to include the line: "Today for lunch we had noodles and cooked fruit. Very good but over-done and too cold."[30] His passion for arranging things also continued unabated and ranged from parceling out among family and friends portions of a hoard of artificial honey acquired from a fellow trainee to sending home a piece of leather from his belt, to be used for repairing shoes. The war was now inflicting real deprivation on civilians, and Heinrich's ability to take care of things was warmly welcomed at home.[31]

Through it all he never tired of tormenting his parents with hints of trouble or reports of his poor health. The family seems to have developed a method for countering his medical scare stories: they began to describe their own illnesses. As flu and other contagious diseases grew more prevalent, it became his turn to worry and seek reassurance, and from then on he showed more caution in chronicling his own ailments.[32]

As the qualification course drew to a close in late August and early September, his apprehension about the future returned. There were rumors that he would be assigned to yet another training program, but he now seems to have been genuinely anxious for a taste of combat, and his eagerness was increased by clear signs that the war in the West was not going well and that, if he was to see action, it might be now or never. On August 4, as he speculated on what might happen when he left Freising, he noted "Many regiments have suffered frightful losses or have been virtually destroyed."[33] Three weeks later, when it seemed clear that his next assignment would be a machine-gun course in Bamberg, he wrote that rumors were flying and that a major had confided to one of the trainees that they faced "the toughest duty that could be asked of a soldier." From his brother too the news was grim, for Gebhard admitted in his laconic way that no quiet and pretty places were left in the West, "not even in Lorraine."[34] It was difficult for Heinrich to remain vegetating in training camp while events at the front came to a head. The feeling that he might be too late once more was accentuated by a letter from an old school friend who had been wounded in action. After describing the writer's experiences the letter closed with the hope that Heinrich's duty in Freising was "still a ball [*recht grossen Spass*]."[35]

The army however took no account of dreams of wartime glory, and in mid-September Heinrich, to his bitter disappointment, was sent to the machine-gun course at Bamberg. He managed to work up some enthusiasm for the field training in weapon operation and deployment, but neither the demands of the course nor his eagerness to finish it interfered with his customary way of life. He had enough free time to make social calls and reserved a number of afternoons and evenings for sightseeing and visits to the opera. During his travels he managed to collect stamps and coins which he sent home with his usual shipments of dirty laundry and scraps of food—and a stern warning that the stamps and coins were for his own collections and were not to be appropriated by the other collectors in the family.[36]

In early October the course in Bamberg ended. After a short leave Heinrich was ordered to return to Regensburg for reassignment and arrived there during the second week of October. While he was awaiting his orders he and Robert Kistler were put to work drilling recruits—Heinrich's only command experience during his brief army career. Both were eager for combat, and their close friendship did not prevent young Himmler from maneuvering to gain special favor with the officers in order to insure his own assignment to the front if there was not room for both of them.[37]

He resumed his old round of social calls and theater visits, but this did not preclude frantic efforts to obtain his orders. For the full gravity of Germany's situation was now clear to him. "I see the political situation as very black, wholly black," he wrote on October 16, "I believe unfortunately with good grounds. I'll tell you when I see you. I will never lose my resolve even if there is a revolution, which is not out of the question."[38] His frustration at this time was aggravated by the fact that his brother Gebhard had received a battlefield promotion to *Fähnrich.*[39]

At last on October 23 he gleefully wrote home that after a long conversation with a *Fähnrich* and a lieutenant who were organizing a replacement company he believed that he would be assigned to the new unit. He had been told that his orders for the front would be through in eight days, and that he could expect a last short leave before they came.[40] But the rising tide of opposition on the homefront and the German collapse in the West delayed the company's departure. Finally, overtaken by the armistice and the revolution which swept Germany out of the war during the first two weeks of November, it was abandoned altogether. Instead of embarking on the long-sought march to glory, Heinrich and most of the officer candidates were bundled off home to save them from the wrath of the revolutionary soldiers' and workers' councils.

Throughout the month of November, while the revolution burned on, Heinrich remained in Landshut, safely out of harm's way, his hope of an officer's career temporarily destroyed. Pressured by his father, he began to prepare for a return to the *Gymnasium,* as if the events of 1918 had been only a wild dream. But as conditions began to return to normal and he heard encouraging reports from those who had remained in Regensburg, his hope and courage revived. Shortly before December 1 he returned to Regensburg and discovered that despite the continued existence of the soldiers' councils the military authorities were in firm control. The field units had not yet returned from the West, the new Republican government had not clarified its plans for the army, and peace negotiations were shrouded in uncertainty. It seemed possible that many men would be kept in the army, and rumors regarding the fate of the officer candidates flew thick and fast; there was a recurring story that many of them would be enrolled in a special war school to be held in Munich early in 1919.[41]

Heinrich lent a hopeful ear to every rumor which offered some prospect of realizing his dream of securing a commission. He stayed in Regensburg and obtained a position at a small salary, working with his cousin Lieutenant Ludwig Zahler in the demobilization records section of the regiment. Along with Zahler (to whom even in his letters home he referred as Lieutenant Zahler rather than Lu) he rented a room in Regensburg and settled down to a pleasant routine. He resumed his social visits in the neighborhood and his regular attendance at the theater. In early December Gebhard returned from the front and the brothers spent many pleasant hours together in Regensburg. It gradually became clear however that the special war school was a mirage, and that there was little or no chance that any officer candidates born after 1899 would be allowed to complete their training. Heinrich, whose age was a year under this limit, began to spend more of his free time studying French and brushing up on the German writers from Otto Ludwig to Gerhart Hauptmann, in the event that after all he would return to the *Gymnasium.*[42]

His uncertainty about the future was increased by the signs of radical social change associated with the revolution. He was unsettled by stories of attacks on officers which had occurred here and there, even in Bavaria, and begged his parents to send him some civilian clothes so that he would be able to travel safely. His passion for inside information made him lend a ready ear to conservative scare stories, which he eagerly passed on to his parents. Thus, after attending a closed meeting of the *Bayerische Volkspartei* (*BVP*), an organization newly formed to rally conservative Bavarians, he was nearly overcome with foreboding. "What one hears is shattering and perhaps twice as bad as I told the Schulers [family friends in Landshut]. Buy all of the coal you can and also all the food, even if you have to buy it by the pound. In 14 days there will be no more coal and no more electric light. . . . Father, you must join the *Bayerische Volkspartei,* it is the only hope." At the end of this letter, written on November 30, he added a private note in shorthand to his father: "Now only for you. I don't know how it is in Landshut. Don't let mother go out alone at night. Not without protection. Be careful in your letters. You can't be sure."[43]

Heinrich's fears were made more bearable by the new opportunities to become involved in behind-the-scenes maneuvering. One of Gebhard's former school friends was a leading *BVP* spokesman in Regensburg, and Heinrich used this opportunity to gather information and flirt with politics. He relished his role, even though much of his involvement and much of the danger which he saw everywhere was imaginary. His ideal is perhaps expressed in the concluding sentence of the shorthand note to his father quoted above: "Have no fears on my account for I am sly as a fox."[44]

In spite of the pleasure he derived from it, however, he could not forever chase rumors in Regensburg. His last chance to gain admission to officers' school was to wait until the regiment arrived from the West and then somehow persuade its commander to retain him in service. When the regiment arrived in the second week of December, Heinrich's request was turned down. On December 17 he was informed that all *Fahnenjunker* of the 1900 age group were to be discharged.[45]

With that Heinrich gave up and returned to Landshut a few days before Christmas. He left the army, frustrated in his dream of acquiring military glory and with the shadowy status of a *Fahnenjunker* who had earned his qualification for yet never attained the rank of *Fähnrich* or received a formal commission. With his own military hopes in ruins and conditions in Germany almost in chaos, his return to Landshut was a sorry ending to a year that had promised so much and produced so little.[46]

Chapter V

A Young Man Groping: 1919

At the time of his entry into military training in January 1918 Heinrich had completed seven years of the nine-year program at the *Gymnasium* and had attended the eighth class for a few weeks. When he returned to Landshut shortly before Christmas 1918, his family's views and his own values made it virtually inevitable that he would resume his education. In spite of this, however, his confusion and frustration might well have undermined his resolve and caused him to drop out, had he been required to go through the normal last two years to obtain his *Abitur* (graduation certificate). But the Education Ministry's emergency regulations covering men returning from service offered him an opportunity to complete his secondary education with a minimum of inconvenience. One of these orders established special *Gymnasium* classes (*Sonderklassen*) for veterans and specified that those who had attended the eighth year prior to entering the service could qualify for graduation after two semesters. As an additional incentive, the semesters were shortened so that a veteran could complete two years of regular work in an intensified six-month course. For Heinrich this meant that, if he completed the two semesters of *Sonderklasse,* he would graduate in the early summer of 1919, the exact time at which he would have graduated if he had never entered the army.[1]

The system of *Sonderklassen* made certain concessions to the special problems and greater maturity of veterans but left the authoritarian atmosphere of the *Gymnasium* untouched. The students were still treated as schoolboys. The curriculum retained its major emphasis on Latin, Greek, and German, and classes in science, history, and religion were merely supplementary. The impression that little had changed was heightened by the fact that the returnees, many of whom had entered the service at the same time, tended to be reunited in the same *Sonderklasse.* Thus when Heinrich enrolled in *Sonderklasse A* in Landshut he found himself with Anton Meier, Falk Zipperer, and many others among his old classmates.[2]

His return to the status of lowly schoolboy was made

unmistakably clear to the young Himmler by the fact that his homeroom teacher for the *Sonderklasse* was none other than his father. This ensured that, though he could hope for special assistance at home and school, there would be no escape from the precise requirements of *Gymnasial* education. Konrektor Himmler prepared the class schedule and the personal records of the *Sonderklasse* students in the same rigid detail that he used for all his other classes. His all-consuming pedantry is revealed in the shorthand entry in his private records appearing under Heinrich's name: "Himmler, Heinrich. Father *Gymnasium Konrektor.* Left the eighth class, Landshut (after 7.10.1917) then *Hilfsdienst.* Since 2.1. *Fahnenjunker* in the 11th I.R. Certificate for the seventh class."[3] In the hands of a father-teacher with this kind of bureaucratic mania, Heinrich can have had no doubt of the status to which he had returned.

In the free time permitted by his heavy class load, Heinrich resumed the familiar interests and activities of his pre-army days. His closest friend was again Falk Zipperer, and the two young men spent much of their time writing poetry. Falk had a genuine poetic touch and his period of military service had helped him to develop his skill and broaden his interests. Following his return from the army a number of his poems were published in the local paper, and the samples of his work which he gave to Heinrich reveal a wide range of subjects and careful craftsmanship. A poem written in March 1919 begins:

> Frühling ist draussen und Sonne
> Und auf die Wiesen Blumen und Tau
> Und es lachen der herzigen Liebsten
> Schelmische Augen so leuchend und blau.*[4]

Heinrich's precisely written poems on the other hand seldom deviated from the theme of war. One poem of his, written about the same time as the lines by Falk quoted above, starts with the following lines:

---

*Spring is outside and sun
And in the meadows flowers and dew.
And the dearest love laughs,
Roguish eyes so shining and blue.[4]

Franzosen, Franzosen, O gebt nur recht acht
Für euch wird kein Pardon gemacht.
Uns're Kugeln pfeifen und sausen
Und verbreiten euch Schrecken und Grauen
Wenn wir da so unheimlich hausen.*[5]

Falk must have been remarkably kind about his friend's endeavors, for Heinrich wrote many verses and apparently never lost his enthusiasm.

Evening strolls, bicycle riding, and various games were among the other earlier pursuits which the young Himmler now resumed. And his interest in Luisa Hager continued, although apparently somewhat cooled by distance and differing pursuits. While in the army he had acquired some new friends and renewed some old acquaintanceships. He kept in touch with his cousin Ludwig Zahler, with whom he had worked in Regensburg. The Zahler family home was in Landshut, and while attending the *Technische Hochschule* in Munich during spring 1919 young Zahler became a close friend of Heinrich's brother Gebhard, who was a student in the same school. A combination of shared army and school experiences drew the three cousins closer together, but Heinrich, two years younger than either Gebhard or Lu, was the junior member of the triumvirate.[6]

In among his school load and his social activities Heinrich also managed some personal reading. He had a passion for adventure stories and was particularly taken with the works of Jules Verne. During the first nine months of 1919 he read twelve volumes of Verne's collected works, including *20,000 Leagues Under the Sea* and *Around the World in Eighty Days.* Near the end of his second term in the *Sonderklasse* he began to read the *Die Entstehung der Erde* (The origin of the earth) by M. Wilhelm Meyer, a late-nineteenth-century scientific popularizer. Meyer mixed together religion, scientific theory, and some of his own exotic notions, such as the suggestion that God had spread life through the universe by means of planets. On finishing this blend of imagination and religious and scientific orthodoxy Heinrich wrote:

---

*Frenchmen, Frenchmen, oh pay close attention
For there will be no pardon for you.
Our bullets will whistle and hiss
Spreading fright and terror among you
As we so sternly chop away.

"Highly interesting, rigidly scientific, philosophic, and religious."[7] Indeed, he was so impressed that he read it again two years later.

His satisfaction with Meyer's position highlights the effort he and his family were making to hold together the old value system which balanced the demands of the new science against the teachings of the church. Despite the chaos and confusion of the war era, which might have led to deep questioning of traditional values and beliefs, this effort was initially quite successful, and Heinrich clung to the old values, apparently untroubled by doubts.

Return to prewar Bavarian political conservatism was far more difficult. The war had upset the political balance at home and altered the form and tone of public life. Its disastrous conclusion, bringing in its train the collapse in the West and the revolution, threw into complete disarray what was left of conservative orthodoxy. Loyalty to the state now had to reconcile itself to the loss of the ruling house in both Bavaria and the German Empire. The conservative had somehow to find his place in a world dominated by the victorious Allies and in a republic dominated by liberals and Social Democrats.

The events of the immediate postwar period, especially the months during which Heinrich was a student in the *Sonderklasse*, graphically illustrated how difficult adjustment to the new situation would be. The six months from January to June 1919 saw the convening of the Paris Peace Conference, the drafting of peace terms which Germans viewed as monstrous, and the republican government's painful decision to sign the treaty. Inside Germany the elections to the constitutional assembly had produced an overwhelming victory for what came to be known as the Weimar coalition of Democrats, moderate Socialists, and the Catholic Center. The constitution that resulted was far too democratic for most conservatives. In Bavaria itself the revolutionary regime was crippled by election defeat and the assassination of its Socialist minister-president, Kurt Eisner; in the resulting confusion the radical Left seized the initiative and on April 6, 1919, proclaimed a Soviet republic in Munich.[8]

Events of this magnitude could not be walled out. Heinrich had already taken an interest in conservative politics while he was in Regensburg. When he returned to Landshut he worked hard to whip up support and recruit members for the conservative *Bayerische Volkspartei* (*BVP*), which he joined toward the end of 1918. For a month or so in late 1918 and early 1919 he corresponded with a young man who was active in party work in Regensburg. Gradually however, as the demands of school increased and the responses from Regensburg became chillier, his active work for the party petered out.[9]

Yet when he was back as a schoolboy, it was impossible for him to ignore the political life that was swirling around him. In early April, during the short vacation between semesters, he received a revealing letter from a fellow student, a rather pathetic little fellow named Adalbert Holzapfel who was suffering from a wartime nervous disorder and had gone home to a village near Rosenheim. The all-pervasive character of the political turmoil and the hostile reaction of Heinrich's circle to the trend of events are obvious in this letter. After the customary greetings, the writer chronicled the failings of the "Red government" and the terror of the "Communist-Spartacist bands" which were active in the neighborhood. He added that he would write an essay for Professor Himmler's Latin class and entitle it "The Ruin of Hannibal and Carthage: A Portrait of Germany's Present Situation."[10]

In mid-April events in Bavaria took a turn which touched Heinrich's political views and his vision of the future at their most sensitive point. A force of regular army units and paramilitary formations was being formed to overthrow the Soviet republic set up in Munich. In Landshut paramilitary organizations and *Freikorps** had existed since the end of the war, one of the major organizers being the pharmacist Gregor Strasser, who later became second in command in the Nazi party. In addition Captain Ernst Röhm, an extreme political activist in the army and subsequently Hitler's chief of the *Sturm Abteilungen* (*SA*), was stationed there at this time.[11] As long as the prospects for political intrigue and part-time soldiering had been dim, Professor Himmler had been able to prevent Heinrich from active participation. But when serious preparations for the attack on Munich began and there was a chance that the paramilitary units would be part of a regular army force, all Heinrich's old military dreams revived.

*Volunteer auxiliaries.

The overthrow of the hated Red regime was a goal with which Professor Himmler was strongly in sympathy. Even so, he did not want his son to throw over his educational program by taking a direct part in the forthcoming struggle. On April 26 the *Rektorat* of the *Gymnasium* prepared a certificate which stressed that Heinrich was a student in the *Sonderklasse*—a step which may have been intended to discourage any sudden impulse to enlist during the vacation. On April 30, the first day of the second term of the *Sonderklasse* and one day after the army units had started their advance on Munich, Heinrich was in his proper place in class.[12] To keep him out of all military activity, however, was impossible. At the end of April he joined the *Freikorps Landshut* and the reserve company of the *Freikorps Oberland.* During May and June, the last two months of the *Sonderklasse* course, he served in both free-corps units and became aid or deputy to the commander of the *Oberland* reserve company. His success in obtaining this position apparently convinced him that there was a real possibility of his resuming a regular army career through service in *Oberland,* even though relations between *Oberland* and the two dominant military figures in Bavaria, Generals Franz Ritter von Epp and Erich Ludendorff, were not very friendly.[13] What made the prospects of an army career seem favorable at this time were the preparations then underway to skirt around the Allies' demobilization orders by absorbing the forces used against the Munich revolutionaries into the regular army. Although Heinrich had not participated in the attack on Munich—the revolutionary regime collapsed after a brief struggle on May 1—the main units of *Oberland* had formed part of the attacking force. In mid-May he made a brief visit to Munich and may have explored the career possibilities while he was there. A month later he wrote to his old regiment requesting that his military records be forwarded to him because he was "joining the *Reichswehr* [regular army] in a few days."[14]

However, the few days passed and the coveted army career still did not materialize. Following the completion of the *Sonderklasse* at the end of June, Heinrich continued his service in the reserve company and carried on a lively correspondence with his friends in the *Oberland* unit serving in Munich. On August 26, however, when the free-corps units were ceremoniously received into the *Reichswehr,* the

Oberland reserve company was not included.[15] As on earlier occasions when Heinrich had sought a place in the army, he was defeated by a combination of parental reservations and his own bad timing.

His military dreams again thwarted and his *Gymnasium* education completed, young Himmler now had to make a basic decision regarding his future training and career. The decision he made (or, probably more accurately, the decision he made in conjunction with his parents) constitutes the most surprising and unpredictable turn in the course of his early life. He decided to train for a career in agriculture by working on a farm for a year or two and then enrolling in the agronomy program at the *Technische Hochschule* in Munich. A period of work as a *Praktikant* prior to classroom study was the accepted procedure in many technical courses. The surprising thing about Heinrich's decision is that he should have wanted to go into agriculture at all. None of the surviving documents contain any hint of his interest in agriculture prior to August 1919, although it should be noted that the documentation for this period is somewhat sparse. Agriculture was not an occupation that accorded well with the Himmlers' views on occupation and social status. It was dangerously close to a manual occupation, and the training program in agriculture was far removed indeed from the family's ideal of a humanistic education. Training in the physical sciences, even in engineering, carried more prestige than training in agriculture. Some idealization of the peasantry and life on the land may well have crept into Professor Himmler's romantic and conservative view of the social order, but, as is apparent from Heinrich's own earlier social attitudes, there had never been any question of associating with peasants.[16] A trained agronomist was certainly not a peasant, but the training as a *Praktikant* and some of the career possibilities would place Heinrich on the fringe of the social position which the Himmlers had considered right and proper. Perhaps Gebhard's earlier decision to abandon humanistic education in favor of a technical career (apparently engineering) and Ernsti's inclination toward applied science, which would subsequently also lead to engineering,* made the decision

*Ernst went on to become an engineer and collaborated on a book on radio jamming: Alfred Dennhardt and Ernst H. Himmler, *Leitfaden der Rundfunkentstörung.*

easier for the family to accept.[17] Yet Heinrich's decision to train for an agricultural career constitutes an abrupt and largely inexplicable break with his own earlier views and his family's ideas of social status.

Once the decision was made, Professor Himmler did his best to make sure that it was carried out as safely and respectably as possible. He had been appointed *Rektor* at the *Gymnasium* in Ingolstadt—a significant promotion from his position as *Konrektor* at Landshut—and planned to move the family there in the late summer of 1919. If Heinrich could do his *Praktikum* near the new family home, the Himmlers would find the situation more agreeable and some family supervision would be possible. An acquaintance, Karl Otto, brought the family into contact with Ökonomierat Winter who owned a sizeable farm in Oberhaunstadt, three kilometers north of Ingolstadt. After careful preparation, including apparently a trip by Heinrich to the farm on July 24, an agreement was concluded whereby he would work on Winter's farm for at least one year, beginning August 1. Heinrich seems to have been enthusiastic about the arrangements, and, as he had done on a previous occasion, spent the last week of July happily notifying relatives and friends of his new job and future plans.[18]

On August 1 he arrived at the farm on schedule and went to work almost immediately. The farm, which grew cereals, predominantly wheat and rye, was worked by a nucleus of regular farm laborers and harvest hands. In addition, there was another *Praktikant,* Joseph Strasser (a relative of the Karl Otto who had recommended Heinrich) who had some experience in farming and helped Heinrich find his way. Young Strasser's similar social background was as welcome to Heinrich as his assistance, and the two got on very well together.[19]

In his letters home Heinrich stressed that he enjoyed his work and that his fellow workers and the overseer were kind and helpful. At the same time he found the work very hard, and the detailed schedule, which he sent home three times during the first ten days, seems formidable enough: "Around 4 a.m. in the horse stall, then coffee at about 5:30. At 6 the real work begins. So far it has been sheaving grain. At 10:30 in the stall again. At 11:30 lunch. At 12:00 the work begins again, in the field or loading straw. 3-3:30 bread and beer, then work until 6:00. At 6 in the Stall. 6:30 dinner. Then to bed around 8:00."[20] For a city boy who had spent the last six months in school it was a grueling pace, and he adds ruefully that he was so tired on Sunday that he fell asleep in church. After a few days, he was happy to report that he had been relieved of his duties in the horse stall.[21]

Through it all, he remained in high spirits and stressed that, though the straw binding tended to fatigue even the most experienced workers, he welcomed it as an opportunity to build up his strength.[22] Perhaps his eagerness for hard physical work affords a clue to his reasons for choosing an agricultural career: it offered him a chance to overcome the feelings of inadequacy arising from his unathletic body and poor health. There is no question that throughout his life he was obsessed by the desire to achieve a fine physique and that he suffered acutely at any revelation of his softness and awkwardness.

If Heinrich moved to Oberhaunstadt primarily in order to attain physical strength, this did not mean that he was prepared to forego the assistance and comfort provided by his family. As in his army years, his letters were filled with lists of items he wanted his mother to send, including blankets, clothing and—above all—food. He admitted the food on the farm was good and the portions generous but pleaded with his mother to send what he called "goodies [*Gutterln*]"; and when a food package arrived his happiness knew no bounds. Sometimes he was embarrassed by his parents' continuous shipment of provisions and tried to send something home in exchange; on his father's name-day he sent a spray of wheat, rye, and barley as a ceremonial gift. But normally the only thing, aside from letters, that arrived from Oberhaunstadt was his dirty laundry.[23]

The Himmlers were not disturbed by his requests; Frau Himmler especially seized the opportunity to do something for him as a means to ease her concern. Both parents were somewhat doubtful about the whole venture and repeatedly requested detailed information about his workload, living conditions, and health. His stress on the amount and difficulty of his toil did little to reassure them, but he did take great pains to say that he was well, comfortable, and happy. More than once he chided his mother for her fears and begged her "not to read between the lines" of his letters.[24] Yet he could not completely break himself of his old wartime habit of describing all his little problems or stifle his need for contact with and support from his parents. Although he often noted that he was so busy that it was impossible for him to write, he sent home at least eight letters and cards during his first three and a half weeks on the farm.[25] Despite his resolve to be strong and independent, he was still a very young nineteen-year-old who wanted and needed a protective hand.

Within a month it became clear that the leap from *Gymnasium* student to field hand had been too abrupt. In the late afternoon of September 2 while following his accustomed work routine he became seriously ill. Through the next day and a half he tried to rest, but the combination of fever, fainting, and intestinal trouble got worse. During the night of September 4 he was taken to the hospital where tests revealed that he was suffering from paratyphus, a bacterial infection similar in many of its symptoms to typhoid fever but not as severe or dangerous. With due allowance for his enjoyment of the role of hospital patient, it is clear that he was seriously ill. He spent more than three weeks in the hospital. The doctors were able to get the disease under control in approximately ten days, however, and during the last part of his convalescence he was required to stay in the hospital only overnight.[26]

The first news of his illness and hospitalization reduced his mother almost to frenzy, partly because she was in the midst of preparations for moving to Ingolstadt and, understandably, somewhat on edge. Her worst fears were soon checked, however, because Rektor Himmler went to Ingolstadt ahead of his family and from September 7 on was able to visit Heinrich once or twice a day. With the dangerous phase of the illness soon over and direct contact with the family restored, Heinrich was able to lie back and enjoy the last part of his hospital stay. He rested, strolled in the garden, and often conversed with the colleagues and friends whom his father brought along on his visits. In between, he wrote letters, chiefly to his mother but also to close friends and relatives. Frau Himmler was spared none of the details about his condition and received current reports on his temperature, bowel movements, aches, and pains. While giving careful descriptions of his condition, interspersed with reassurances that he was fine and the food excellent, he also chided her for worrying. On September 9 he began his letter to her with three or four items of general interest, then added, "Now as to how it goes with me—I can see you, dear mother, fidgeting with impatience."[27]

The obvious pleasure that he derived from playing invalid could not completely obscure the unpleasant consequences of his illness. His condition precluded any prospect of continuing his *Praktikum* in the near future, and for reasons that are not clear on September 15 he severed his connections with the overseer in Oberhaunstadt after an unpleasant last conversation. In addition, although the paratyphus was cured, his general physical condition did not satisfy his doctors, and the possibility of more serious trouble emerged. On September 24, the day after Frau Himmler and Ernsti completed the family move to Ingolstadt, Heinrich went to Munich to be examined by Dr. Quenstedt, the doctor who had delivered him as a baby and treated him during his serious illness in Passau seventeen years earlier.* After the examination Quenstedt wrote his father that Heinrich had a hypertrophied (enlarged) heart due to overexertion during his military service. He added that, if Heinrich avoided strenuous activity for a year and restricted himself to light exercise, he would recover.[28]

Diagnoses of heart hypertrophy were very common following World War I, and the illness was usually attributed to wartime overexertion. Today most doctors scoff at this opinion and write off the whole episode as one of mistaken diagnosis. However that may be, it is certain that many of Heinrich's contemporaries were ill in the immediate postwar period; Falk Zipperer, for example, was recuperating in the mountains at the time that Heinrich was in hospital.[29] Whether all this physical disability was due to poor physical conditions and nervous strain, it is now impossible to say. The doctor in September 1919 claimed that Heinrich had a hypertrophied heart, and in consequence his parents anticipated trouble from this condition and remained anxious and protective throughout the following years. Current medical opinion suggests that in all probability there was nothing wrong with Heinrich's heart and that, aside from the consequences of wartime shortages and the need to recuperate from an illness, he was probably in reasonably good health. For Heinrich and his family, however, the

*Dr. Quenstedt had a long professional career. He was still listed as a practicing physician in the Munich Telephone Book for 1932.

diagnosis in the fall of 1919 was one more link in the chain that led from his childhood illnesses through his youthful frustrations in the army to his adult condition of nervous hypochondriac.

For the immediate future the Himmlers had to consider an alternative to the planned year of work on the farm. A possible course of action was to enroll Heinrich in the *Technische Hochschule* in October and defer the *Praktikum,* if he could, for another year. In the meantime he was to rest and as far as possible avoid physical strain.

The weeks in the hospital and the subsequent period of convalescence gave Heinrich an excellent opportunity for sustained reading, of which he took full advantage. Between August and mid-October he read a total of twenty-eight volumes, some of which he had started earlier and only finished off during this period.[30] Many of the books were probably chosen by his father, but it is not only the selection but also the comments which he jotted down about his reading that provide an excellent opportunity to assess his literary taste and his intellectual values. As might have been expected of a young convalescent, he read numerous adventure stories, including seven more works by Jules Verne. He also read a number of German classics, such as the second part of *Faust,* and works that in Bavaria had assumed the position of near classics, especially the popular tales of Maximilian Schmidt. There was a sprinkling of old-fashioned novels including Ottilie Wildermuth's *Frauenleben* (Women's lives), religious stories, and such collections of amusing trifles as Gustav Blumröder's *Geist und Welt bei Tische, humoristische Vorlesungen über Esskunst* (The spirit and world of the table, humorous lectures on the art of dining), which in view of Heinrich's love of food must have afforded him particular pleasure. Only one fairly current novel was included, Thomas Mann's *Königliche Hoheit* (Royal Highness), and he did not like it. "A novel that is terribly dull at the beginning but more exciting at the end. Too naturalistic,"[31] he noted. The remaining titles were concerned with World War I and the current political situation, and ranged from Henrietta Brey's sentimental *Mein Bruder bist du!* (You are my brother!), written for wounded soldiers in 1918, to Friedrich Wichtl's hate-filled tract, *Weltfreimauerei, Weltrevolution, Weltrepublik. Eine Untersuchung über Ursprung und Endziele des Weltkrieges*

(World Freemasonry, world revolution and a world republic: an investigation of the origin and purpose of the world war).[32]

Heinrich's comments reveal a mechanical reader, very deferent to the authority of the written word and completely convinced that good books are those that present important truths in a didactic manner. Often he describes books as "intellectual" and "educational" or vaguely expresses his feeling that a work is significant by noting that it is "worthy of recommendation."[33] His comment on Ludwig Aurbacher's *Volksbüchlein* (People's book) epitomizes his longing for significance in one short sentence: "Something one must read, [it] is part of an education."[34]

If a book expounded conventional moral lessons or patriotic sentiments, it automatically became significant. Regarding Brey's *Mein Bruder bist du!* he writes, "Moral, elevating, a book which a German must feel and understand."[35] He was somewhat uneasy about his love for adventure stories because they did not have obvious educational value. He did not write comments on each and every one of the weightier tomes he read; not a single one of the numerous Jules Verne stories received any comment at all. When he found an exciting book which included what he considered useful features, he was especially pleased. Commenting on Heinrich Schmidt's *Seeschlachten und Abenteuer* (Sea battles and adventures), he writes: "Very interesting and extremely exciting, but at the same time historically instructive."[36]

Not all of his comments are conventional and bland; he is very critical of what he considers dull fiction. Thomas Mann is criticized on this count as are the pious tales of Heinrich Federer which are stigmatized as "incomprehensible and dull" even though Heinrich usually enjoyed stories of Catholic piety.[37] He also finds fault with Ossian's *Fingal* and *Temora* because "the translation is too literal for prose," although he grants that they are "interesting." He makes no reference to the question of Ossian's authenticity.[38]

In the last part of September and the first part of October books about war and politics engaged more of his attention. Some of his comments reveal the degree to which he was still dominated by the moderate patriotic and conservative values of the prewar period. His enthusiasm for Brey's book is one example, and his comments on Schrott-Fiechtl's *Sonnseitige*

Menschen (People on the sunny side) illustrate the same commitment to traditional social morality. "An excellent novel of the Tyrol," he writes, "resolves the problem of the worker in an agrarian state very well. A lofty hymn to morality, work and religion."[39]

Yet there were also clear signs that under the impact of recent changes and the onrush of events he was having difficulty in applying the old values and was casting about for new ones. Wichtl's book on Freemasonry, published by the Pan-German Lehmann press, provided an intelligible bridge from the old to the new. Catholic authorities had long attacked Freemasons as anti-Catholic, liberal, and potentially subversive. Wichtl's book stressed the view that the Masons were republican revolutionaries, centered in England, who had engineered World War I as part of their plot to destroy monarchies. Its treatment of the subject was very anti-Semitic and portrayed Jews, Masons, and Democrats as the core of the revolutionary plot.* Wichtl made generous use of anti-Semitic anecdotes and carefully cited the anti-Semitic literature (including the *Protocols of the Wise Men of Zion*). Heinrich was impressed by the book, though he makes no mention of the specifics in Wichtl's argument. His comment reads, "A book that explains everything and tells us whom we must fight against next time."[40] This might suggest that he had already made the leap to a radical anti-Semitic position, but such an interpretation would probably overstate the case. The comment in question does not fit easily into the available space and may have been tucked in later. More important, it does not make clear whether Heinrich's hostility stopped at Freemasons or accepted Wichtl's argument and went on to embrace Jews and even the English. From some of his comments in late 1919 and 1920 it seems probable that he had not yet accepted the Jewish conspiracy doctrine although he was moving in that direction and harbored a considerable amount of conservative antipathy to Jews.

---

*A fascinating parallel to Wichtl's book is the work of an Englishwoman Nesta H. Webster, *Secret Societies and Subversive Movements,* originally published in the 1920s. This work equates Jews-Freemasons-revolutionaries and German nationalists, laying stress on the evil plots of Bavarian groups such as the *Einwohnerwehr* and the *Organization Escherich.* The latter were the very groups which found Wichtl's theory of an English-Jewish-Freemason-republican conspiracy most attractive. Incidentally, Heinrich Himmler later joined the *Einwohnerwehr* and enthusiastically read the publications of *Escherich.*

Item number 19 in his reading list provides a tantalizing hint that his explorations in this direction were in full swing. This item, which he read in mid-September, consisted of the first eight numbers of *Pro-Palästina Schriften* (Pro-Palestine papers), a series of Zionist pamphlets published in 1918 and 1919 and devoted to expounding the virtues of the Palestinian settlement, discussing the economic problems of Palestine, and exploring sensitive topics such as the movement of Eastern European Jews into Germany. To the despair of future investigators, Heinrich meticulously wrote down all the publication details of the series, including the address of the publishers—the "German Committee for the Encouragement of Jewish Settlement in Palestine"[41]—but made no comment on what he read.

In the absence of a definite statement of his position, it is impossible to say with certainty how far the radicalization of his political ideas had gone by the fall of 1919. It seems probable that he was exploring the theory of a Jewish conspiracy expounded by the radical Right, and that he found it attractive. His inclination in this direction should not be surprising. There had long been an undertone of anti-Semitism in Bavaria, especially in conservative circles, and during the war and the period immediately following the war anti-Semitic agitation had increased in both quantity and scurrility. For many conservative Catholics, the linking of the long-suspect Freemasons with a Jewish conspiracy occasioned little difficulty. Even more important, the idea of a Jewish conspiracy offered an explanation for all the defeats and the humiliations of recent years and provided a theory, or *Weltanschauung,* for those desperately seeking a means of dealing with prevailing conditions. Yet the very traditionalism that made it difficult for such individuals to accept the postwar situation also worked against any quick resolve to seize extreme solutions, even if these were logical developments of their conservatism.

Caution and a lack of willingness to break with the past were characteristic of Heinrich's personality and outlook. The whole pattern of his life was based on conventionality, on a desire to do the right thing and think the right thoughts. Now however he was at the crossroads between the old and the new. Just as he was uncertain which path to follow in his education and career, so also in the evolution of his thinking about the world around him he was pulled between the old ways in which he believed and the demand that he adopt new ways in place of those he knew and loved. In October 1919 all aspects of his life, from his reading habits to his occupational plans, were in a state of flux.

Chapter VI

The Student

On October 18, 1919, Heinrich visited Dr. Quenstedt who had been in consultation with other doctors concerning his case. Much to his patient's relief, Quenstedt's conclusion was that if he spent the year 1919-20 in study and deferred his *Praktikum* till later, he could continue his training for a career in agriculture. The doctor warned, however, that in the forthcoming year he should avoid becoming nervous and should restrict himself to moderate social activities, such as dancing. Heinrich was further encouraged by the fact that on the same day he completed his matriculation at the *Technische Hochschule.* With these two obstacles removed, he was able to escape from the limbo to which his illness had relegated him and prepare for a year of study.[1]

After a short stay at home in Ingolstadt he returned to Munich and on October 28 began his life as a student. A degree in agriculture called for six semesters at the *Technische Hochschule* plus a minimum of one year of *Praktikum.* The curriculum during the first year emphasized the physical sciences and included chemistry, physics, and botany. Many of these courses were offered by the University of Munich rather than the *Technische Hochscule.* Especially in the first year and to a lesser degree later Heinrich did much of his classroom work at the university.[2]

At the start Heinrich stayed with his brother in a room at Schellingstrasse 5. It was not until the end of November that he began to search out a place for himself, finally locating a room near the university at Amalienstrasse 28/4 which he kept until he began his *Praktikum* in summer 1920. He took his meals in the home of Frau Loritz, the widow of a singer, who offered board and in some cases residence, on a business basis, to students at Jägerstrasse 8, near the Odeons Platz. In company with her two daughters, Kaethe and Maja, Frau Loritz provided a well-chaperoned environment where students could have a homelike atmosphere and a chance to socialize while taking their meals.[3]

Within a week after his arrival, Heinrich, his brother Gebhard, and his cousin Ludwig Zahler joined the Fourteenth Alarm Company of the Twenty-first *Schützenbrigade,* one of the ready reserve units of the *Reichswehr* that had grown out of the attack on revolutionary Munich in the spring of 1919. Heinrich had the rank of *Fahnenjunker,* Gebhard that of *Fähnrich,* and Zahler that of *Fähnrich* or perhaps lieutenant. Like other units of the Twenty-first *Schützenbrigade,* the Fourteenth Alarm Company underwent weekend training sessions, including target practice, and kept in a state of readiness for emergencies. The unit could be placed on active service at a moment's notice, and its members were required to remain as much as possible in the Munich area. If they left, they had to secure a pass or leave beforehand and furnish an address where they could be contacted if the unit should be called into active service. At least twice in the year 1919-20 the company was placed on active duty and used to patrol the streets during periods when the authorities believed there was danger of revolutionary activity.[4]

The opportunity to be a student at two institutions of higher learning, and simultaneously to play the part of a soldier was the fulfillment of Heinrich's fondest dreams. He was proud of his status as a student and took advantage of his dual university and *Technische Hochschule* enrollment to involve himself in such activities as the *Allgemeiner Studenten Ausschuss* (General Student Committee) and the *Reichs Kriegsteilnehmer Verband* (Imperial War Veterans League). But the chance to be a soldier again, even if only on weekend training exercises, pleased him even more. "Today I have put the uniform on again," he wrote in his diary on December 1. "For me it is always the most precious clothing one can wear."[6] By building his life round the twin pillars of student status and part-time military service he was able to adjust to the outward demands of his new environment and, through the give-and-take with his fellow students, to strengthen his self-confidence.

The center of his social life was the Loritz home, where he went for meals and often stayed to meet and chat with people he knew and liked. Frau Loritz was the personification of traditional propriety, and the atmosphere of her home corresponded closely to the way of life Heinrich had enjoyed with his parents. The singer's widow valued "the finer things in life," and the cultural emphasis of the household was on good books, serious discussion, and impromptu music recitals. At the time Heinrich arrived in Munich his brother Gebhard was much attracted to the elder

Loritz daughter, Kaethe. She too was a pianist, and their joint interest in music was the basis for their budding romance. Ludwig Zahler, the cousin of the Himmlers, was also a frequent visitor to the Loritz home, and he and Kaethe's younger sister, Maja, were caught up in a similar romance. In the meantime Heinrich had an opportunity to develop his relations with Luisa Hager who was residing with her parents in Munich.[7]

Within a few weeks of Heinrich's joining the Loritz circle, however, a major realignment of romantic interests took place. The younger Himmler soon became disenchanted with Luisa Hager whom he found too introverted and immature, while Ludwig found his attention wandering from the younger Loritz girl to her elder sister. Kaethe responded warmly to this new interest, Gebhard was gradually eased out, and Heinrich turned his attention to Maja. These shifts in romantic interest produced changes in the individuals concerned. After Heinrich had overcome his initial reservations about Lu's conduct in the affair, he and Lu were drawn more closely together. The bonds between the Himmler brothers were correspondingly weakened, and Heinrich's earlier admiration and partial jealousy of Gebhard were largely replaced by criticism and veiled condescension. Gebhard gradually disappears from Heinrich's letters and diary, and his place as close confidant and companion is taken by Lu. Meanwhile the romantic side of the new alignment developed unevenly. For Kaethe and Lu the first stirrings of mutual interest gradually expanded into a full-scale romance, culminating in a courtship and secret engagement in the spring of 1920. Heinrich did not fare so well with Maja. He seems to have been genuinely taken with her, and for a few weeks his diary is filled with references to her. They read together hand in hand and exchanged a kiss or two, but by the end of the year 1919 it was clear that for Maja it was not very serious. When she left the city in January 1920 for a year of *Praktikum* as part of her own educational program, all prospects of a romance had faded.[8]

In his relations with people his own age Heinrich was self-conscious and wary of circumstances which might tear away his protective veil and show him as weak, awkward, or incapable. He assumed an outward posture of self-assurance that bordered on aggressiveness and nearly always tried to seize the initiative in conversations with his peers. Yet the difficulty of maintaining this stance gnawed away at him. He was frequently torn by self-doubt and had repeated periods of severe depression in which he despaired of himself and his future and snapped at friends and acquaintances. In the spring of 1920 his ill temper led to a long feud with his parents. The situation was so tense that Lu and Kaethe overlooked the moody carping which he directed at them and urged him to cheer up and at all costs to improve his relations with his parents.[9]

Although his inner torment was never completely stilled, he was strengthened by a second important element in his personality—faith in the effectiveness of will power and personal struggle. Frequently in the midst of one of his deepest depressions he would pick himself up by means of a mixture of piety and resolve to fight on to the end. Typical of this was the conclusion he reached as he reflected on the complications that had resulted from his break with Luisa: "God will direct everything to a good end. However, I will not weakly put myself at the mercy of fate, but will steer myself through the best way I can."[10] To endure rebuffs and disappointment and still keep struggling forward was his highest ideal. On viewing his first student duel, he noted characteristically, "It strengthens the nerves and one can thereby learn to take a wound calmly."[11] In his reading too he sought out edifying examples of those who had overcome obstacles and emerged victorious. On finishing Verner von Heidenstam's *Kampf und Tod Karls des Zwölften* (The struggle and death of Charles XII), he wrote: "The story of an iron man, who with his spirit and will power, wanted everything for his people and until his dying day drove them on to be heroes. A man such as we need so badly now."[12] The need for a "man of iron," patterned after Bismarck, was a common theme among conservatives at this time; but Heinrich's need was for a "man of iron" as a personal ideal to sustain him through his daily life.

The conflict between his self-doubt and his belief in will power modified some of the personality traits which he had manifested earlier. He still loved to "arrange things" and often cast himself in the role of the good fellow who solved other people's problems. The performance of minor good deeds, such as distributing "goodies" among friends or assisting drunken fellow students home from a party, gave him great satisfaction. He especially relished the opportunity to be the secret helpmate, as when he acted as clandestine ambassador between Kaethe and Lu at the time of their engagement.[13] In addition to enjoying the role of one who could get things done he was increasingly attracted by the picture of himself as a person who practiced self-sacrifice for the sake of others. In part, this was a consequence of his family's Catholic piety; he had often been encouraged by his parents to do good deeds for those in need. But when he was in his moods of deepest depression it was the vision of the hero who escaped from his problems through martyrdom which held his imagination. Once, after a long discussion with Gebhard and Lu of the fun they would have had if they had all fought in the army together, he noted morosely in his diary, "Perhaps then I would not exist now—one less fighting heart."[14]

His morbid moods were usually shortlived. But the desire to sacrifice himself for a great cause was never far from his thoughts. Increasingly he judged other people by the measure of their devotion and willingness to give of themselves. It was Maja's initial display of self-sacrifice in agreeing to copy some of his zoology notes that touched him most deeply, and in Rudolf Binding's *Der Opfergang* (The way of sacrifice) it was the heroine's "sensitive and all-pervading high ideal of sacrifice" that he found most worthy of comment.[15]

The strains of adjustment gradually altered some aspects of his personality and sometimes led him to lose himself in rather wild fantasies. But it would be a mistake to overemphasize the negative features of this process. By and large he adjusted to the life of a student quite well and preserved many of his distinctive personal traits. He was still deeply attracted by his family's secure and stable life and welcomed any opportunity to go home and rejoin that close circle. In part this was due to his overdependence on his parents and his irrepressible urge to look to them for the satisfaction of all his daily wants. Throughout the period he was in Munich his mother kept him supplied with clean laundry. In response to his requests, tobacco, "goodies," and even writing paper were mailed to him from Ingolstadt. He was always sure of a sympathetic hearing at home for his fears about his health, which now included the problem of his heart in addition to the earlier concern about his eyes and stomach. And his periodic outbursts of enthusiasm about a noteworthy meal struck a responsive chord in all the

Himmlers. But more important than the tangible benefits of family life was the inner peace that he usually enjoyed when he was with his parents. Such family traditions as the lighting of the Christmas tree and the exchange of presents touched him deeply and despite occasional family differences his diary and letters repeatedly speak of the happiness he felt when he could go home.[16]

His contentment with the old ways embodied in the life of his family was paralleled by his success in preserving in his daily life as a student many of the traditional relationships and social mores. Besides enjoying the conservative, bourgeois atmosphere of the Loritz home, he sought out and passed many hours with a number of old family friends in Munich. In contrast to most adolescents, he was able to relax in the company of adults; in fact, in many ways he felt more at home with members of the older generation than he did with his own peers. Some of the most enthusiastic comments in his diaries and letters are those connected with social calls on old friends of his father or periodic visits to his former nurse Thilda, who now lived in Munich and could be counted on for happy conversation, large pieces of cake, and a genuine interest in his activities. Well attuned to formal social life by his parents' careful training, he always strove to fulfill all the demands of propriety. When he first arrived in Munich and again when he was temporarily on active duty with the Fourteenth Alarm Company, the first thing he asked his mother to send was an ample supply of visiting cards.[17]

He fitted well into the formal routine that still prevailed in most of the social life of university students. Dr. Quenstedt had encouraged him to learn dancing as an activity appropriate to his supposed heart condition, and Heinrich recognized that it was also essential for the social milieu in which he would live. Initially he was apprehensive about revealing his awkwardness and was forced to confess that the first attempts were "disastrous."[18] Prodded on, however, by his own resolve to fight it through and by the careful coaching of his friends (Maja gave him instructions on the proper way to bow) he began to improve, and by the Christmas holidays he felt secure enough to use his new-found skill at parties. In the spring term he frequently went to dances and was pleased by the social assurance he had attained.[19]

His adjustment to student life was enhanced also by his

success in joining a fraternity. Three weeks after arriving in Munich he was accepted by the *Bund Apollo.* Though not one of the most select fraternities, this organization still enjoyed the reputation in the Munich area of being an old and well-regarded fraternity. It had just been designated a *Burschenschaft* (a type of fraternity whose prestige was equaled only by the Corps) and was part of the *Rothenburger Verband Schwarzer Verbindungen* which united fraternities from universities and *Technische Hochschulen* all over Germany. In the first months, as a mere *Fuchs* (pledge) Heinrich was allowed few of the privileges of membership and had to suffer the petty humiliations traditionally handed out to new members of student organizations. Although *Bund Apollo* was a dueling fraternity, a *Fuchs* was not allowed to take any part in dueling during his first semester, and it was only in the spring of 1920 that Heinrich began a period of training and practice in the traditional art of refined bloodletting.[20] Even then, he was not allowed to do any actual dueling, and it was not until he returned from his *Praktikum* in 1921-22 that he acquired the long-sought scars of fraternal battle.

As a *Fuchs,* he participated in the *Kneipen,* the periodic get-togethers devoted to speeches, songs, and vast quantities of beer, and in the *Mittagtische* (regular luncheons) of the fraternity which were held two or three times a month. In addition there were special *Füchsestunden* for the new members and a round of social outings sponsored by the *Bund,* consisting of dances, bowling nights, and short excursions to nearby resorts. Heinrich was eager to participate in all the meetings and social activities for which he was eligible and derived much pleasure and pride from his membership. Some of the older members of the *Bund* were privately amused by his exaggerated eagerness to prove himself as well as by his stiffness and his penchant for reciting old-fashioned poetry at *Kneipen.* But by and large he fitted in quite well and made some lasting friendships among his fraternity brothers.[21]

That he felt at home in this particular fraternity was not surprising, for it numbered among its members and *Alte Herren* (alumni) many representatives of families closely tied to *Gymnasium* instruction. Among them were one of the Dicknethers, Professor Rauschmayer, and other family friends; and Professor Himmler himself had been a member during his university days and was still an active *Alter Herr*. Heinrich's status as a second-generation member of Apollo and close relations with many of its alumni and senior members facilitated his acceptance and gave him a feeling that in this most traditional of all German academic institutions he really belonged.[22]

Outside the *Bund* also the social contacts he made in consequence of his father's past and present positions made his path smoother. He made new contacts through his father's post in Ingolstadt, and the children of many of his father's colleagues were among his fellow students at the university and *Technische Hochschule* in Munich. And over and above all this he had a large number of acquaintances among his own former classmates in Munich and Landshut. Rarely did he go to a party or dance that he did not come upon some former school friend or family acquaintance. His old companion Falk Zipperer was in Munich too, and on occasion the two boys resumed their poetic endeavors. The presence of so many familiar faces made it easier for him to feel at home and to avoid pangs of anxiety and loneliness.[23]

Yet there were many evenings when the Loritz family and his brother Gebhard, all of whom were members of another student group, the *Akademische Gesang Verein,* went off together to a dance or concert and Heinrich was left alone to study and brood about himself and his future. During his whole first year as a student, in the quiet moments that he had to himself he came back again and again to the question of what was to become of him. Despite his general success in keeping his frustrations under control and finding a pleasant social niche, he relapsed repeatedly into anxiety about what lay ahead of him.

One of the major causes of his worry was money. The inflation which had started during the war years progressed by fits and starts, and Professor Himmler's fixed income was beginning to show the strain. Burdened with the expense of putting three boys through a higher education, both the professor and his wife were becoming more exacting about the money that Heinrich and Gebhard spent while away from home. The boys were required to keep detailed records of their expenditures, and their requests for extra money encountered increasing resistance. In spring 1920 Heinrich paid his tuition in six small installments. This may have been due to a shortage of ready cash. At the same time he took a part-time job as a teacher's aid in the writing program of the *Akademische Arbeiterkurse,* a special education program which offered secondary school education to members of the lower classes. His need of money may have been as important a motive as the desire to do something for the working class.[24]

More significant than the temporary inconvenience which resulted from the tightened money situation was his rising apprehension about whether there would be enough money to see him through the next three years of his education. The inflation struck at the heart of the security and self-confidence of members of the professional middle class by revealing how dependent they were on forces they could not control and often did not understand. But if the ground was shaky under the feet of middle-class adults, their adolescent offspring were even more sharply threatened; should the money for their education fail, they ran the risk of falling permanently out of their proper class and finding themselves helpless in an unaccustomed world of impoverishment and uncertainty.

Heinrich's apprehension about the future was indirectly heightened by his worry and confusion regarding sex. Puritanical as he was, he repeatedly voiced his devotion to the ideal of sexual abstinence and ardently sought a formal friendship with a girl in order to mask his own self-doubt. On the one hand he wanted the security of a long, formal courtship, on the other he was afraid that, if he actually became serious about a girl, it might lead to early marriage and thus rule out any possibility of the extended training necessary for a successful career. After his disappointing romances with Luisa Hager and Maja Loritz he was more on guard against close relations with girls. He put on the armor of politeness and avoided going beyond amenities or discussions of the characteristics of the ideal woman or of the differences between males and females.[25]

Underneath this social veneer he was bothered by his own developing sex drive and his first encounters with people who had a freer attitude toward sexual relations. His ignorance about sex heightened both his interest and his fears. He was inclined to seek enlightenment through books and guarded discussions with his friends. One night he and a fellow student were approached by a prostitute on their way home. The description of the incident given in his diary is quick to point out that her efforts were "of course without success" but adds "the incident was very interesting however."[26] In his reading he sought examples of chaste relations between young men and women and of models of female virtue. If he found them, he was ready to put aside all doubts in order to draw inspiration from what he read. Ludwig Finckh's *Der Rosen Doktor* stressed that the author was a radical democrat, a fact that would usually have called Heinrich's critical faculties into play; but since it painted a picture of a happy young couple who scrupulously avoided any immorality, he was overjoyed by it. "A book full of high ideals," he comments, "great, often only too valid truths. A lofty hymn, a well-warranted lofty hymn to women. I was satisfied as I have not been for a long time."[27]

Other books disturbed him and inclined him to reexamine some of his attitudes. When he finished Margarete Böhme's *Tagebuch einer Verlorenen* (Diary of a lost soul), a rather farfetched exposé of the plight of a prostitute, his comment shows some doubts about the scorn he usually poured on those who had wandered from the path of virtue. "A book that gives one a glimpse of the frightful fate of people," he writes, "and leads one to look at many prostitutes from a very different point of view."[28] Yet it was not to encounter new ideas or fresh doubts that he sought books on sex but to find encouragement in his effort to maintain the established code. His greatest success came when he read Hans Wegener's *Wir jungen Männer, das Sexuelle Problem des gebildeten jungen Mannes vor der Ehe* (We young men: the sexual problem of the educated young man prior to marriage), an appeal for male chastity aimed at young men of Heinrich's class and age. Wegener based his case on the physical and personality damage that allegedly arose from promiscuity rather than on the authority of religious commandments. Heinrich raced through the book in two days and received so much solace from it that he failed to note the absence of his favorite religious and moral arguments. His comments exude pleasure and increased confidence: "A book of the highest ideals. Elevated but rich and surely right. Certainly the most beautiful book that I have read on this question."[29]

Despite the temporary support that he gained from his reading, he was still plagued by doubts; and when he stumbled on some unfamiliar aspect of sexual life, such as homosexuality, he sank to new depths of confusion and near despair. On a Sunday evening in March 1920 he picked up Oscar Wilde's short defense of homosexuality *The Priest and the Acolyte,* and the result was devastating. His brief comment shows his shocked disapproval: "An idealization of homosexual men. Awful pictures." In addition he notes, "10:30 at night, I'm in a dreadful mood."[30]

In his internal struggle over sex, marriage, and the future he tried to gain security by abiding by the teachings of the church and holding firmly to his religious faith. But here again problems arose from the new situations which he confronted as a student, and he fell into periods of religious doubt. The major threat to his faith did not come from any uncertainties about the compatibility of religion and the scientific lessons he was receiving; far from being tempted by philosophical materialism, he viewed the scientific picture of life in the universe as the detailed record of God's design. It was as a result of his social life that he experienced his first religious uncertainty. He was concerned lest fraternity dueling might conflict with the teachings of the church. Since his membership in Apollo was very important to him, he was seriously troubled. A short sermon he heard on the day after Christmas 1919 during a celebration in a Catholic club in Ingolstadt brought these doubts to a head: "During the sermon I had to endure an inner struggle more serious than any before. The dueling business constantly keeps cropping up. In the evening I prayed. I had, of course, earlier partly overcome it. God will continue to help me to overcome my doubts."[31]

Heinrich's religious struggle over dueling seems inconsistent with some of his other activities. Faced with a similar, if potentially much more serious conflict of belief when he went into the army, he had easily reconciled the demands of war with his religious faith. Moreover a letter to his parents while he was on duty in the Fourteenth Alarm Company in spring 1920, written on his return from a patrol through Munich in an armoured car at the time of the Kapp-Lüttwitz *Putsch** shows that he was still free from religious doubts about his army service. "This morning we had a military church service which was very nice," he writes. General absolution and the Communion for the three of us [Heinrich, Gebhard, and Lu]."[32] On the basis of the available

*An abortive effort by conservative army and civilian groups to overthrow the Weimar Republic.

evidence it is impossible to explain how he could have been free from doubt when he might have to kill and still be severely troubled by the prospect of dueling which left scars but rarely produced serious injury. Yet it would be a mistake to regard Heinrich's religious struggle on this score as silly. It is clear that he was upset by what he saw as conflicting obligations to his fraternity and his faith. Only very gradually, after much inner soul-searching and after reassuring talks with his father, was he able to free himself from his torment and feel completely at ease in the *Bund.*[33]

The depth of his anguish while torn by religious doubt reveals how important his faith was to him. He not only attended church regularly and tried to observe the moral commandments of his religion but he frequently sought help and comfort in prayer. His faith was his most important support in meeting daily problems and enduring inner struggles. In times of distress he would call out for support, "Turbulent is the heart, until it rests in Thee O Lord." Often he recovered his resolve only because he believed that his cry had been answered and felt that "God will continue to help me."[34] Yet neither his personal anxieties nor his faith completely submerged his critical faculty. He still enjoyed pious stories such as Sienkiewicz's *Ihm lasst uns folgen* (Let us follow Him) and tales of World War I which combined loyal army service with religious faith.[35] But he was alert for signs of proreligious bias in descriptive writing and his comments criticize works which he considers to be "too one-sidedly Christian" or as having a "one-sidedly Catholic point of view."[36]

In political matters too he was becoming more critical of the position of the church. He was, for example, highly incensed by the disparaging remarks about Prussia he heard in a sermon delivered at Ingolstadt. More important, he was disillusioned with the activities of the *Bayerische Volkspartei* (*BVP*), especially with the indications that in the dark days after the war the *BVP* had toyed with the idea of separating Bavaria from the rest of Germany. Since the *BVP* was closely tied to the church, occupying the position held by the Catholic Center Party in the rest of the Reich, he found himself in opposition to the political position of most orthodox Catholics, including his parents.[37]

Alienation from conservative political Catholicism was merely one aspect of Heinrich's gradual movement during this year in the direction of rightwing radicalism. His political evolution, like his religious doubts and his problems concerning sex and inflation, tended to make him apprehensive about the future and uncertain in his adjustment to student life. He still held conservative and rather optimistic opinions about the rightness of the social order. Even from so biting a denunciation of the social system as Ibsen's *Pillars of Society* he could draw a cheerful moral. "Shows the lies and deceptions on which society is built," he writes but then adds, "However, it also shows the good that exists in society which comes to the surface and is victorious in some individuals."[38]

The immediate political developments, however, troubled him. During the year 1919-20, in an attempt to enforce the conditions of the Versailles settlement, the Allies were demanding that the German armed forces be trimmed and that plebiscites be held in Schleswig and Upper Silesia. These pressures aroused bitter opposition in Germany. At the same time the republican government was making little headway against the problems of defeat, inflation, and popular dissatisfaction with the postwar world. Spring 1920 saw the rightist Kapp-Lüttwitz *Putsch;* shortly after its suppression disorders occurred in the Ruhr which most conservatives viewed as the first stirrings of another communist or Spartacist attempt to seize power. In the general elections in June the moderate parties in the coalition lost heavily, and the newly formed government made a clear, if modest, move to the Right.

Heinrich carefully followed the newspaper accounts of these events and made a large collection of clippings, with heavy emphasis on articles that described German humiliations and the failures of the existing government. From time to time he was overcome by foreboding. On November 4 he notes in his diary: "In the evening we were in the back room. I was awfully serious and depressed. I believe very bad times are coming, or does it mean something else? "[39] Usually the hope that the day of reckoning with Germany's enemies was approaching and that he would be able to take part in it helped him to snap back. "Perhaps in a few years I'll be involved in war and struggle," he writes on November 14. "I'd be so happy with a war of liberation, and would go along if I can still move a limb."[40] His scorn for Germany's enemies was unbounded. Even *Die Kreuzritter*

(The Crusaders) by Sienkiewicz, a Catholic writer whom he liked, did not escape his wrath; " . . . seen through the eyes of Polish arrogance and rage," he comments. "The Poles painted in white and the Germans in black."[41]

His service with the Fourteenth Alarm Company kept his military enthusiasms alive and sharpened his fears about the internal threats to Germany's future, for whenever the authorities became apprehensive they placed the company on active service. He believed all reports of imminent danger and dutifully passed them on to his parents. In a letter home on March 3 he wrote: "At the start of next week the danger of a general strike is *very great.* * . . . The general feeling prevails however that the Bolsheviks, even if they don't rise up this time, will raise their heads in a month or two and then it will come to a bloody and hard struggle."[42] His belief in an immediate showdown combined with his love of soldiering to lessen his doubts about serving a government which he found too liberal and not sufficiently devoted to the nationalistic cause. On March 24, when the Alarm Company was on duty once more because of the Kapp-Lüttwitz *Putsch,* Gebhard, Heinrich, and Lu wrote a joint letter to the Himmlers in Ingolstadt. Gebhard was at great pains to make clear that he was sorry they were missing Easter at home and explained that the military authorities would not let them go. Lu added a couple of lines, filled with joking thanks for his share of a box of "goodies" that Frau Himmler had sent. But Heinrich, who had virtually no sense of humor, was not about to joke or make others responsible for his situation. His contribution to the joint letter read: "Dearest Parents. I also send you the most loving greetings. I remain here because I believe it is my absolute sacred duty to do so. Your Heinrich."[43]

His sense of duty and his dislike of the republican regime forced him to walk a narrow path between service and opposition. In January 1920 he took part in a mass demonstration at the University of Munich to protest the death sentence passed on Count Anton Arco-Valley, the rightwing assassin of Kurt Eisner. He was also involved in a nebulous plan for military action if Arco-Valley were not reprieved. To his father he wrote that Professor Himmler would have been proud of the patriotism shown by the student demonstrators, but in his diary, after noting that the

---

*Underlined in original.

government had reprieved Arco-Valley and thus eliminated any chance for military action or a coup, he commented sadly, "Well, then some other time."[44]

His military ardor helped to paper over his doubts about serving the regime, but it did not prevent a gradual radicalization of his political ideas. He was convinced of German greatness, present frustrations and humiliations notwithstanding, and he had no patience with peaceful or pacifist sentiments. After reading Bertha von Suttner's pacifist novel *Die Waffen nieder!* (Ground arms!) he describes the heroine as "an hysterical woman" and adds that the book "disgusted" him.[45] But it was in his attitude to anti-Freemason and anti-Semitic sentiments that the change was most apparent. In December 1919 he read Albert L. Daiber's pamphlet *Elf Jahre Freimaurer!* (Eleven years a Freemason!), hoping apparently to find more evidence of a secret plot involving Masons and Jews. His disappointment when he discovered that Daiber considered the Masons silly rather than dangerous is evident in his comments. "A book that doesn't reveal anything especially new about Masonry and portrays it as frightfully (*furchtbar*) harmless," he writes, and then adds, "I might seriously doubt from which side the book was written."[46] In his reading of fiction he showed increased receptivity to anti-Semitic stereotypes. Concerning Friedrich Spielhagen's nineteenth-century novel *Ultimo* which featured an unscrupulous and evil Jewish banker he notes: "Certainly not a worthless novel. It shows many experiences of life and characterized the Jews very well."[47]

A discussion about "Jews" is mentioned in Heinrich's diary in December 1919.[48] And a letter from Lu, written in September 1920, suggests that there were other such incidents. Lu writes that he has obtained a copy of Wilhelm Meister's *Judas Schuldbuch* (Book of Jewish guilt), a chronicle of the supposed racial characteristics and misdeeds of Jews which the anti-Semitic (later Nazi) press *Deutscher Volksverlag* issued in many editions in the immediate postwar years. He also notes that he has "long been interested" in it and that he has "discussed this book with you [Heinrich] once in Munich."[49] This constitutes a rather important indication of young Himmler's mood and the tone of his discussions at this time. He himself did not read the book until a year and a half later.[50] He was, however, obviously playing with the idea of a Jewish scapegoat, then very popular in young conservative circles, and in the process was absorbing increasingly anti-Semitic attitudes. But he had not yet made the leap to complete acceptance.

Where he stood by April 1920 is revealed most clearly in his comments on Arthur Dinter's novel *Die Sünde wider das Blut* (The sin against the blood), a classic of racial anti-Semitism which contained a long appendix of documents for the reader's further enlightenment. Heinrich's notes on the book read: "A book that introduces one to the Jewish question with shocking clarity and causes one to approach this situation with extreme distrust. However, at the same time [it inclines one] to investigate the documents on which the novel is based. Then the middle way may truly be the right one. I believe the author is blinded by his rage against the Jews. The novel is a purely polemical novel, with anti-Semitic lectures."[51] He was held back by his conservatism and his belief in academic caution, although there is no indication that he ever actually investigated Dinter's sources. The appeal of Dinter's message was obviously very strong, and Heinrich's suspicion of fanaticism and vulgarity was a fragile defense against the rising tide of radical anti-Semitism.

In view of his increasingly difficult struggle to maintain an orthodox conservatism in politics, of the pressure on other aspects of his value system, and of his own personal torment, it is not surprising that Heinrich was frequently tempted to throw up his hands and flee. From the time he first arrived in Munich, he had tried to learn the Russian language, not because it was required in his course of study (he had already filled his language requirements) but because he had a plan to emigrate to the East and become a farmer. His study and his eagerness to find a girl friend were intertwined in his mind with the notion of leaving Germany and going to Russia, which, although still in the midst of the Red-White struggle, seemed to offer prospects for a farmer. In one of his early moods of depression he noted in his diary: "At the moment I don't know why I am working. I work because it is my duty, because I find peace in work, and for my German life's companion with whom one day in the East I'll live and fight through my life as a German, far from dear Germany."[52] A month later, when his chances with Maja looked dim, he wrote: "Today, inside myself, I have cut loose from everyone and now depend on myself alone. If I don't find a girl whose character suits mine and who loves me, I'll go to Russia alone."[53]

His dream of life in Russia was not the only indication that he longed to escape. Despite his sense of duty and the joy of serving as a part-time soldier, he had not surrendered the hope of someday obtaining a commission and going off to war. He followed the lure of military service wherever it led. When in late spring 1920 the Allies forced the Reich government to dissolve the *Schützenbrigade,* including the Fourteenth Alarm Company, Heinrich immediately joined the *Einwohnerwehr,* Bavaria's newest device to escape the disarmament clauses of the treaty. He also became a member of the *Schützengesellschaft Freiweg,* one of the numerous groupings of former military men who continued to undergo military training and to plan for the day when the state or the cause of German liberation, would require their services once more. No opportunity, no matter how remote, to advance his military prospects escaped his attention. The first time the Fourteenth Alarm Company was placed on active service he went immediately to the War Ministry "in uniform." Apparently he was trying to get someone to listen to his request for the rank of *Fähnrich* and thus finally to attain the status of junior commissioned officer.[54]

The important goal, however, was not the mere attainment of the commission but the chance to participate as an officer in a renewal of hostilities and thus escape from his existing situation. His diary notes abound with expressions of his hope that soon there will be a "war of liberation" or "another war" and that he will be able to take part.[55] A letter to his parents written during the 1920 spring vacation explains that there is a good chance of action in the immediate future and adds: "If the thing breaks out right away it would be great. If it doesn't I'll come home and then return to school here and work and study with all my might."[56] Apparently his parents were becoming weary of his military dreams and feared that his studies were suffering.

Yet Heinrich's military activity and the perennial attraction of war were more than a youthful diversion. He had tried hard to adjust to the conventional life of a student, joining the right groups, reading the proper books, participating in *Fasching* (pre-Lenten) parties, and dutifully studying. But the drastically different world situation coupled with his own inner confusion and torment robbed him of the confidence and sense of security that he needed to carry on with the game. Throughout his first year as a student discouragement and confusion alternated with the desire to escape; if he had been forced to continue on through the established sequence of study, in the end he would very probably have broken or run away.

He was saved by his unfailing knack of looking out for his own interest and his well-developed talent for courting the right people and achieving what he wanted. In a series of petitions he convinced the officials of the *Technische Hochschule* that because he was a veteran he should be exempted from some of the requirements of the program and should be allowed to take his preparatory examinations early. He was also permitted to register for courses during the same period in the school year 1920-21 in which he planned to take his *Praktikum.* These special arrangements would enable him to complete the six-semester degree program and the required year of *Praktikum* in three years.[57] The only problem that remained was the need to find a pleasant and not-too-demanding location for his *Praktikum.* Characteristically, he began early in 1920 to sound out associates of his father. Then he received a bonanza from an unexpected source. Some Loritz family relatives by the name of Rehrl operated a farm at Fridolfing, near the Himmlers' old summer home in Tittmoning and adjacent to the Austrian border. Frau Loritz consented to act as intermediary with the Rehrls and, after brief negotiations and a pair of short inspection trips by Heinrich, arrangements for his *Praktikum,* beginning September 1, were completed.[58]

The circumstances surrounding Heinrich's *Praktikum* with the Rehrls were ideal for everyone concerned. The Himmler family was assured by Herr Rehrl that the workload would not be strenuous and reassured by the location of the farm at Fridolfing, close to many family friends. Herr Rehrl was guaranteed a hard-working, reliable young farmer who would work for room and board. Heinrich himself stood to benefit even more: the family atmosphere promised to be congenial, his workload would allow ample time for study, and Herr Rehrl assured him that he would gain experience in many aspects of farming. But above all else the *Praktikum* meant escape from his discouraging and tormented life as a student. At Fridolfing he would not be subject to the constant demands of social life or under pressure to determine who he was and where he was going. Perhaps, with a quiet year "in the country," these questions would take care of themselves.

Chapter VII

The Young Farmer

Throughout the last weeks of August 1920 Heinrich eagerly prepared for his departure from Munich. He said goodbye to relatives and old friends and visited points of interest in the city, as if he were about to embark upon the Grand Tour. In his eyes, the year of *Praktikum* was no burden, it was an opportunity to escape to high adventure. His excitement was enhanced by the acquisition of a motorbike, of which he was extremely proud. The Himmlers apparently hoped this machine would lessen some of the expense of the *Praktikum,* but Heinrich saw it as a passport to freedom and exploration.[1]

In the first week of September he pulled on a heavy pack, mounted his motorbike, and headed for his new life in Fridolfing. Much to his joy, he encountered a severe storm and was forced to fight his way through pounding rain and flooded roads. As he gleefully reported to friends and relatives, he was advised not to travel at night because the flooding was dangerous and he did not know the roads. But he pushed ahead anyway and finally reached Fridolfing, like a motorized Columbus, drenched but happy.[2]

Once on the farm, he immediately plunged into the role of child of nature. "Realize," states a letter to his parents written soon after his arrival, "that it is a year in which nerves and soul can be rested in nature and in the seriousness and joy of the agricultural life. Where the body will be strengthened by a precious peace and made tougher through hard work. . . ."[3] His picture of himself was pretentious, but he wanted to believe it, and with all the enthusiasm of his twenty years he did everything he could to make it true. He liked the work and sent Lu and Kaethe as well as his mother detailed descriptions of his labors. As in the previous year at Oberhaunstadt, he reached Fridolfing during the harvest season, and much of his time was spent shocking and binding grain.[4]

Rehrl's farm comprised a modest 120 acres and required diversified work and much improvisation at this time of year. Heinrich was often busy running farm machinery and in addition had to tackle special tasks such as redirecting an irrigation ditch to prevent flooding. He also worked at Rehrl's small mill, sacking and hauling bags of flour and doing other tedious chores, as well as gaining experience in mill operation.[5]

He liked Rehrl, whom he described as a kindly man, "extremely well informed . . . on all subjects. A man such as one finds so rarely today,"[6] and spent long hours with him, discussing the details of farm management and the state of the world. Over and over again his letters mention that the Rehrls treat him as part of the family. He enjoyed participating in their daily activities, took his meals with them, and often spent the evenings in their home reading, talking, or playing cards. His living quarters, however, were in an outbuilding, where he could enjoy some privacy. Frau Rehrl did his laundry, and Heinrich reported to his mother that his clothes were returned in "perfect" condition. Frau Himmler may have been a little chagrined that her son no longer required some of her skills, but she cannot but have been reassured by his description of the food as "excellent and abundant" and of his room as "cozy" and warm.[7]

Heinrich had some hard work to do, but his circumstances were akin to those of a young gentleman. He was not required to perform routine or unpleasant tasks, such as cleaning the stable. A cleaning woman, paid for by his parents, took care of his room, and he had no housekeeping chores to do in the Rehrl household. Occasionally he assisted Frau Rehrl when she was preparing for an important social event—for example, he helped her set the table for her daughter's wedding dinner—but this merely illustrated the degree to which he had been accepted into the family circle. In the field labor Rehrl made certain that he did not overstrain himself or remain on any task to the point of tedium. Heinrich was able to assure his parents that he was busy but not overworked and that his health was excellent. His closest approach to illness was a struggle with hay fever in the summer of 1921, but this did not seriously impede his work.[8]

Heinrich's enjoyment of country life went beyond his interest in the work of the farm and his feeling that he was part of the Rehrl family. The social life of the Rehrls involved him in the simple, old-fashioned diversions which still prevailed in country districts. He was closer to the way of life which he had known as a child, a way of life which those who found fault with the conditions and governmental system of republican Germany were coming to idealize as "the good old days." The simple traditionalism gave Heinrich great pleasure and the opportunity to rid himself of much of the tension and foreboding that had developed during his year in Munich.

Herr Rehrl took Heinrich with him wherever he went. They visited exhibitions of local fruits and vegetables, attended performances of a neighborhood theater group, and even went to the sessions of the local historical association. Since Herr Rehrl was a member of a singing club, Heinrich joined too, though his voice was somewhat shaky so that, when he wrote to his parents that he had also joined the church choir, he asked them not to laugh. He conscientiously attended the club's practice sessions, took part in its performances, and as he had done earlier in the *Bund Apollo,* seized the opportunity it offered to recite poetry. The pastoral poems of Karl Stieler and others he chose for these occasions reflected the interests of the audience as well as his own enjoyment of the simple, homely poetry of an earlier generation.[9] In spring he joined Herr Rehrl on long walks through the countryside. Sometimes they went hunting or fishing together—outings which were quickly followed by reassurances to his parents that he was perfectly safe and there was no danger that he would be shot or get lost in the woods.[10]

His interest in peasant traditions seems to have been strengthened by his experience in Fridolfing. He took more note of peasant customs and collected local songs and sayings, which he promised to share with his father when he returned to Ingolstadt. The appeal of peasant life, however, never broke down his consciousness of class and social distance, nor did it mean that he could forsake his background as an academically trained observer. His basic approach is reflected in his comment on Jeremias Gotthelf's *Uli der Knecht,* an early nineteenth-century account of peasant life which his father had obtained for him: "An excellent book on the characteristics of the peasant mind. One should read it more than once. Especially as an agriculturalist, one can get a lot from it."[11]

His devotion to correct form and traditional mores also seems to have been reinforced by his experiences in Fridolfing. He was especially anxious that his mother fulfill the demands of gracious propriety when Frau Rehrl visited Ingolstadt. The prospect of missing his family's Christmas celebration filled him with such gloom that he finally decided to go to Ingolstadt for the holidays. Later he was disturbed that he could not participate in a *Fasching* party at the Loritz home, which he had greatly enjoyed the year before. His desire to be a part of these festivities arose from something more than mere homesickness; it was due to the strong appeal that established ways held for him. His letters home were full of questions about the activities of *Bund Apollo* and its members and rarely failed to request his parents transmit his greetings to "the fraternity brothers in Ingolstadt" although he was not on particularly friendly terms with any of them.[12]

Similarly, upon receiving news that enrollment in the Ingolstadt *Gymnasium* had sharply increased he wrote his father that this made him "very happy" because "it will show the gentlemen of the *Realschule* that they cannot say that humanism is one of those aged and too-conservative things that is destined to die."[13] This opinion was no mere gesture in his father's direction; it was an expression of his own devotion to the "good old days," even though his own occupational goals had led him in a different direction.

Heinrich also found great pleasure in the country church. He regularly attended mass and sang in the church choir. Confession and communion were important events in his life, and he frequently mentioned them in his letters to his parents. On his short sightseeing trips he visited important churches, as he had done with the family during his childhood vacations. In one letter describing to his mother a trip which he had made to Salzburg he starts to recount the places he has visited but finally gives up the attempt and merely notes that he has seen "lots of churches."[14] He read more religious books than he had while he was in Munich and devoted particular attention to the works of the popular prewar Catholic apologist Conrad von Bolanden. His comments on these works show his gratitude for new arguments to support his faith and for an "edifying hymn to Christianity."[15] His serious torment about his faith had largely disappeared, and he could note shortcomings in the church, such as the low quality of local sermons, without feeling personally threatened. In his reading, even though he seized on points that would strengthen his belief, he did not hesitate to attack arguments which he found doubtful. After granting that Bolanden's *Wider Kaiser und Reich* (Against Kaiser and Reich) is "a very good apology," he adds that it is "too polemical. I doubt that the Protestant religion is so lacking in content, for if that was so, it would not have been able to last through the centuries. On the contrary it must have good ingredients, but Bolanden won't credit Protestantism with anything good. We should be happy when this grave division is healed." [16]

His increasing self-satisfaction and the pleasantness of his life in Fridolfing did not lead him to curl up in isolated contentment. It was as if his new life had set him free and emboldened him to recover his earlier mood of activity. Armed with a new inner peace and his motorbike, he bustled around the Fridolfing area calling on old friends and making new acquaintances. He often went to Tittmoning to visit the Lindners, a family he had known intimately during the Himmlers' prewar vacations there. He also frequently visited two married members of *Bund Apollo* who had completed their schooling and were now employed close to Fridolfing. Bundesbruder Rind, a veterinarian residing near Tittmoning, was especially friendly, and Heinrich spent many evenings with his family. From time to time Georg Schorskl, a fellow student whose home was also in Ingolstadt, came to visit him on the farm and usually stayed a few days. The two young men would wander through the countryside or make short excursions, while Schorskl filled in Heinrich on all the news and gossip from Munich. In addition young Himmler was kept in touch with events through the steady stream of letters he received from Lu and Kaethe and the news he got from the Rehrls who were in direct communication with the Loritz family. [17]

His motorbike allowed Heinrich to extend his journeys and social contacts beyond the immediate neighborhood. Three or four times during the year he went to Munich for short stays, ostensibly to take care of business at the *Technische Hochschule* but also to spend time with his friends and take in a performance at the opera or a *Kneipe* at his fraternity. He made several extended trips to the Austrian Alps and toured through much of the back country of Southeastern Germany. An eager sightseer, he joined both the German Touring Club and the *Alpen Verein,* and made a careful study of his touring guide before starting on an expedition. He visited all the important sights, traveled through the different country districts, and recounted his adventures in "the beautiful German Fatherland."[18] When he did stay home on the farm, he was seldom by himself for a number of relatives and old family friends, including the Dicknethers and Uncle Hennenberger, made social calls in Fridolfing.[19]

The combination of trips and contacts with people in surrounding areas gave him ample opportunity to indulge his love of searching out bargains and making special deals. He found an inexpensive tailor across the border in Austria and persuaded his parents to send money for him to have a suit made. He carefully saved the scraps of material that were left over and sent them home to his mother along with his regular shipments of what he described as "junk," including such things as old books and worn-out underwear. These packages were usually accompanied by requests for return shipments, with heavy emphasis on new clothes, tobacco, and plenty of "goodies." In summer 1921 he got on the track of a cache of inexpensive potatoes and urged his mother to allow him to make the deal and arrange to have the potatoes shipped to Ingolstadt. Account should, however, be taken of the steadily rising inflation which made it increasingly difficult for the Himmlers to make ends meet.[20]

Heinrich's enthusiasm for these operations and the pedantry and penchant for precise record keeping that he displayed while engaged in them revealed an important aspect of his personality. His bookkeeper's mentality was most clearly shown in the way he handled the mail he received from Lu and Kaethe. (The letters he received from his family have not been preserved.) On each item he wrote not only the date of receipt but even the precise hour and minute when the letter reached his hands. Since many of these items were birthday greetings and the like, his pedantry went beyond absurdity; it was as if he had suffered a relapse, as if his manner of life and most obvious characteristics had returned to the pattern of his year in the army.[21]

In his relations with his family he also showed some signs of the tone that had prevailed while he was in Regensburg. In his references to his brother Ernsti in particular he resumed his earlier mocking, scolding approach. His letters to him abounded with admonitions that he "shouldn't be so vain" or that he "should always be good and pleasant" so as to please his parents.[22] These remarks were often followed by mock insults: "I won't even speak of Ernst. . . . he is small, insignificant, and dreadful."[23] Much of this was youthful bravado, and there are signs that he had a genuine affection for his younger brother. He looked forward to the time when Ernsti could join him in practicing gymnastic exercises and from time to time sent him small mementoes from his travels. But overall Heinrich treated the fifteen-year-old Ernsti as if he were a baby and took great pleasure in looking down at him from the lofty height of his own twenty years.[24]

Some of the same patronizing tone showed up in his relations with his parents. There had been instances of this when he was in the army, especially when he played games with them about his health and the importance of his military duties. But in Fridolfing it was much more obvious. He again complains about lack of mail, but the appeals have become more subtle and suggest that he is in the dominant position. His standard opening line to his mother is, "Since you haven't written to me, I'll have to write to you."[25] In his words of thanks and affection the same tone appears; after expressing his gratitude for a box his mother has sent he adds, "Be aware that I will always be faithful to you and try to please you, even though I am a grown man now."[26] The state of his father's health also holds his attention, and on a number of occasions he urges Frau Himmler to make certain that "Vati" does not work too hard.[27] Perhaps the best example of his affection, dashed with pomposity, is to be found in the birthday greetings he sent to his father in May 1921:

> From a heart filled with devotion, let me wish all the conceivable good that one can wish for a father. May you soon experience—and you will surely experience it—that our German Fatherland is again great and strong. That is my first wish, since the Fatherland is to us, next to God, the first and highest. Then for my second [wish] may you experience many joys with us and live long and happily with our good mother. . . . And for the third, that you can work long and as prosperously in your position as you have up until now.[28]

If Ernsti and his parents received generous doses of this kind of preaching, his brother Gebhard bore the full brunt of his criticism and caustic comment. The main complaint was that Gebhard was too easygoing, too ready to adjust to circumstances, and insufficiently imbued with the "heroic" ideal. In addition Gebhard seems to have escaped much of the family mania for orderliness and precision, and his alleged carelessness was a frequent target for Heinrich's snide remarks. Ludwig Zahler was often sarcastic at Gebhard's expense, but even he was on one occasion forced to urge moderation on Heinrich, for the younger brother's attacks had become vitriolic. "You are two different natures," Lu wrote, and he went on to advise Heinrich to be cautious, for Gebhard had been "deeply hurt" by his latest onslaught.[29]

In part Heinrich seems to have been motivated by jealousy and spite, for Gebhard was passing through his training with little difficulty and no sign of the deep inner torment which afflicted the younger brother. Gebhard also adjusted more easily to female company and in the spring of 1921 was successfully courting a distant cousin; there were clear signs that his approaches were warmly received and that marriage might result. In May 1921 he was belatedly awarded the Iron Cross First Class, one of Germany's highest military decorations, for heroic service during the last days of the war. This must have been very difficult for Heinrich to bear. He appeared unable to accept the fact that it was Gebhard who, with his easygoing manner and ability to accommodate himself, won the honors as well as the girls and at the same time managed to make easy progress toward his educational goal. He continued to carp at Gebhard's alleged failings, as if to prove that without the inner confusion and need to struggle which characterized his own experience, life was not worth living and trophies were somehow tainted.[30]

Heinrich's friends also noted his harshness and inability to compromise. Lu often wrote him that he was too rigid and far too ready to condemn weaknesses in others. During one of his trips to Munich Heinrich became embroiled in a nasty scene with Kaethe, and references to this encounter kept cropping up in their correspondence. Kaethe was a highly emotional young lady, given to sentimental outbursts and periods of moroseness, but her complaint against Heinrich was the same as Lu's: he was simply too hard and rigid and pressed people's soft spots too ruthlessly.[31]

Lu and Kaethe were making the final preparations for their marriage, while he finished his thesis and she worked as a piano teacher, and were less tolerant of Heinrich's iron rules of behavior and constant pontificating. Yet they still liked him and by seeking his advice often fed the flames of his bossiness. Differences, however, were always patched up, and the basic friendship remained, for despite his failings Heinrich was in many ways an excellent friend and companion. He was interested in people and eager to help them, never passing over a birthday or name-day without sending a note or a carefully chosen present. He wanted to be liked and usually tried to be pleasant. Even when he had been rebuffed, he managed to hide his chagrin and salvage appearances. When informed that Maja was to be married, for example, he did not consult his own hurt feelings but sent her immediate congratulations.[32] And when he was with little children or old people and felt it was acceptable to show warmth and a sense of fun, his external toughness dropped away.

Serene though life in the country might be, Fridolfing was not sufficiently distant from the kaleidoscopic changes taking place in Germany to afford Heinrich complete security. It was money that made the most direct intrusion into his sanctuary. Prices were rising rapidly, and the expenses of his education, his *Praktikum,* and his peripatetic social life led to repeated quibbling with his parents. All his activities were important to him and, in his eyes, worth the money; but he was also aware of the financial burden they placed on his parents, and this genuinely bothered him. Nearly every letter home included a request for money, and he often expressed his chagrin that he had to come begging. "Don't be angry with me that I come to you again [for money]," he writes on February 18, 1921. "For me too, it is so hard to do."[33] Caught between his wants and his embarrassment, he sometimes resorted to questionable tactics, such as borrowing cash from Herr Rehrl and then asking his parents to reimburse him. On other occasions he became quite self-righteous and indignant when his requests were not satisfied. When the Himmlers balked at his plans to go to Salzburg to buy Christmas presents in early December 1920, he wrote a long justification of his past expenditures and then added sulkily: "I will not go to Salzburg next Sunday . . . But how will it go with me if we are suddenly called in [to service] and I only have 50 or 60 marks!"[34] Such scenes were usually followed by apologies from Heinrich ("Don't be angry with me . . . "), and in the end the money was invariably sent.[35] But the hassles upset him, and the careful record of his expenditures demanded by his parents emphasized his dependence and inability to take care of himself. Only one of his regular trimonthly expenditure records has been preserved among his letters, but this item, dated July 10, 1921, is revealing. At the top of each page he lists the amount of money he has and below that the daily expenditures for the period in question. The start of page two, covering June 1921, reads as follows:

> Carry over 249.00 m.
>
> 10.6.21 Map 1.00 m.
> Stamps 1.20 m.
> Cigarettes 1.00 m.
>
> 19.6.21. Trip to Tittmon[ing] 5.00 m.
> Beer and sausage 8.00 m.
> Stamps and picture postcards 1.80 m.[36]

It is not difficult to understand how a twenty-year-old, required to account for every pack of cigarettes and each picture postcard, would become frustrated and somewhat dissatisfied with his lot.

In contrast to the disquiet he felt on the score of direct and pressing financial demands, Heinrich's concern about political and military questions grew somewhat less acute while he was in Fridolfing. From the point of view of his own beliefs and dreams for the future, the situation in Germany was still grim, but he did not take it quite as seriously as he had done the year before. This was partly the result of the peaceful atmosphere and the stronger hold of the prewar way of life in Fridolfing for, despite his harping on the need to stand alone and fight for the good cause, Heinrich was very much at the mercy of his environment. His second letter home after arriving on the farm stressed his satisfaction with the old-fashioned patriotism of his fellow farmworkers.[37] In the hectic atmosphere of Munich he had continuously voiced his forebodings about Germany's future, while his parents and friends played the role of optimists who attempted to show him a brighter side. In Fridolfing, although he occasionally foresaw bad times, he became more philosophical and optimistic about the situation and often struck a more cheerful note. "Hopefully things are going well for you in this miserable time," he wrote his parents in November 1920, "but this will bring us happy and much desired benefits in the days that are coming."[38] Instead of running to his family with tales of woe, he often had to reassure Lu or his father. In March 1921, when the communists attempted a rising in central Germany, Professor Himmler became panicky about his son's safety in the event of a "Bolshevik attack from Austria."[39] In his reply Heinrich stressed that there was very little chance of this eventuality and, even if it did materialize, he would probably be ordered to report to his *Einwohnerwehr* unit in Munich. Despite this show of comparative realism and good sense, he could not entirely resist the temptation to play military conspirator and he added in shorthand: "By the way, don't write often about such things. An unregistered letter may get lost and that would be embarrassing."[40]

His direct involvement was kept alive during this period only by his participation in military organizations and his hopes for a commission and for an opportunity to enter the regular army. He attended *Einwohnerwehr* meetings and took target practice with a unit near Fridolfing, but when the *Einwohnerwehr* was abolished in June he was not particularly disturbed. Partly because of Lu's pessimistic reports, his other paramilitary involvement, membership in the *Schützengesellschaft Freiweg,* had cooled even earlier; when he was visiting in Munich, he made little attempt to attend its meetings.[41]

About his application for a commission he was more serious, though he was forced to admit that his military future seemed bleak. On one occasion he toyed with the notion of going to Upper Silesia to join the free-corps fighting there, but he was quickly dissuaded by Lu's opinion that the situation was a "mess" and had no prospect of success.[42] Heinrich seems to have agreed with Lu's conclusion that there was little chance for serious military activity as long as the "impossible" republican regime continued to exist.[43]

His progress toward rightwing radicalism seems to have been slowed down by the type of reading he did during the year 1920-21. Since he had little exposure to student discussion of anti-Semitic or radical themes and no supply of new publications, he read the books that were available in the libraries of his father or the Rehrls. With ample time to read, especially during the long winter on the farm, he pored over their collections of old-fashioned historical studies, pious tracts, and novels. The chief aims of his reading no matter what the subject of the work, were moral edification and the acquisition of useful information. He continued to make critical comments on the literary and interpretive failings which he detected, but his academic caution was easily washed away by a gripping adventure story or a tale embodying "high ideals."[44] He made careful note of any references to the danger of Freemasonry which appeared in some of the prewar religious books and jotted down appreciative comments, such as "The clear presentation of Freemasonry was especially good."[45] No anti-Semitic references appear in his comments on his reading during this period, however, and he was not especially anxious to draw analogies with current conditions. Possible parallels between past and present revolutions alone attracted his interest, but even then he failed to make clear any historical analogies that he might have found.[46]

The dominant theme in his comments was his desire to develop a personal philosophy of life. He read some of the German classics customarily used to guide youth, such as the works of Schiller, and he reread Meyer's *Entstehung der Erde.*[47] Dabbling for the first time in occult and spiritualist writings, he was at first attracted by Mathius Fidler's *Die Toten Leben!* (The dead live!). He noted that Fidler might have used trick photography but concluded: "I believe however that the material is authentic. If this is the case, there are meaningful new grounds [for believing] in the transmigration of souls."[48] The major source of his inspiration, however, was not the occult but collections of reflections and significant quotations, especially Schopenhauer's *Über Lesen und Bücher* (On reading and books). For three months during the winter of 1921 he pondered Schopenhauer's quotations and comments. He also wrote down long passages from the book, together with quotations from Ibsen, Schiller, and the nineteenth-century conservative nationalist, Emanuel Geibel, who was one of his favorite poets.[49] His final comment on Schopenhauer's book makes it clear that he was trying to gain guidance from those whom he considered deep and serious thinkers. "The book has given me a great deal," he writes, "and also confirmed many of my own ideas."[50]

His eagerness to find important personal truths also appeared in the attraction he felt to Ibsen. He was especially fascinated by *Brand,* noting that "It is a deep insight into morality and the strengthening of the will. One of the best and most idealistic dramas I know of. *It is the book of the will** and of life without compromise."[51] When he was unable to apply himself sufficiently to uncover a personal message in a book which he considered important, he refrained from comment rather than run the risk of overlooking something. For example, after struggling for three days with Ibsen's involved handling of morality and power in *The Pretenders* he gave up, merely noting, "I'm not able to make a judgement now and don't have time for a deeper study."[52] Such confessions of failure were rare however, for he was determined to strengthen himself by discovering the real truth. In late May he even enrolled in a correspondence course to improve his thinking ability and strengthen his memory. He dutifully worked on the assignments for the course even after his return to the *Technische Hochschule* in the fall and jotted down on scraps of paper such words as "intelligence," "character," and "energy," as if they could somehow be arranged to provide the revelation he sought.[53]

Judging from the nearly twenty pages of quotations which he copied as well as his comments on the books he read at this time, the central point in his emerging personal *Weltanschauung* was the importance of will power and of obedience to a personal code of honor. He had used this idea as a prop before, but now he buttressed it with philosophic arguments from the masters and emphasized the gap existing between the honorable determined man and society in general. Examples of unsung heroes, unappreciated by their peers, show up frequently in his collection of quotations. At the same time caustic references to the ignorance and stupidity of the majority of the people or rabble (*Pöbel*), abound.[54]

This combination of ideas offered a solution of sorts to the difficulty of applying traditional values to existing conditions. The prevailing atmosphere of uncertainty and the leading doctrines of liberalism, pacificism, and social democracy were intolerable to him; yet his fundamental conservatism made it extremely difficult for him to embrace the cause of radical change. By wrapping himself in the protective mantle of the superior moralist who perseveres through an act of will and is unaffected by the ignorant

*Words in italics are underlined in the original.

masses who surround him he was able to maintain his beliefs and to avoid the dilemma implicit in revolutionary conservatism. He was thus able to justify his personal rigidity and continue his "highly moral" reserve toward the opposite sex. And he could sustain his belief in the superiority of the class from which he came simply by equating the values of his own group with the characteristics of the dominant and moral man.

In later years this line of thinking may well have made him more susceptible to the elitist doctrines of the radical Right. For the time being, however, it was undermined by his attitude toward personal social success. For all his talk about the heroic man who scorned the mob, he measured personal success by the traditional standards of wealth, social esteem, and professional status. With his faith in the power of the will, it was essential that he act upon his belief and achieve some visible success. Even while in Fridolfing, he understood that more was at stake in his academic work than the customary pursuit of a good record. Again aided by the light winter workload on the farm, he studied very hard and passed his preparatory examinations in April 1921, a full year ahead of schedule.[55]

Side by side with his regular assignments he also tried to teach himself Spanish. Probably because of the Soviets' success in the civil war, he had become discouraged about the chances of emigrating to Russia and had shifted his attention to Latin America. Spanish now became his insurance policy against possible failure to obtain a position which would satisfy his need to prove that he could fight things through alone. The more he learned from friends that attractive positions were hard to find, even for someone with a good school record and social connections, the more he clutched at the possibility of emigration as a means of escape.

By the time his *Praktikum* ended in August 1921 he could look back on a year that had made subtle but significant changes in his manner of life and his view of himself. He was stronger and healthier, and in Fridolfing he now possessed a haven to which he could return when he needed rest and encouragement amid the trials of the outside world. Possibilities for permanent escape from the existing social order, however, had been sharply diminished. Except for the remote chance of a commission and the last resort of emigration, all he had was his new resolve to scorn the mob and hold on to the old way. Surveying the republican system with foreboding and extreme distaste, he was convinced that he would have to achieve success by his own efforts and in spite of society.[56]

Fortified by this new resolve and armed with a sheaf of recommendations by Rehrl, he decided not to return to Munich immediately but to go instead to Ingolstadt, where his parents had arranged for him a two-month *Praktikum* with a farm machinery company.[57] Again, he worked hard and gained additional confidence from the knowledge that he was preparing himself to make his way as an experienced and well-trained agronomist. The only obstacle that remained was the last year of training at the *Technische Hochschule.* If he could get through this without weakening in his resolution, and if the world would stand still and refrain from overwhelming him with new doubts until he had found a satisfactory position, then all would be well. But if at any of these points he failed, the elaborate *Weltanschauung* he had assembled in Fridolfing would collapse, and he would be left defenseless and alone.

Freitag, den 26.5.22.

[illegible] ich finde das in dem Alter von 3 Jahren [illegible] dem Kind [illegible] beibringen soll nicht für richtig. Um 10 ins Bett. Gut geschlafen.

Samstag, den 27.~~22~~ 5. 1922.

½ 8 [illegible]

Selection from Heinrich Himmler's Diaries

Friday, 26.5.22. Irmgard jumped around naked before going to bed. I don't think this is proper for a three-year-old at a time when one should teach a child a sense of shame. Went to bed about 10. Slept well.

Saturday, 27.5.1922. Up at 7:30. Hugo had come in during the night. He was very nice and was very happy that I was there. Lots of consulting room business. His practice is very good. Friedl is extremely able and industrious both in the pharmacy and at doing the housework. Hitched up the horse about 10:00 and went with Hugo on his rounds. Irmgard also went along. It was uphill and down hill through the woods to Birkland. The villages around here . . .

Translation of facing page

PROFESSOR AND FRAU HIMMLER

Frischauer, *Himmler*

Frischauer, *Himmler*

HEINRICH AND GEBHARD JR. DURING WORLD WAR I

RFSS, Roll 99, Frame 2620357

SKETCHES OF HEINRICH HIMMLER MADE IN 1919 BY A FELLOW STUDENT

Die Geschichte eines Hochverräters, Munich, Zentralverlag der NSDAP, 1934

HEINRICH HIMMLER (FLAG BEARER) BEFORE KRIEGSMINISTERIUM, MUNICH, 9 NOVEMBER 1923

Professor Joe Dixon, Weber State College, Ogden, Utah

Nazi leaders. Landshut 1925/26. Three central figures (first row), left to right: Gregor Strasser (without cap), Pfeffer von Soloman, Heinrich Himmler

Chapter VIII

Last Year as a Student, 1921-22

Early in November 1921 Heinrich returned to Munich for his final year of study. With the help of his parents he found a room at a comparatively low rent in the house of an old family acquaintance, Frau Wolff, who resided at Briennerstrasse III, a few blocks from the university and the *Technische Hochschule.* He was able to take his mid-day meals and many of his suppers with Frau Wolff. She also let him prepare his own breakfast and occasionally his other meals too, which further reduced his living costs. It was not long before he acquired from his mother a cache of potatoes, meat, and "goodies" on which he drew when he was short of cash.[1]

Under the fixed system of room and board provided by Frau Wolff it was impossible for him to return to his previous routine of eating and socializing at the Loritz home; he still dropped in occasionally, but it was no longer the center of his life. In other ways too his situation was now markedly different from that during his first year as a student in Munich. A number of his senior fraternity brothers in the *Bund Apollo* had completed their schooling and left the city while he was in Fridolfing, and he found little of the paternalistic support that he had received when he was a *Fuchs.* As a senior member of Apollo, he now had to make his way like everyone else. His brother Gebhard was working in a factory in Ingolstadt to gain additional experience before his return to school in 1922-23. Other friends and acquaintances had also left the city, including Falk Zipperer who had been involved in an undetermined scandal in the previous school term. Heinrich's closest friend, Ludwig Zahler, was still there but was largely cut off from student life; in a desperate attempt to earn enough money to marry Kaethe Loritz he was working in a bank.[2]

The changes in Heinrich's daily routine and the absence of some of his closest friends removed most of the subtle pressures which had helped keep his attention focused on his studies. Now that he was more on his own, much of his academic devotion evaporated. He was thus free to involve himself in the activities he liked best. While his conventionality and naiveté ensured that these activities would offer no grounds for moral strictures, his love of good food, idle chatter, and philosophic discussions overpowered his desire to personify the virtues of triumphant will power.

As soon as he was settled in his new quarters, he set off on a round of social calls to old friends and relatives. Prompted partly by his parents and partly by his own gregariousness and desire to keep up useful contacts, he visited the Hagers, the Dicknethers, the Kastls and other families he had known over the years. Twice he called on Princess Arnulf, with whom he discussed the old days and the wretchedness of present conditions. Although sometimes troubled by the fact that his visits were not "idealistically" motivated (he hoped someday to turn these connections to his advantage), he thoroughly enjoyed the old-fashioned formality as well as the cookies and cakes. Anxious to maintain the proper demeanor on all occasions, he was apprehensive about his social savoir-faire, not because he did not know what to do, but because his clumsiness often got in the way. His diary records a series of incidents in which he lost his coat or the coat check or his notebook and then had to recover himself amid embarrassment and apologies.[3]

Incidents of this kind, however, did little to dampen his social enthusiasm or his sincere joy in renewing contacts with friends and acquaintances his own age. During his first months back in the city he encountered at every turn companions from school or from his military and paramilitary units, fraternity brothers, and people he had known in Fridolfing. Such meetings provided gratifying opportunities for long chats over coffee or reminiscences amid cigar smoke in a friend's *Bude* (study), but their potential usefulness in gaining favors or aiding his career was also never far from his thoughts. Every chance contact with persons who had significant positions or titles—even the presence of a prince at a large party he attended—appears both in his diary and in his letters home.[4]

Self-interest was a determining factor in Heinrich's participation in organized social activities. Among the many organizations to which he belonged were the *Alpen Verein,* various associations of agriculturists, the *Allgemeiner Studenten Ausschuss,* the officers' association of his old regiment, and—most important—his fraternity. He made a heroic effort to attend as many of the meetings and social gatherings of these groups as possible and spent a substantial part of his time on the social circuit. His dancing skill was sufficient to eliminate any fear of embarrassment, and he seldom missed an opportunity to display his confidence on the dance floor. Especially during *Fasching* he went from one dance party to another, and his diary records the enjoyment he derived from returning day after day to Frau Wolff's in the early morning hours between 1:30 and 5:00 a.m.[5]

His favorite parties and celebrations were those sponsored by his fraternity and its closely allied groups. Perhaps because the *Bund* was no longer simply a well-regulated sanctuary but had become a place where he had to make his own mark, he threw himself completely into its activities. He regularly practiced dueling and was often present as an observer when his fraternity brothers had matches. After frustrating delays in arranging a bout for himself, he finally fought a duel in June 1922 and proudly endured the ministrations which would guarantee him the honored scars.[6]

The traditional *Kameradschaft* of the *Bund* had a deep appeal for him, and he took his responsibilities to his fraternity brothers very seriously. He visited sick Apolloneans and sought out members and alumni wherever he went. The parallel between the *Kameradschaft* of the *Bund* and the esprit de corps of a military unit pleased him. In the *Bund* he found an expression of the "genuine German" spirit.[7] An additional appeal lay in the unlimited opportunities it offered for maneuvering and in-group politics. Its relations with other fraternities, membership in a larger federation, and intricate rituals and affairs of honor kept its members in a continuous uproar. Heinrich organized factions, gossiped with small cliques on every petty detail, and in general waded with gusto into the middle of the turmoil.[8]

Yet, in spite of his enthusiasm for the *Bund* and the vast amount of time that he devoted to it, he was not completely satisfied. He found, especially among the younger members, a lack of devotion to the old ways and to the ideal of fellowship. The very factionalism that excited his interest and participation also led him to doubt the continuation of the traditions which he cherished. In addition, even though Apollo was animated by a deep conservatism and had little sympathy with the new republican system, it was insufficiently committed to rightist opposition to satisfy him.[9]

In addition to being subject to these reservations and doubts he was troubled by the fact that he was not very popular with his fraternity brothers, some of whom quite openly expressed their lack of confidence in him. The fixity of his ideas and his continuous organizing and gossiping did nothing to break down the barriers to his social acceptance. His difficulty in getting a dueling match arose in part from coolness on the part on other Apollo members. When he tried to obtain the post of *Fuchsmajor* (the *Bund* officer who supervised new members), he was rebuffed. The reserve with which many of the members treated him did not dampen his enthusiasm for participation in *Bund* affairs but it did cause him many hours of self-evaluation in which he scolded himself for talking too much and being a busybody.[10]

The resistance Heinrich encountered in the *Bund* was his most obvious but by no means his only experience of this kind. The whole panorama of his frantic social activity was shadowed by disappointments and unhappiness. Unwilling to go beyond established and safe routines in his relations with people, he constantly retreated behind a mask of conventionality and formality. The rigidity of his beliefs, which had been increased in Fridolfing, was now reinforced by a similar stiffening of the social conventions in which he shrouded himself. His ideal was to give an appearance of cordiality and closeness while remaining safely within the barriers of politeness and correct social form. Nearly everyone he met he categorized and fitted into some such conventional slot as "a good fellow," "an honest man," or a "patriot and a Catholic."[11] In moments of crisis he was quick to avail himself of a cliché that offered a solution to the problem or provided guidance for the future. In June 1922, for example, after recounting in his diary that he has made a mistake about the time and date of a meeting, he writes, "A warning–one must never misread announcements."[12]

The detailed descriptions of his social life which appear in his diaries depend on capsule stereotypes, such as "arrogant Prussian" or "genuine Northerner, quiet, calm, large, blond, blue-eyed."[13] The girls he met were invariably characterized by such standard descriptive phrases as "virtuous," "a simple Gretchen," and–his favorite–"good and beautiful."[14] The tone of his descriptions clearly indicates that, even though he wanted warm relations with people, his fears and self-doubts forced him to erect strong defensive walls.

It was in his social relations with girls that he experienced the strongest attraction and at the same time the greatest fear and need to hold aloof. In contrast to his earlier, guarded comments, his diary for this period is replete with references to his feelings about sex and his eagerness to discuss sexual questions with other students. On the one hand, he saw himself as a person with a strong sex drive who "should marry young" because the sexual drive was so intense.[15] On the other hand, he was restrained by a whole series of factors. The traditional prohibition of premarital sexual relations which his family stressed in combination with the church's prescriptive code had a strong hold on him. He was firm enough in his resolve even to admit to adults that he was a virgin and would try to remain so. On occasions when he imagined that a girl might be receptive he admonished himself, "I cannot have sexual relations."[16]

His prudery went deeper than this prohibition, however, and he was easily shocked by what he considered loose behavior in others. Even a couple whose enlightened attitudes he admired invited his strictures when they permitted their infant daughter to run around the house naked, for he felt she needed to be taught "a sense of shame."[17] The ignorance of sex which accompanied this rigid code also helped to enforce his abstinence, and he frequently gave voice to his fears about the great mystery.[18]

To preserve his chaste ideal and avoid the dangers inherent in his own drives and the temptations posed by female companionship, Heinrich assumed the role of the good, earnest fellow who is always polite but respects girls too much to seek any intimacies. At parties he danced with all the girls and prided himself on how well he conversed with them, but when the party was over he made certain that the relationship ended there. During the whole year he never had a date and, if he escorted a girl home from a party, it was in company with one of his fraternity brothers. Occasionally, as in the *Fasching* parties at the Loritz home it was difficult to maintain this distance. He was terrified by the dangers involved, and after one party he needed a long walk and reassuring conversation with Lu to recover. The stereotyped categories under which he catalogued the dozens of girls whom he met helped to keep the whole question on an abstract and less threatening plane.[19]

The very abstractness of his defense, however, tended to isolate him from reality and increased the pressure exerted by his fantasies. He categorized not only the girls he met but even those he saw at a distance; a soloist at a concert was "temperamental and sweet," and another singer was "a fine, sympathetic girl, above all, spiritual."[20] As the year progressed, he became more concerned with the sexual habits of the girls he observed; he concluded, for instance, that a young woman he met on the train "was innocent," while a girl friend of one of his old army buddies "could be had."[21] The appeal of uncontrolled passion interested him in the abstract, and in his reading and discussion the question of a natural sex life and nakedness (especially in the Orient) kept cropping up. The frequency with which he discussed sex and sexual problems with his close male friends suggests that he was having trouble with his defenses.[22]

Homosexuality he found particularly disturbing. He contrived to associate it with the degeneration and lack of morality which he thought were rampant in postwar Germany. After a discussion of homosexuality with one of his fraternity brothers he borrowed Hans Blüher's *Die Rolle der Erotik in der männlichen Gesellschaft* (The role of the erotic in male society) in which the author argued that physical attraction between males was a natural outgrowth of the male companionship which animated organizations such as student fraternities and military units. This thesis was particularly threatening to Heinrich, and his comments on the book clearly reveal his confusion:

> The man has certainly penetrated colossally deep into the male erotic, and has grasped it psychologically and philosophically [?]. Still he uses too much vague philosophy in order for it to convince me, even though much of it is wrapped up in learned language. That there must be male societies is clear. If one can call them erotic, I doubt. In any case the pure physical homosexuality is an error of degenerate individualism that is contrary to nature.[23]

To some observers such comments may betoken latent homosexuality. But in view of his other sexual torments and of his ignorance about sex it seems likely that in his anxiety to find an abstract and academic explanation he had fallen into new confusion.

He wanted the unattainable: the excitement of sexual interest but without any risk. His reading, his long discussions, and even his self-appointed position as a ghostwriter of love letters for Frau Wolff's son, Alphonse, could not solve his problem.[24] In the process of trying to find a solution, however, his rigid formal pose put so much distance between himself and the opposite sex that there was soon little danger that his chastity would be threatened.

His struggle over sex was only one phase of the torment which he endured during this year. His tendency to be hard and rigid in his relations with other people became more pronounced, and he projected the image of an arrogant young man who knew what was good for everyone. The inevitable result was a long series of battles with friends and relatives which left hard feelings on all sides. Gebhard was a prime target for his onslaughts, even though much of the attack had to be carried out by letter or in diary notes. His jealousy and resentment of Gebhard's easygoing attitude were of long standing, and he seized the occasion of his brother's formal engagement to make nasty remarks and patronizing innuendoes about his character and prospects. At various times he berated both Gebhard and his mother for not being sufficiently self-controlled. The tone of his remarks became increasingly haughty.[25]

In March 1922 his brother and his mother were anxious to obtain a room for Gebhard for the coming school year. Though his assistance had not been asked, Heinrich managed to involve himself in the business. On March 3 he wrote his mother a mocking and sarcastic letter in which he criticized their efforts and announced that he was taking a direct hand in the matter. In reply, Gebhard and Frau Himmler apparently expressed their shock and indignation. Heinrich then sent a long letter which reads in part:

> Many thanks for your dear letter. I am neither angry, nor have I become agitated, I have merely noticed that you two [Gebhard and his mother] have fallen into a very strong, but unnecessary agitation. . . . I will now be completely open. I find it completely incomprehensible that a whole family could fall into that kind of tumult over such a ludicrous affair. . . . I find it a sin when one manufactures an issue out of that kind of thing. . . . Do not be angry that I write you, however I cannot do otherwise [*ich kann aber nicht anders*].[26]

The conscious or unconscious paraphrasing of Luther at Worms which ends this section of the letter is an example of his pretentiousness at its worst.

His combination of cold formality and omniscience produced strained relations also with people of his own age. He made pronouncements on everyone he met and seems to have been as brusk and haughty in conversation as he was in his diary comments. Even Lu was not exempt from his strictures: after a long discussion on inflation, birth control, and other matters Heinrich criticized the "moral laxness" he had discovered in his friend.[27] Fraternity brothers also received a full complement of insulting remarks, and much of his unpopularity in the *Bund* arose from these incidents. The major force of his wrath, however, was reserved for Frau Loritz and Kaethe with whom he quarreled repeatedly.

Heinrich's aggressiveness in projecting his own standards on other people had now become an important feature of his makeup. Yet he was seriously troubled by the unhappiness and hurt feelings that resulted. His own anger usually passed quickly, and the faintest sign of sympathy or desire for reconciliation by the recipient of his abuse would bring forth expressions of devotion. His fights with Kaethe, in the midst of which he registers his belief that there is an "unbridgeable gulf" between them, are soon followed by scenes of family affection in which he expresses his fidelity to his "sister."[28]

During the periods when his aggressiveness had alienated others from him, he was racked by self-doubt and remorse. In place of his earlier long periods of depression, he now gave way to fits of self-recrimination in which he scolded himself for a wide assortment of failings. The central charge in his self-indictment was the inability to stop talking—a vague cloak for his aggressiveness and intolerance. Literally dozens of his diary entries during the year included sections in which he berated himself for this failing. "I just can't keep my mouth shut," he notes on one occasion. At another time he asks sadly, "When will I stop talking too much?"[29] His inability to hold back mocking comments also bothered him. "I told an awful lot of jokes, talked and mocked a lot," he writes in recounting a family stroll in Ingolstadt, and then adds repentantly, "I just can't stop it."[30]

His eagerness to judge other people also led to periods of remorse, especially if he had an opportunity to talk with someone he had criticized. After a conversation with Princess

Arnulf he concluded that the old ruling class was not as insensitive to the problems of its subjects as he had thought and noted in his diary, "A lesson—one should not think ill of anyone unless he is sure of the facts."[31] He had no sympathy for young people who knew everything and were free with their judgments on people and events. His conclusion on the lamentations of a fraternity alumnus who was unhappy with his son is typical: "The son . . . lets no one tell him anything, knows everything, makes judgments on everything. A genuine child of his time."[32] There is no sign of realization that the traits which most bothered him in others were the very ones that caused him so much dissatisfaction with himself.

Heinrich tried to gain help by invoking his favorite doctrine of the effectiveness of will power in overcoming obstacles. In early November he reread parts of Ibsen's *Brand* in an attempt to recapture the determination he had built up in Fridolfing. He also sought inspiration in fictional characters who demonstrated the positive effects of will power, for example, the heroine of Jacob Christoph Heer's *Laubgewinde* (Garland) who faced personal problems "which she alone had to fight through."[33] From further work in the correspondence course that purported to improve thought processes and memory he hoped to derive additional self-confidence. One day in mid-November, after a visit to the office of Herr Paehlmann, the man who ran the program, he noted enviously that Paehlmann "has a classic calmness and [sense of] security."[34]

None of his efforts to ascend to heroic heights were very successful, and occasionally after a bout of self-chastisement he would behave as though he were very tired of being a young man, as though nothing would please him more than to be old and free from torment. On other occasions he would gain great satisfaction from being able to grasp the prerogative of childhood and pour out his troubles to his parents. After a conversation with his father in May 1922 he wrote in his diary, "To father . . . we had a good conversation and told each other everything."[35]

For one major failing, however, he got no sympathy from his family—his tendency to fritter away in socializing and gossiping time that should have been devoted to study. His parents were seriously alarmed lest he had turned into a gadabout and believed that he was headed for academic trouble. They were also uneasy about some of his companions, especially Alphonse Wolff whom one of Heinrich's letters had imprudently described as a "girl chaser."[36] Perhaps to protect himself from further indiscretions of this nature, he wrote home much less frequently. But the lack of letters seems to have awakened new suspicions.

When he did write, he tried to convince the family that he was a diligent student. On January 20, 1922, he wrote his mother but forgot to send greetings for her birthday. Near the end of his diary entry for that day he notes, "Forgot Mom's birthday!" Early the following morning he set out to repair the damage. The result was a masterpiece of self-justification. "My dear little mother," he begins, "Please do not be angry with me that I didn't write to you! Hopefully, you weren't really hurt that nothing came from your Heini!" Then, after extending his best wishes for her birthday he continues, "However you must not think I forgot because of thoughtlessness or a big time at *Fasching*. Oh no, on the contrary, I haven't done anything on *Fasching*, only worked." Then, fearing that he may have awakened his mother's apprehensions about his health, he adds, "Still I'm careful to get seven hours of sleep every night so you can be calm on that score." In a final effort to prove his devotion both to his studies and to her he writes: "I gave the letter to Lindemeier about 8:50. However, you should not think that it [her birthday] first dawned on me this morning, for I remembered it last night while I was studying physics."[37]

Despite the artistic merit of such explanations (he had in fact spent half the day gossiping with his fraternity brothers and watching duels) his parents still insisted that he get to work. He was studying little and was missing lectures, even though most of his courses were on the specialized agricultural subjects which should have fitted his interests. Just before his preparatory examinations in March and again before his final examinations in July he studied very hard. Both of these bursts were successful and he passed the examinations. Until the results were safely in, however, he was in serious doubt. In fact, before he took the preparatory examinations he was so worried that he persuaded one of the examiners to narrow the range of the questions he would ask. His father was not impressed by his periodic flurries of activity and the fact that he actually passed the tests. When Heinrich began to toy with the notion of staying in Munich for another year of schooling and mentioned his hope that, if he remained, he could play an important role in Apollo, his father told him bluntly that, if he was to continue his education, his participation in fraternity life would have to be cut to a minimum.[38]

Professor Himmler's hard line on study was chiefly due to the ever-mounting inflation which was playing havoc with the family finances. The mark had lost half its value by the end of World War I and had continued to lose ground in subsequent years. After ranging between 40 and 90 marks to the dollar, it had tumbled to 270 by November 1921, the time Heinrich's school year began. During 1921-22 the pace of inflation quickened. By July 1922 the mark had fallen to 493 to the dollar, and in August it stood at 1,200.

The threat that had been implicit in the instability and periodic slippage during previous years now became a terrifying reality: Germany was in the midst of a runaway inflation and there was no end in sight. The year 1921-22 slashed the purchasing power of Professor Himmler's salary and virtually annihilated his savings. With no indication that the government would be able to stem the tide, he, like the rest of the professional middle class, was on the verge of despair.

In spring 1922 Professor Himmler was appointed *Rektor* of the *Wittelsbach Gymnasium* in Munich. He left the rest of the family in Ingolstadt and occupied temporary quarters until the family could join him in the fall. Between May and August 1922, while living alone in Munich, he frequently met Heinrich for dinner, and the young Himmler's diary accounts of these meetings dwell on his father's deep depression about the condition of Germany and the fate which awaited the family.[39]

Professor Himmler repeatedly urged Heinrich to be careful with money and to cut down his expenses. In the correspondence between Heinrich and his mother, the same theme crops up over and over again: costs are going up, and the amount the family has budgeted for his expenses is insufficient. Despite his assurances that he was doing the best he could and hated to ask for money, his parents demanded that the screw be tightened further and pointed to the cost of his extracurricular activities as the logical place to begin. Thus on both academic and financial grounds Heinrich's social life and poor study habits were under parental attack.[40]

The most serious element in the whole issue was the question it posed about his future. At the start of the school term in November 1921 he had intended to complete his education as quickly as possible and find a job in farming either in Germany or abroad. On occasion the old dream of a military career still flitted through his mind, but in general he was far more settled in his decision to become a farm administrator than he had been before. As the weeks went by, however, his social life—despite its torments—and the discouraging results of his first soundings for a job inclined him to favor the idea of remaining in school for another year. In late May 1922 he sought admission to the Political Science Department of the University of Munich and requested that he be relieved of tuition costs for the year 1922-23. In early June he was notified that both requests had been granted.[41] This did not settle things, however, for there remained the question of where the money would come from to support both Heinrich and his brother during another year of school. The problem of money and all its implications for his future cast a shadow over his life. In late June 1922, after meeting his father and once again having to beg for money, he noted gloomily, "Father would be so good if I didn't have to plague him [for money] any more and was self-supporting."[42]

As in the past, external events combined with his personal problems to accelerate his movement toward the radical Right. At the beginning of the school year his political views had tended toward a comparatively restrained conservatism. His reading interest centered mainly on fiction, and he seems to have avoided radical political tracts, although a short gap in his book list at this time makes it impossible to speak with certainty. By early 1922, however, his reading, opinions, and activities had clearly taken a more radical turn.

During his last eight months at the *Technische Hochschule* twenty-five volumes appeared in his reading list. Fourteen of these were novels and adventure stories which he read on vacations. Of the eleven books which he read while actually in Munich one was a novel, one a book on sex, and nine were works on politics and military history. Four books and pamphlets in this last group were published by Lehmann's Pan-German Press, and two others were radically anti-Semitic.[43]

The rapid radicalization of his political views shows up clearly in both his reading notes and his diary entries. He resented the Allies' treatment of Germany, and, especially against France, his bitterness was very deep. Hermann Bauer's denunciation of the French in *Die Sizilianische Vesper* (The Sicilian vespers), published by Lehmann, brought forth the comment, " . . . it shows us that the French have always been the same people that they are today."[44] The alleged threat of Bolshevism also troubled him, and in January he had long discussions on this subject with one of his elderly aunts. His communications with friends and acquaintances betray the sorrow, felt by many conservative Germans, over the loss of German-speaking territories, particularly the transfer of the South Tyrol from Austria to Italy.[45]

But it was his attitude toward internal developments and especially the need to identify a scapegoat at home that showed the clearest change. Freemasons tended to slip into the background, and for the first time his comments focused directly on Jews. In January 1922 he finally read *Judas Schuldbuch,* the volume he had discussed with Ludwig Zahler two years earlier. Much of his comment is illegible, but his concluding words are clear enough: "What one suspects, but continually forgets. A splendid collection of sources."[46] On February 11, 1922, he read Houston Stewart Chamberlain's pamphlet *Rasse und Nation* (Race and nation) with great relish because "It is true and one has the impression that it is objective, not just hate filled anti-Semitism. Because of this it has more effect. These terrible Jews."[47] In early August he finished *Erinnerungen des Kronprinz Wilhelm* (Memoirs of the Crown Prince William). He thought the prince was "A good person, with a good heart and sound, clear vision" who had been maligned by "propaganda." However, he could not condone the fact that the prince did not produce the book himself but let "the Jews do it."[48]

His diary entries during the same period abound with references to conversations in which "the Jewish question" played a prominent part. His description of the topics discussed indicates that the real issue was the alleged role of Jews in the contemporary troubles. On January 12 he talked over "Politics, anti-Semitism, and the situation of Germans in Austria" with some friends of his father. A month later, in a discussion with Lu the topics were "The Jewish question, capitalism, Stinnes [Hugo Stinnes, a prominent industrialist], capital, and the making of money." In early March he explored "Land reform, degeneration, homosexuality, and the Jewish question" with a fraternity brother. On June 15 he and his father conversed with some people in a beer hall about "the past, the war, revolution, the Jews, harassment of officers, the Red period, liberation."[49]

Heinrich was developing an eye for detecting Jews among the people with whom he came in contact. About a lawyer he met while running an errand for his father in January 1922 he notes, "he cannot deny his Jewishness . . . this thing lies in the blood of these people."[50] At a meeting of agriculturists in Nuremberg he is quick to note "the Jewish features"[51] of one of the participants. On one occasion, while visiting a cabaret with Alphonse Wolff, he made anti-Semitic remarks to a young dancer whom Alphonse knew and then discovered she was Jewish. His diary account of this incident records his embarrassment at the turn of events and includes a long laudatory comment on the girl, who "deserved respect."[52] This apparent exception to his anti-Semitic development should not carry much weight, however, for he often softened his harsh judgements when a girl showed an inclination to be nice to him. Moreover on this occasion he was intrigued by the supposed open sexuality of "Oriental women," and this may have combined with his embarrassment to give her the benefit of the doubt. The sweet, sensual Jewish girl was often portrayed with sympathy in anti-Semitic literature, even though she was accused of being the unwitting tool of malevolent Judaism.[53]

When he suspected that an individual who was involved in democratic or leftist political activities also had "Jewish blood," Heinrich had no mercy. One of his old friends from the *Wilhelms Gymnasium* was active in a democratic organization at Munich University (Democratic Students Opposed to the Black-White-Red Terror), and for this he was denounced by Heinrich as "Jewboy" and a "Jewish louse."[54] The happy times they had had together in school counted for nothing when compared with an alleged Jewish origin and democratic politics.

Heinrich's occasional references to blood and race in connection with Jews indicate that he was slipping into a full racist syndrome. Here and there in his diary and book comments there are vague references to the importance of race. He praises Hermann Burte, the author of *Wiltfeber, der ewige Deutsche* (Wiltfeber, the eternal German), for being a "racial German."[55] After a long conversation during a stroll with Lu in June he gave classic expression to his acceptance of the racist creed "How thick-headed [*dumm*] we genuine Aryans are," runs the entry in his diary, "and thank God we are so thick-headed."[56]

His reading coupled with his continuous discussions on radical political themes influenced the way he regarded himself and the world. On the front page of the diary which he began in June 1922 he copied the first few lines from Emanuel Geibel's *Fahnentreu* (True to the flag):

> Ob sie dich durchboren,
> Trutze drum und ficht,
> Gib dich selbst verloren,
> Doch das Banner nicht.*[57]

At first glance the poem seems merely to reflect his old belief in the force of will power; he had in fact copied part of it while in Fridolfing the year before. But the version he used in June 1922 was transcribed from the last page of *Judas Schuldbuch* and included all the minor alterations which Wilhelm Meister had made in the original text.[58] This incident suggests that he was now tending to seek inspiration, not in the traditional "serious" thinkers and writers, but rather in radical political propaganda. Another sign of this trend had been his choice in February 1922 of material for reading aloud to the boarders assembled for dinner at Frau Loritz's home. On previous occasions when he had indulged his love of public recitation he had read old-fashioned poetry. This time the text was *Karthagos Untergang* (Ruin of Carthage) which offered clear parallels with Germany's plight at that time. He noted with satisfaction that its "nationalistic tone received great applause."[59]

Expressions of nationalism found a welcome among all the people with whom he associated, but his increasing sympathy for action against "the enemies" at home sometimes encountered resistance. Heinrich was pleased by the assassination of Walter Rathenau† on June 24 and described

---

*Although they may pierce you,
Fight, resist, stand by,
You yourself may perish
But keep the banner high.

†A German Jewish industrialist, largely responsible for Germany's World War I economic planning, who played a prominent role in the early Weimar Republic.

the murdered man as a "scoundrel."[60] When he voiced sentiments of this kind at Frau Wolff's dinner table, he was horrified to discover that most of those present disagreed and commented sadly in his diary, "O blind people."[61] A week later he had an "unpleasant conversation"[62] of a similar kind at Frau Wolff's home. In between these two incidents he noted in his diary that "it is not good to speak with Kaethe [Loritz] about the rightist parties."[63] During this same period he found the *Bund Apollo* lacking in nationalistic fervor (see p. 126).

He was not, however, entirely alone in his radical opinions. The Kastl family, whom the Himmlers had known for years, held views close to his, and during June and July Heinrich had a number of political discussions in their home. Herr Kastl persuaded him to circulate petitions demanding that Germany adopt the old, imperial red-white-black banner in place of the hated black-red-gold flag of the republic. Heinrich took his petition sheet with him and solicited signatures wherever he went. He was particularly successful in early July at a meeting of the *Schützengesellschaft Freiweg*. In view of the fact that this occasion provided a meeting point for ex-soldiers and former free-corps members this is not surprising.[64]

Membership in the *Freiweg* was Heinrich's nearest approach to serious implementation of his radical beliefs. But it is not altogether clear what was going on inside that organization. Two entries in his diary refer to target practice, on one occasion with a machine gun, but give no details. Since by this time the other paramilitary groups to which he had belonged had been dissolved, it is probable that some of their members used *Freiweg* for military organization and training, and that it was there that Heinrich got his target practice.[65] It is clear that he had sources of information about the secret military and ultrarightist organizations in Munich. He discussed these secret societies with his father in June, and his diary comment on the capture of Rathenau's assassins ("Organization 'C' [Consul].* Awful if everything should become known.") suggests that he had some idea of what was going on.[66] That his source of information may have been the *Freiweg* is suggested by the fact that on July 5

*A secret rightist organization formed in Bavaria in 1921 which "executed" political opponents (Waite, *Vanguard of Nazism*, pp. 212-27).

he approached its head, Obermeier, and volunteered "for special assignments."[67]

Even if this diary entry exaggerates his involvement and, perhaps, the role of the *Freiweg,* there were other sources from which he could have picked up information. Persons like Ernst Röhm who were most deeply involved in the plots and secret organizations kept in close touch with various regimental officers' clubs, including that of the Eleventh, to which Heinrich belonged. In late January Röhm attended a meeting of this club, and Heinrich chatted with him there. The tone of the diary account suggests that this was not their first meeting: "Captain Röhm and Major Angerer were also there; very friendly. Röhm pessimistic about Bolshevism."[68] This Major Angerer had been Heinrich's company commander in the old Fourteenth Alarm Company, an organization that Röhm had helped to establish when serving as General von Epp's deputy in the *Schützenbrigade* system. Angerer was also a student at the *Technische Hochschule,* the source of many recruits for rightist organizations during 1923. An indication that this institution already had a distinctly rightist coloration is the fact that in June 1922, when the *Bund Apollo* refused to take part in a demonstration against Germany's war guilt, Heinrich joined a large delegation that represented the *Technische Hochschule.* Thus by the summer of 1922 young Himmler's radical political views were edging closer to active involvement and the groups with which he was in contact hovered in a shadowy no-man's land between conspiratorial politics and active military service.[69]

All Heinrich's earlier longing to join the regular army now returned with redoubled force. For a year it had been a mere hopeful undercurrent in his thinking, but now he saw the revival of German military power as the remedy for the nation's ills, and, even more, as offering a solution to his own problems with regard to politics and his personal future. Any chance encounter with military pageantry reawakened his deep emotional attachment to the soldier's life. As he walked down the street in late February, a detachment of troops marched past; his diary entry on this reads, "Military went past—O my God!"[70] In November he had at last received his certification as a *Fähnrich,* but his efforts to obtain active service were unsuccessful. He was encouraged by any rumor which suggested that Germany might defy the disarmament clauses or decide on war. When in June he met a lieutenant in the Twentieth Infantry Regiment, his reaction was a combination of jealousy, hope, and curiosity. "I'm awfully sorry that I'm no longer a part of it [the service] and that I had to get out. Who knows, perhaps I'll get back in. I'm really curious about what will become of me."[71]

His calmness on this occasion was belied by his deeply troubled attitude toward the future. As he had done in Fridolfing, he tried to gain some comfort from philosophic reflection, but, in spite of his reading and in spite of hours spent "thinking and dreaming," he gained little inner peace.[72] Once again he revived his plan to emigrate, even though he had abandoned his study of Spanish, as he had earlier given up Russian. The locations he was now considering were more exotic and included Peru, Georgian Russia, and Turkey. This last possibility was kept alive in his mind by a Turkish student of his acquaintance, and he even discussed it with Herr Rehrl.[73]

By the time Heinrich had completed his final examinations and received his diploma on August 1, his ideas about his future and his political and social attitudes were in complete disarray. His tentative inquiries about an agricultural job in Germany had produced nothing. His idea of emigrating to operate a large farm abroad was a dream and nothing more. Meanwhile the radicalism of his political views was drawing him closer to groups of rightist conspirators, even as it was isolating him from some of his old friends. But this kind of political identification offered no prospects of employment in the summer of 1922. And even if an opportunity for such employment had presented itself, it seems doubtful that he would have been ready to cast his lot with any group at this time. For despite his politicking, and his torment about himself and his future, many of his habits and old ways, including church attendance, social calls, fraternity dances, and shipments of dirty laundry to Ingolstadt, still held fast.

As the moment for his decision about his future approached, the appeal of life in Munich grew stronger. His feeling that he was not completely accepted by others and his terrible uncertainty about sex and marriage remained; but these emotions paled into insignificance when compared with the sorrow he felt at the prospect of ending his life as a student and embarking on a rather humdrum career. The award of a tuition-free scholarship for study at the university seemed to give him what he wanted but failed to eliminate the money obstacle. The family's savings had been liquidated by the inflation, and Heinrich's own small reserve, which appears to have consisted of the residue of Princess Arnulf's gift in 1917 and perhaps an inheritance from his grandmother, had likewise disappeared. Some idea of the inflation's impact on the family's position and Heinrich's opportunities may be gained from the fact that Princess Arnulf's gift of 1,000 marks which had seemed so generous in 1917 was in August 1922 worth a mere two dollars.

In whatever direction he looked, the road seemed blocked. His only chance appeared to lie in finding a summer job sufficiently highly paid to enable him to go to school for another year. But in an economy reeling under inflation there was little hope of this. Then, on August 16, he received a windfall. Once again when he was faced with a personal crisis the old system of contacts and influence paid off. A letter reached him from one of his former teachers at the Munich *Gymnasium,* Professor Huolezeck, passing on to him the offer of a job with a nitrogen fertilizer company in Schleissheim.[74]

The offer originated with Professor Huolezeck's brother who was an official of the company. The job was that of technical assistant, carried a monthly wage of 4,000 marks, and was available immediately.[75] The salary lost more than half its purchasing power in the month of August alone, slipping from the equivalent of $8.00 a month to $3.80, but the job was still the best opportunity open to Heinrich, and he quickly accepted it. He could hope for an adjustment in salary if the inflation continued, and the job would yield at least some earnings to help him weather the storm. Once conditions settled down, he could look for other possibilities; in the meantime he would be gaining additional experience in agricultural work. Moreover Schleissheim was only a few miles north of Munich, and he would be able to keep in close touch with his family, now settled in Munich, and with his various political and social contacts.

The final arrangements for his move to Schleissheim were worked out within a few days, and on September 1 he reported for work at the old army remount depot where the company's headquarters were located. At the time of his departure, he can have had little idea that this would prove to be perhaps the most important decision he had yet made. In

August 1922 all he appeared to be gaining was a temporary respite; but in fact the road that led to Schleissheim would in the next year lead on to a period of military service, membership in the Nazi party, and an irrevocable commitment to radical politics.

Chapter IX

To the Feldherrnhalle and Beyond

Once on the job in Schleissheim, Heinrich was assigned to work on the company's research on manure, a project which was apparently designed to discover new agricultural uses for nitrogen products. He proved a conscientious, hard-working, and useful employee with a high degree of company loyalty; the firm was satisfied with his attitude, practical knowledge, and professional competence. The work seems to have interested him insofar as it broadened his knowledge of agricultural chemistry, but some of its features were not to his liking. Manure experimentation was not exactly what he had had in mind when he envisioned his future life as a farmer, and the prospects of pay and promotion were not promising. He did his work with competence, but his main interest and concern were focused elsewhere.[1]

The rising tide of inflation kept him in constant agitation during 1922-23. As costs skyrocketed, the company raised his salary; but wage increases lagged behind prices and did nothing to offset the feeling that rampant madness was in control and that no one could escape. The rapidity of the changes and the unreality of the atmosphere may be gauged from the amounts Heinrich contributed to the employees' insurance program. In September his insurance was 80 marks, in December it was 2,340 marks—more than half his total salary during his first month on the job. In a desperate effort to survive, Heinrich and his mother worked out a plan to take advantage of temporary price lags in Schleissheim and Munich, but the constant changes in prices made rational purchasing difficult. On November 7 his mother wrote that she had managed to buy a quantity of flour at prices ranging from 120 to 140 marks a pound and that, if he bought flour, he was not to pay more than 140 marks per pound or buy more than half a kilo "because we do not have enough money."[2]

Efforts of this kind could not keep pace with the inflation. By mid-November the mark stood at 8,000 to the U.S. dollar; by January 1923 it had fallen to 18,000. On January 11 the French and Belgian governments sent troops into the Ruhr, on the ground that Germany had not fulfilled her reparation obligations. The Reich government countered by declaring passive resistance in the Ruhr, and the new pressure on the mark increased the rate of the inflation. By the end of January the mark reached 50,000 to the dollar and then continued its upward leap through hundreds of thousands, millions, billions, and even trillions to the dollar until in mid-October 1923 the government surrendered, repudiated the old mark, and replaced it with the Renten mark. While it lasted the inflation overturned stable incomes, wiped out savings, and brought in its train widespread ruin or severe deprivation. In the process it gripped the population in an atmosphere of dread which corroded away much of the remaining support for and confidence in the republican system.

The triple impact of the inflation, the republic's loss of prestige, and the need to resist the foreign occupation of the Ruhr intensified and accelerated the activities of rightist organizations committed to radical change. In Bavaria in particular numerous paramilitary and rightwing (*völkisch*) groups had been in existence prior to the occupation of the Ruhr. During his last year in the *Technische Hochschule* Heinrich had close contacts with a number of these organizations. Schleissheim also proved to be a center of right-wing activity, and the Schleissheim area contained an unusually large number of paramilitary groups. Heinrich lost no time in joining the *Reichsflagge,* one of the groups under the leadership of Ernst Röhm.[3] Like countless others, this organization was made up of men who entertained vague hopes of someday reversing the defeat of 1918 and getting rid of the republican regime, and wished to participate in some kind of military formation. These rightist groups constituted a labyrinth of intrigue and shifting political views, but they were at one in their love of soldiering and their dissatisfaction with the present.

Ever since 1918, fearing the possibility of communist or Spartacist revolution and committed to the desirability of a large military force, the Reich government had made periodic use of free-corps formations. It had also secretly encouraged a close connection between the *Reichswehr* and the various paramilitary groups. The Bavarian government had gone even further in this direction. It had largely organized, staffed, and paid for various semiofficial formations of the type Heinrich had joined between 1919 and 1922, and, after these formations had been suppressed in consequence of Allied pressure, it had continued to maintain a liaison between the free corps and the Bavarian units of the *Reichswehr.* Important roles in this liaison were played by General von Epp and Captain Röhm who were regular *Reichswehr* officers.[4]

In November 1922 Bavarian officials united seven paramilitary groups into the *Vereinigte Vaterländische Verbände Bayerns* (*VVVB*). In the weeks following the occupation of the Ruhr they took various measures designed to strengthen the position of the *VVVB,* including drawing up plans for the absorption of its units into the Bavarian *Reichswehr* in the event of mobilization. The Bavarian government also took an interest in the caches of World War I weapons which were indispensable for completing the armament of the paramilitary units in time of emergency and had been secreted in various parts of Bavaria to escape Allied detection. These weapons were placed under the control of the *Reichswehr,* the costs being shared by the government and a group representing Bavarian heavy industry. Plans were also made for the construction of secret factories to provide the necessary ammunition when the day of decision should arrive.[5]

The renewed military and paramilitary concern of the Bavarian authorities also led to the creation of many new free-corps units. In these units factions and people with whom Heinrich had been in touch, such as Röhm and the regimental veterans clubs, played a major role. The *Technische Hochschule* in Munich was a favorite recruiting ground, and at least one of the new units, *Bund Blücher,* had its headquarters in Schleissheim.[6]

In an atmosphere and area so favorable to paramilitary activity it was virtually inevitable that Heinrich would play some part. The new opportunities for rightist politics also guaranteed that he would become enmeshed in the factional fights and in the struggles which quickly developed over tactics, goals, and leadership. Three main issues animated and divided Bavarian rightists: the desirability of armed resistance in the Ruhr, the possibility of overthrowing the republican government in Berlin, and the need for Bavaria to achieve a degree of home rule under a restored monarchy. Nearly every rightist political and paramilitary organization had some sympathy for each of these alternatives; the main divisive ts had to do with priorities and the strategy and tactics be used to realize their aims. The Bavarian government, hich was controlled by the *Bayerische Volkspartei* (*BVP*), vas predominantly concerned with the protection of onservative Bavarian interests; on the question of whether esistance to the French or a radical change in Berlin was the nore important, its attitude was shifting and subject to change. The leaders of paramilitary groups in the *VVVB* usually hewed to the political line pursued by the Bavarian government.

This emphasis on Bavarian interests led to an almost immediate counterthrust by the leaders of some paramilitary and radical rightist groups. Two weeks after the French entered the Ruhr a second federation of Bavarian paramilitary groups was formed. The new organization, the *Arbeitsgemeinschaft der Vaterländischen Kampfverbände*, embraced six paramilitary groups which had withdrawn from the *VVVB*, including *Wiking*, *Oberland* and *Reichsflagge*, the group to which Heinrich belonged. The political leader of the *Arbeitsgemeinschaft* (and its successor, the *Kampfbund*, formed in September 1923) was Adolf Hitler, whose *Nationalsozialistische Deutsche Arbeiterpartei* (*NSDAP*) with its paramilitary arm, the *Sturm Abteilungen* (*SA*), played an important role in both organizations. The Nazis had steadily increased in size and influence since 1920, but they were merely one radical group among many, albeit a very dynamic one. Hitler was forced to play coalition politics with other organizations and leaders; the result was the *Arbeitsgemeinschaft* in which he was supported by Röhm, Dr. Weber of *Oberland*, and to a degree General Ludendorff. Hitler demanded that separatism be rejected and the Ruhr issue be deemphasized in favor of an attack on Berlin. But even Hitler occasionally toyed with the idea of pushing Bavarian issues to the forefront, and to some of the secondary leaders of the *Arbeitsgemeinschaft* Bavarian interests and Ruhr resistance often seemed more important than the overthrow of the Berlin government.

On a number of occasions in the course of 1923 the *VVVB* lined up on one side and the *Arbeitsgemeinschaft* on the other. The most dramatic confrontation occurred on May 1 when the *Arbeitsgemeinschaft* planned to take direct action against the Social Democrats during the May Day celebration. The *VVVB* refused to cooperate in this scheme and supported the efforts of the Bavarian government to keep the peace.

Young Himmler was pulled first one way and then the other. Of the seven units in the *VVVB,* he had at one time or another been affiliated with three. But he had also had close relations with or membership in five of the *Arbeitsgemeinschaft* groups.[8] All he could do was bow his head and hope that some way or another the conflict would be resolved before it came to blows. On May 1, he escaped the ultimate dilemma, because the *Arbeitsgemeinschaft* backed down at the last minute. But the basic question of which direction to follow still remained. In an effort to find his way he seized upon the simplest of expedients and identified himself with the person of Ernst Röhm, following wherever Röhm led. But Röhm also was being driven by events; and by the summer of 1923 he had thrown in his lot with the *NSDAP.* All Heinrich could do was stumble along behind his leader. In August he too joined the *NSDAP,* receiving membership card No. 42404.[9]

In early October Röhm became embroiled in a new conflict, this time over control of the *Reichsflagge.* The upshot was that a separate organization, the *Reichskriegsflagge,* was formed under his leadership. Heinrich once again followed Röhm, dropping out of the older unit to take his place among Röhm's stalwarts in the *Reichskriegsflagge.*[10] Thus by the early fall his position at last seemed settled. He was committed to the *Reichskriegsflagge* and Röhm. Röhm in turn was tied to the *Arbeitsgemeinschaft* and Hitler. Heinrich waited to see which way the political winds would blow his leaders and himself.

On many issues the Hitler-Röhm group and the Bavarian government were sharply divided by October 1923. One development, however, temporarily reunited them. The Bavarian government had become involved in a fight with Berlin over insulting remarks which the Nazis had printed in the *Völkischer Beobachter* about the commander of the *Reichswehr,* General Hans von Seeckt. The Bavarians refused to accede to Berlin's demand that they silence the *Völkischer Beobachter,* and the *Reichswehr* commander in Bavaria followed the lead of the local authorities. Bavaria's position bordered on rebellion and seemed to unite all the Bavarian rightist groups against Berlin.

The reconciliation of the rightist factions in Bavaria was

strengthened by new signs of danger from outside. While Berlin was uttering dire threats and desperately trying to settle the situation in the Ruhr, Bavaria's neighbor Thuringia began to move to the left. In Munich this was viewed as the prelude to another communist revolution, and on an impulse of wild reaction some Bavarian *Freikorps* and *Reichswehr* units were rushed to the northern border. With the Bavarian government thus apparently committed to an anticommunist and anti-Berlin position, the members of the *Arbeitsgemeinschaft* could feel more at ease.

For Heinrich this was a particularly happy development which led to what he regarded as a golden opportunity. The Bavarian *Reichswehr* decided on partial implementation of its mobilization plan in order to form replacements for the units which had been sent north. The most important of these replacement units was Company Werner which was organized as a volunteer Fourth company of the First battalion of the Nineteenth Infantry Regiment and drew much of its manpower from existing paramilitary formations. A number of the men had some contact with the *Technische Hochschule* in Munich. On September 1 he quit his job in Schleissheim, in part perhaps because he thought there was some chance for military service in the near future. On September 15 he was accepted into Company Werner. After many trials and disappointments his old dream of once more putting on "the soldier's coat" had been realized, and he was again part of the German army.[11]

The course of political events, however, soon dampened his enthusiasm. As the Reich government made progress toward liquidating the inflation and the occupation of the Ruhr, it began to seem possible that the Bavarian government would have to make its peace with Berlin. Thus throughout October and early November Hitler, Röhm, and their supporters tried to drive the Bavarian government into a more uncompromising stand; at the same time they were apprehensive that the Bavarians might choose to sacrifice Hitler and his fellows in order to save themselves. In the heightening tension which followed, Hitler and his allies struck first.

During the now famous Hitler *Putsch* of 8-9 November 1923, the *VVVB* backed the government while the *Arbeitsgemeinschaft* supported Hitler. The police units of the Bavarian state and the bulk of the Bavarian *Reichswehr* remained loyal. Only one army unit seriously wavered–Company Werner, the unit Heinrich had joined. After long consideration, however, it decided to remain neutral and agreed to the army's demand that it disarm and be dissolved. Thus after a mere seven weeks Heinrich's new military career came to an abrupt close.[12]

For Heinrich's personal future Company Werner's decision was opportune, because he had already decided to support Röhm. While Hitler was taking over the *Bürgerbräukeller,* Röhm and the *Reichskriegsflagge* were holding a "social gathering" in the *Augustinerkeller,* anxiously awaiting orders authorizing military action. As soon as Hitler's men attacked, orders were sent to Röhm to seize the War Ministry buildings on the Leopoldstrasse. The *Reichskriegsflagge*'s social evening thereupon ended in a burst of enthusiasm, and fully armed, the unit marched through Munich in the direction of the War Ministry. In the ranks of the *Reichskriegsflagge* were many of Heinrich's friends from Schleissheim and his brother Gebhard. At the head of the column bearing the ensign of the unit, the old imperial war flag (not the swastika), was Heinrich Himmler.[13]

On attempting to seize the War Ministry Röhm's men were refused entry by *Reichswehr* officials. Uncertain what course to take, Röhm surrounded the building and threw up a light, barbed-wire barricade in front of it. On the morning of November 9 Röhm and his men found themselves in the unenviable position of surrounding the building while themselves being surrounded by the police. By noon Hitler's effort to relieve Röhm had ended in the famous debacle at the Feldherrnhalle, and the Hitler *Putsch* was over. For Röhm's men, still waiting behind their barricade, there was nothing to do but surrender. The *Reichskriegsflagge* leaders were taken into custody; the rank and file gave up their weapons, identified themselves to the police, and went home.[14]

During months immediately following the *Putsch* Heinrich's political hopes were at their nadir. Like many of the participants in the *Putsch,* Heinrich believed that it would succeed and he gloried in his role as flag bearer before the War Ministry. To have all this swept away was hard for him to bear, as were the subsequent measures which the Bavarian government took against the *Kampfbund.* All the organizations to which he had belonged were banned, Röhm and Hitler were in custody, and his erstwhile immediate superiors in the *Reichskriegsflagge* were in hiding. Toward the authorities, especially his friends in the *Bayerische Volkspartei,* Heinrich was very bitter, his mood alternating between imaginary fears of his own arrest and disappointment that the government was not interested in him. He did his best to keep in touch with the *Reichskriegsflagge* members who were in hiding or in jail and set up a series of mail drops through which those being sought by police could communicate with each other. These activities awakened fears that he was being watched and was in imminent danger.[15] On one occasion he warned a correspondent to be careful because he believed his mail was being opened. In late January 1924 he wrote to a *Reichskriegsflagge* member in hiding: "As a friend, and especially as a soldier and devoted member of the *völkisch* movement, I will never run from danger, but we have a duty to each other and to the movement to hold ourselves in readiness for the struggle."[16]

As *völkisch* organizations to replace the banned Nazi party began to take shape, Heinrich's courage and interest revived. In the middle of February he visited Röhm in Stadelheim prison and familiarized himself with his leader's thinking about the political situation.[17] Since the paramilitary organizations had been effectively quashed by the government but *völkisch* political activity was still legal, he focused his attention on *völkisch* party work. There were factional fights in the *völkisch* movement, partly inspired by Hitler's jealousy of any organization which he did not directly control, but in early 1924 many of the rank and file rallied to the *Nationalsozialistische Freiheitsbewegung* led by General Ludendorff and Gregor Strasser of Landshut.

Heinrich worked hard for the *völkisch* cause, studying political issues and using every opporunity to disseminate *völkisch* propaganda among his friends and acquaintances. In February 1924 he delivered speeches in the small towns of northern Bavaria and also wrote short articles on *völkisch* activities for sympathetic rural newspapers. He relished the self-sacrifice involved, noting in his diary on February 24, "This service to the people is bitterly hard and full of heartaches."[18] But he cannot but have been encouraged by the signs of *völkisch* success and especially by the large vote won by the *völkisch* block in the *Reichstag* elections in May.

Among the thirty-two successful *völkisch* candidates was Ernst Röhm, recently released from Stadelheim prison.

As the government's apprehension about a revival of the *Arbeitsgemeinschaft* became less acute, Heinrich was able to resume paramilitary activity. He attended meetings of the *Verein Deutscher Offiziere,* which however was too closely tied to the *BVP* to give him much pleasure. The hostility he now felt toward the *BVP* strained many of his social contacts and even his relations with members of his own family.[19]

A little later he joined the newly formed *Deutschvölkische Offiziersbund* (*DVOB*).* On May 26 he attended a formal meeting of the *DVOB*, and he noted gleefully how nice it was to be "in uniform again," for on this occasion too he carried his unit's flag.[20] Thus by spring 1924 he was participating in many activities of the extreme wing of the *völkisch* and paramilitary activists in Bavaria.

Heinrich's deepening *völkisch* involvement was only one of the factors which ultimately led him to commit himself body and soul to the movement. At the time he was engaged in steadily increasing political activity he was also encountering serious problems regarding his professional future. When he quit his job in Schleissheim, these problems were glossed over by his brief period of *Reichswehr* service and the excitement and hope generated by the attempted *Putsch.* But even then he was trying to locate a job in agriculture which would be interesting and offer a chance for advancement. In the hope of locating an attractive position in Turkey he kept up a steady correspondence with a young Turkish student whom he had met at the *Technische Hochschule.*[21]

After the failure of the *Putsch* his job hunting became more serious since the lack of any immediate prospects left him in an embarrassing position. He was living with his parents who were unimpressed by his conspiratorial games and his prolonged idleness. Aside from trips to his mail contacts, chats with friends, *völkisch* activity, and extended reading, there was little for him to do except look for work. He studied French (his third venture at learning a modern language) and attended French conversation classes twice a week at the Berlitz school. Yet life was rather empty, and he amused himself, as he wrote to one of his old *Reichskriegsflagge* comrades, "studying, reading, and

*An organization, nominally under Ludendorff's direction, which brought together ex-officers with *völkisch* sympathies.

wandering around."[22] The resulting pressure to find work led him into wilder fantasies about employment opportunities. The number of letters to and from Turkey increased, and he followed up the slenderest leads. In February he sounded out the possibilities of work in the Caucasus and on February 12 even wrote to the Soviet Embassy to inquire if there was any chance of going to the Ukraine. This idea, so inconsistent with his anti-Communism, appears the more outlandish in light of the fact that he wrote the letter in the midst of preparations to go on a *völkisch* propaganda tour in northern Bavaria.[23]

The inquiry at the Soviet Embassy may raise some questions about Heinrich's repeated references in his book list to loyalty (*Treue*). In fact, however, it highlights how desperate he was to find work. He carefully combed through his list of acquaintances, relatives, and former teachers in a search for some connection that would turn up a job. All his talents in using people and social connections came once more to the fore, and he showed that he still possessed his old skills as a courtier. He made a social call on Falk Zipperer and his parents, and, although not calling on the Zipperers for employment help (he needed editorial advice from Falk) he noted in his diary, "I hold this acquaintanceship with Falk to be very useful."[24]

Despite these efforts he failed to uncover an attractive job. He wanted a position as a farm administrator, but he was informed by those who made inquiries on his behalf that he was too young and lacked the requisite experience. When his Turkish friend finally located a job for him in Turkey, the low pay and the fact that he had not learned Turkish seem to have combined to make him reject the offer.[25] His efforts to learn French while applying for a job in Turkey suggest that his plans to emigrate had always contained more romance than determination.

The constant inquiring and begging tended to embarrass him, especially when the replies included unintentional affronts. In June he wrote to his old army comrade Robert Kistler, who was then working in Milan, and asked about employment opportunities in northern Italy. Kistler's reply was friendly but pessimistic. He suggested that Heinrich try the "colonial areas" such as the Ukraine or Persia; since Heinrich had given up on Turkey and had apparently never received a reply from the Soviet Embassy, this was little help.

The letter concluded with an unintentional wound: "As a simple farm administrator, you can in the last resort get work in Germany."[26] This was just what Heinrich had not been able to do.

By summer 1924 the long series of frustrations and fruitless soundings had left him impatient and anxious to seize on anything that would offer escape. His hopes and ambitions did not fit his circumstances or prevailing conditions, and the depth of his devotion to the *völkisch* cause compounded his troubles. It was hard to find the perfect job while remaining convinced that it was necessary to overthrow the existing order. The events of 8-9 November had completed his change from conservative to radical revolutionary and had intensified his problem of trying to fit into a society which he abhorred. Even in cultivating job contacts his radical position on politics caused trouble. Many old family friends and relatives whose help he could well have used were *BVP* conservatives to whom his position as a *völkisch* activist gave pause. His political activity also weakened his connections with the *Bund Apollo,* many of whose members were staunch supporters of the Bavarian government.[27]

Other friends had simply drifted out of Heinrich's orbit. Lu and Kaethe were married in 1923 and had a baby girl in February of 1924. Lu gave Heinrich some help during the period when the authorities kept *Reichskriegsflagge* members under close surveillance, but the Zahlers were concerned with their own family life and had little time or opportunity for Heinrich. Perhaps in part because of Kaethe's hostility to rightist political activity, by the spring of 1924 the friendship had definitely cooled.[28] Heinrich for his part was no longer attracted by the type of social life he had led earlier. In February, for instance, he went to a gathering at the Loritz home and, even though the occasion was pleasant enough, he found it dull, merely noting in his diary that it had been "harmless."[29]

In a letter which he received in early August 1924, Mariele Rauschmayer, a girl he had known since childhood, put her finger on the root of his social difficulties: he had become a fanatic. She pointed out that she also had *völkisch* sympathies but could not completely commit herself to one faction or group "and speak of 'we' and 'us.' " For her the *völkisch* ideal was the life of the hero, not just "anti-Semitism and opposition to the *BVP.*" Politics are fine, she cautioned Heinrich, but he should remember that "there is so little that one can trust unconditionally."[30] Her points were well taken, but they had no effect on him, for his thinking had evolved beyond the vague endorsement of heroic ideals to a total commitment to a radical anti-Semitic ideology. His political activity in 1923-24 was based on a foundation of anti-Semitic and *völkisch* readings which became progressively more uncompromising and more extreme as the months went by.

During his employment at Schleissheim and during the eleven months of unemployment which succeeded it Heinrich had had ample time and opportunity to read and follow up his political and racist ideas. Between August 1922 and July 1924 he read eighty-one books; thirty-seven of these either led him to write down anti-Semitic comments in his notes or can be identified as anti-Semitic and *völkisch* in content.

One of the themes that appears most frequently in his notes is that of German virtue and superiority. On the *Nibelungenlied* he comments that it contains "unexcelled beauty, language, depth, and Germandom."[31] Although troubled by the difficult names in Klopstock's poetry, he memorized many passages and concludes that it "embodied endlessly beautiful language and German poetry . . . the man was a German."[32] His devotion to Germandom muted some of his former social and regional biases. On Joachim Nettelbeck's *Bürger zu Coberg* (Citizen of Coberg) he comments: "A genuine Prussian. A good old German *Bürger* (meant in the honorable sense)."*[33] Similarly he notes that a collection of nineteenth-century military poetry shows "the ethical strength and inner worth of the Prussian army and Prussian history."[34]

Nevertheless not everything which he encountered in his literary excursions into the German past pleased him. After finishing Nettelbeck's book he reflects that "there were enough *Spiessbürger* then too";[35] but his general conclusion is the glory of the German heritage. He particularly welcomed any work that touched on German domination of other people. Rudolf Bartsch's novel about German landlords in Slavic lands, for example, he describes as a "wonderfully pretty and clear German story."[36]

*Parentheses in the original.

Books which dealt with peasant life and showed the virtues and strengths of *Das Volk* always received favorable comment. He was especially grateful for Gustav Frenssen's novel, *Jörn Uhl,* set in Frisia, ending his note with the remark, "It is an excellent work which brings these kinds of characters and people before the eyes of the reader."[37] To Heinrich, as to many *völkisch* sympathizers, the essence of Germandom lay in devotion to the heroic ideal and a code of personal loyalty. After finishing Werner Jansen's *Das Buch Treue* (The book of loyalty), a reworking of the *Nibelungen* theme, he writes, "One of the most wonderful German books that I have read. The German loyalty [*Treue*] problem . . . wonderfully presented."[38] The hero who was true to his racial characteristics and fought against weakness and compromise was his highest ideal. Martin Otto Johannes' novel *Adel Verpflichtet* (noblesse oblige) described a German family in eastern Europe devoted to the maintenance of racial purity and the avoidance of the mixing of blood. Heinrich's comment on the work consists of one line: "This book presents my ideals and describes them."[39] Hans Günther's *Ritter, Tod und Teufel* (The knight, death, and the devil), a *völkisch* tract which glorified the conservative hero who struggled against fate, was another of his favorites. On this book too, he writes only a one-line note: "A book which expresses in pleasing words and sentences what I have felt and thought since I began to think."[40]

The language as well as the content of Heinrich's comments reveal his commitment to the racist ideal. Terms such as "nordic" and "Aryan" appear without explanation, as if they were integral parts of his thought pattern. The heroine of Björstjerne Björnson's *Mary* he describes as "a pure nordic and Germanic woman" even though the author has described her as of Spanish and Dutch descent.[41] Because she was "pure, strong and noble" she receives the honored racial attributes. Heinrich's racist commitment shows up also in his abhorrence of the Negro troops which the French had stationed in the Rhineland; tales exposing the actions of "black rapists" received his warmest praise.[42]

The center of his racist thinking was an intensified anti-Semitism. Descriptions of Jewish failings and crimes invariably draw favorable comment from him. Sometimes he makes only vague allusion to these themes, for example, by referring to "the rise of the Jews,"[43] but he also seeks out extreme anti-Semitic propaganda, and when he finds a tract which reviles Jews he is strengthened in his belief and in his desire to spread the faith. Theodor Fritsch's viciously anti-Semitic *Handbuch der Judenfrage* (Handbook of the Jewish question) elicits the comment: "It is a handbook in which one can find all the relevant material. Even an initiate is shaken when he reads all this with understanding. If only some of the eternally blind could have it put before their eyes."[44] On the eve of the November 1923 *Putsch* attempt he was pursuing his anti-Semitic studies by struggling through a nineteenth-century book about Yiddish. His comment on this work combines a hatred of Jews and suspicion of those who do not share his views. "One sees that Yiddish is a form of middle high German," he writes. "Shame to our beautiful language. The author seems to understand the Jews, it is true, however, he appears to be a man who has perhaps been advanced by the Jews. In any case, no hater of Jews."[45] Hatred of the Jews which a few years earlier had aroused his suspicions and academic reservations, had by this time become a touchstone of certainty.

The alleged sexuality and sexual misdeeds of Jews which threatened German racial purity attracted his interest. His comment on Eduard Stilgebauer's *Das Liebesnest* (The love nest), is rather bland—"Jewish blood and Jewish sensuality well depicted"[46]—but the trend of his thinking is revealed more clearly when he notes of Erich Kühn's novel *Rasse?* (Race?): "Naturally it is concerned with the Aryan and Jewish race problem. Especially good is the description of the leading astray and seduction of this German girl."[47] As might have been expected from a novel produced by the *Deutscher Volksverlag,* the evil Jewish villain exploited all the modern paraphernalia from automobiles to movies in order to corrupt the Germanic heroine.

Much of Heinrich's anti-Semitism had a markedly sexual character, and this played an important part in his continuing worried interest in sex. His devotion to rigid chastity remained as strong as ever, but he still speculated about the morals of girls whom he met and was quick to seize on erotic literature whenever it was available.[48] While visiting old friends in 1924 he found in their library Carl Felix Schlichtegroll's *Ein Sadist im Priesterrock* (A sadist in priestly attire) which had been banned in Germany in 1904. He raced through it in one day and noted that it was a "story of the corruption of girls and women in a sadistic manner in Paris."[49] On the same day he also read *Das Lustwäldchen* (The grove of joy), a generously illustrated volume of eighteenth-century erotic poetry. After completing the work he wrote: "Love poems that are concerned only with sexual love. The rhyme is often good. All told, however, as a picture, the poetry of decay."[50]

Heinrich's equation of eroticism with decay was another example of the degree to which he intertwined his own responses to sex with his *völkisch* ideology, for modern degeneracy was an established *völkisch* theme. His book comments include numerous references to the failings of "cultured men" and "decadent people."[51] This line of thought not only paralleled his idealization of the peasants and *Das Volk,* it also led to doubts about the excellence of the prewar system. Some of his notes stress the weaknesses of monarchy, and he is sharply critical of Kaiser Wilhelm's memoirs on the grounds that "someone else was always to blame."[52] Sexual failings also played a part in his doubts about the old order. His comment on Theodor Ewald's *Die Stiefel-Kathrine* (The girl in boots) reads: "A dreadful picture of immorality and pictures of monarchy and absolutism which could be used to denounce them. The old and oft-repeated story of base overrefined human beings such as we meet daily and are ourselves."[53]

Not all of the old order was adversely criticized. He describes the setting of a novel which covered the period before the war as "Germany's best time."[54] Wartime leaders who represented strong chauvinistic positions were eulogized. One such was Admiral Alfred von Tirpitz whom he characterizes as "a great organizer, an inventor, a good politician, and a good and great character."[55] Ludendorff, who had the twin virtues of wartime militancy and a postwar career as a *völkisch* leader, receives ringing praise for his war memoirs: "My total impression is only one of wonder, pride, sadness, and yet hope."[56] Bethmann-Hollweg and the Kaiser were usually the villains in the prewar piece, but even they escaped censure in some of his comments. Germany's enemies, past and present, are repeatedly denounced, however; France especially is attacked on the score of alleged internal corruption and the conduct of her forces in the Ruhr.[57]

Another element in German life which had earlier received

Heinrich's strong support was the church. Now it too came in for sharp criticism. His previous religious doubts had been somewhat vague and had arisen chiefly over the relatively trivial issue of dueling. But especially after the *Putsch* his reading comments not only reflect religious doubts but sometimes include attacks on the church. Books on Catholicism are criticized for being "too doctrinaire" or because he feels they embody a "fanatical Catholic spirit."[58] On completing Heinrich Böhmer's *Die Jesuiten* he notes that "it is now clearer to me than ever that it was a beneficial act of Bismarck's when he expelled the Jesuits."[59] Anti-Semitism reinforced his unorthodox view of organized Christianity. He enjoyed Renan's *Life of Jesus,* but it had one major flaw: "Renan believed that Jesus was a Jew, and he is from all appearances a friend of the Jews. However, he proves to me by his whole book that Jesus was no Jew, and that Christianity was and is the most important protest of the Aryans against the Jews, of good against evil."[60] The argument that Jesus was not a Jew was a recurrent theme in *völkisch* writing and indicates the problems which many *völkisch* sympathizers encountered in deciding on their attitude toward the church.

Heinrich continued to attend mass during 1923 and 1924 although he was not as regular as he had been earlier. In his reading comments he reveals a sharp hostility to any idea that smacks of materialism or atheism. The first portion of Ernst Häckel's *Die Welträtsel* (The world riddles), which outlines current scientific theories on the universe, pleases him greatly, but he flatly rejects the author's attacks on Christianity: "the section that begins about the middle of the book and concerns his suppositions and attack on, and denial of, a personal God, is just terrible."[61]

Spiritualism offered him an opportunity to hold on to his belief in the supernatural and escape his doubts about the church, and his reading indicates a greater interest and sympathy for spiritualism and the occult. He greets occult ideas as "unbelievably deep and significant"[62] and is especially appreciative of Karl du Prel's *Der Spiritismus* (Spiritualism) because it "really lets me believe in spiritualism and introduced me to it correctly for the first time."[63]

His emerging reservations about Catholicism were intensified by the events of 8-9 November. The *BVP* which was closely tied to the church not only controlled the

Bavarian government at that time but also represented the forces which in the months that followed imprisoned and tried Heinrich's paramilitary and *völkisch* friends. Just as anti-Semitism began to color his view of Catholic theology, so his opposition to the *BVP* tended to increase his doubts about the church and its leaders. A number of his diary entries show a greater sympathy for people who, while respecting Catholicism, stand outside the church.[64] The intertwining of political hostility and religious doubt is apparent in his comments on Alfred Miller's *Ultramontanes Schuldbuch* (The ledger of Ultramontane guilt), a sharply anti-Catholic attack on the Center Party by a *völkisch* writer. Heinrich swallowed without comment *völkisch* arguments identifying Protestantism with Germandom and reserved his wrath for Catholics sympathetic to the republic. "A new and frightening view of the workshop of the enemy," he writes. "The most bitter part comes when one reads all of this. . . . What enemies of the Christian religion of love these men are."[65]

Even though his reading sometimes took him far afield,* his primary interest continued to be *völkisch* propaganda and ideological tracts. In addition to the anti-Semitic works already mentioned, he read works which glorified *völkisch* heroes and developed the *völkisch* program. Two of his favorites were Adolf Viktor von Koerber's pamphlet *Adolf Hitler, sein Leben und seine Reden* (Adolf Hitler, his life and speeches) and Dietrich Eckart's *Der Bolschewismus von Moses bis Lenin* (Bolshevism from Moses to Lenin). On the latter work he notes that "it gives one perspective on all times and places. . . . I shall read this often."[66] The Koerber pamphlet was the source of recitations to sympathetic friends, and his short comment contains the only direct mention of Hitler to be found in the documents for 1924: "He [Hitler] is truly a great man, and above all a genuine and pure one. His speeches are splendid works of Germandom and Aryanism."[67]

---

*The wide range of titles in Himmler's book list suggests that he frequently read whatever was available, but improbable titles sometimes bore a relation to his political and racist views. Item 209 in his list was Dostoievsky's *House of the Dead,* and his bland comment sounds as if it had been a random selection. However, the work which he read immediately before this book was Dietrich Eckart's *Der Bolschewismus von Moses bis Lenin* which drew anti-Semitic lessons from incidents described in *House of the Dead.*

The emphasis on purity and the pretentious vagueness of this note are typical of Heinrich's book comments during this period. At this time Hitler was evidently an important symbol to Heinrich, but there is no sign that he held any special personal magnetism for him. Perhaps Himmler's later veneration of the *Führer* arose from the fact that throughout these years Hitler was taking his place among the abstract *völkisch* symbols with which the young Himmler was furnishing his ideological home. By 1926, when Heinrich first came into close contact with Hitler, this symbolism had been so firmly established and was so important to him that he protected it by never going beyond fawning adulation.

In 1924, however, he still lacked this degree of confidence and tried to master the philosophic works which were supposed to provide the conceptual basis of the movement. Unfortunately he usually chose the wrong books. Instead of Comte de Gobineau's *Inequality of the Human Races* he read the same author's *The Renaissance;* instead of Houston Stewart Chamberlain's *Foundations of the 19th Century* he struggled through *Richard Wagner.* His comments on the "higher German spirit" and the "spiritual richness" of Chamberlain's book indicate that he tried very hard to gain some edification from these works.[68] But even though he read the more popular writings of the masters, he had to confess that much of the content was beyond him. Tucked in with his praise of Chamberlain and Wagner are the sentences: "There are many portions of the book that are hard to understand. In fact the whole thing is hard to read."[69]

It seems clear that it was not the philosophic works of *völkisch* thinkers that captured Heinrich for the movement. The major factor which pointed him toward the *völkisch* camp was the interaction of his own value crisis and the circumstances in which he found himself. Reading and study played a part in intensifying his beliefs and helping him knit them together, but they were primarily aids to his development rather than its initiators. As Hitler in *Mein Kampf* was soon to advise his readers to do, Heinrich tried to read books in order to strengthen his faith. He had to choose his books carefully however. His old worship of the printed word remained and this sometimes came into conflict with his need for ideological assistance so that he was not always certain about the proper line to take. While giving a speech in February 1924 he was apparently somewhat concerned because his talk and that of his companion "bordered very closely on National Bolshevism."*[70] But these problems were peripheral; concerning the central issues of paramilitary activity, anti-Semitism, and German recovery he was firmly rooted in the *völkisch* ideology.

In the light of his feverish activity on behalf of the *völkisch* cause and his ideological commitment it is not surprising that the years 1923-24 showed rather marked changes in his behavior and personality traits. He did not undergo a Jekyll and Hyde transformation. His way of doing things and his likes and dislikes remained essentially unchanged. The pedantry was still there, as was the love of socializing and the use of rigid personality defenses to protect his feelings. He still embodied many of the homely virtues—helpfulness, love of family, and kindness to little children. But the most unpleasant features of his makeup, which had begun to surface clearly during his last year in the *Technische Hochschule,* were now more sharply defined and were intensified by his image of himself as a warrior in the *völkisch* cause. As a student he had relished the pose of omniscient hardness which enabled him to dominate other people in social situations and triumph over their opinions in discussions. At the same time he had been eager to classify people and to affix labels that would enable him to moralize about the behavior and failings of others. By 1923-24 these features of his personality had deepened. The lines which separated him from people with other opinions had become more rigid. The omniscience had been reinforced by ruthlessness in imposing his views and destroying opposition. The hardness was no longer simply a social mask; it had become a tool to be used to compel others to yield to his ideas.

A brief account of his involvement in the relations between his brother Gebhard and Gebhard's fiancée Paula in the course of 1923-24 will illustrate the degree to which he

*Heinrich's ideological ambivalence which seems so intensely personal was frequently merely a reflection of the confusion and desperate search for answers which prevailed in rightist literature. How could a young man of Himmler's modest thinking ability find ideological security when rightist writers were themselves so confused? Klemens von Klemperer's characterization of National Bolshevism as an approximation of the equation "anti-West equals anti-capitalism equals pro-East equals pro-Bolshevism" indicates the scale of the problem facing a young rightist seeker after truth and clarity (Klemens von Klemperer, *Germany's New Conservatism,* p. 140).

had developed into an arrogant and ruthless combatant. The trouble between Paula and Gebhard concerned the former's alleged infidelity. How serious her indiscretions were it is impossible to say, and the question is in any case unimportant. What is clear is that she did not conform to Heinrich's ideal of a shy, retiring, and chaste Gretchen. He had been somewhat uneasy about her free-and-easy attitude at the time of the engagement in 1922, but it was not until March 1923 that an incident occurred which brought his suspicions and desire to intervene into active play. Apparently Paula had committed an indiscretion, and Gebhard wrote Heinrich imploring him to go to Paula's home to help them settle the question.[71] Heinrich went, as requested, but what occurred while he was there is not clear. A month later, however, he drafted a letter to Paula which gives a glimpse of the way his mind was working. Paula had apparently made four pledges of her past and future fidelity, and this was the point Heinrich chose to attack:

> I will gladly believe that you will uphold these four things, especially as long as Gebhard works directly on you through his personal presence. But that is not enough. A man must have certainty from his bride, even if he is not present for years, and doesn't see her and they don't hear anything from each other for a long time (which in the coming terrible war years only too easily could be the case) that she herself with no word, no glance, no kiss, no gesture and no thought will be untrue to him. . . . You have a test which you should and *must** be able to withstand, and have in a shameful manner not withstood. . . . If your union is to be a happy one for you two and for the health of *das Volk*–which must be built on sound, moral families–you must control yourself with *barbaric** strength. Since you do not handle yourself strongly and firmly, and only control yourself to a small degree, and since your future husband, as I have already said, is too good for you, and possesses too little understanding of people and can't learn it since this age won't let it be learned, someone else must do it. Since you both approached me on this affair and drew me in, I feel myself obligated to do it.[72]

*Underlined in the original.

Although the document from which the above passage is taken was a draft, it is clear that a letter with approximately this tone and content was sent to Paula, for in early July she replied. Considering the kind of missive she had received, her letter was masterly. With only mild sarcasm she thanked him for his strictures which had helped jolt her out of a period of weakness and depression; but she stressed that she had never invited him to become involved, and she closed her letter with the polite but firm request that he mind his own business.[73]

For seven months after this Heinrich at least avoided outright meddling, but in February 1924 he somehow obtained information that convinced him that Paula had again strayed from the path of virtue. Without informing Gebhard, he immediately began to badger his father and mother in order to convince them that the family honor demanded an end to the engagement. After bringing Frau Himmler to tearful and reluctant agreement with his views, he managed to persuade his father as well. Only after this operation was completed did he confront Gebhard directly. When Gebhard agreed to go along and allowed the engagement to end, Heinrich was triumphant and at the same time scornful of his brother's lack of resistance. It was he said, "as if he [Gebhard] had absolutely no soul."[74] The termination of the engagement was especially distasteful to the Himmlers. In addition to the embarrassment of formal nullification there was the added fact that Paula's family was distantly related to the Himmlers. Yet whenever his parents or Gebhard showed any reluctance about going through with the break, Heinrich was ready to apply more pressure. He visited mutual friends to explain why the engagement must end and in the process tore the girl's reputation to shreds. When a letter arrived from Paula, his response was to stress the need to "stand firm and not let oneself be deterred by doubts."[75]

The formal announcement ending the engagement was finally sent, and Heinrich got his wish that, in order to stress the finality of the break all the presents which had been exchanged be returned. Paula's father tried to put a good face on the business and suggested that they end the engagement by mutual consent, adding that he felt the return of presents was silly. Once again Heinrich's hard line triumphed, and the Himmlers rejected all compromise. Paula still tried to be friendly with Gebhard; her only criticism of him was that he paid attention to Heinrich. "Your brother, who is two years younger than you are, takes it upon himself to educate me for you," she wrote, and then added, "You yourself could not find his letter to me proper."[76]

The whole unpleasant incident should now have ended. But Heinrich was still not prepared to let things be. It may be that Paula's rebuke stung him to renewed action; certainly it did not produce remorse. On March 9 he hired a private detective named Max Blüml instructing him to uncover any information on immoral or illegal activities on the part of Paula or her family. On March 12 he wrote to an acquaintance who was living in Paula's home town asking him to pass on any compromising information he could discover on the girl or her parents. He frankly admitted that he was making this request "without the knowledge of my brother" and claimed that it was necessary in case Paula's father, whom he described as "very sly and nimble," decided to make trouble. After assuring his correspondent that he would only use the information in case of direst need, he added that he would appreciate hearing any stories "that you have heard and which you can *prove*!"*[77]

The reply to this letter included no damaging information against Paula, but on March 14 he received from the private detective a collection of stories and gossip that might have been compromising. Armed with this report he seems to have felt that he could let the affair run its course. Five days later he sent back more gifts which he had received from Paula's parents during the preceding two years, claiming that he had forgotten to send them earlier. As a final slap, he apparently sent no letter but merely enclosed one of his visiting cards in the package. Yet even then he kept his ears open for any hint that Paula or her family might try to defend themselves. His final onslaught came two months later in a letter to mutual friends. He asks them to tell Paula to stop saying nasty things about the Himmlers and adds the warning that, although he is a nice fellow, "I will be completely different if anyone forces me to it. Then, I will not be stopped by any false sense of pity until the opponent is socially and morally ousted from the ranks of society."[78]

---

*Underlined in the original.

This was Heinrich's last blast in this long drawn-out episode. It is clear that from beginning to end he was talking himself into a position of vindictive ruthlessness. Yet, in contrast to his earlier behavior, in 1923-24 he not only talked, he also acted and sustained his action over a period of thirteen months. Although this incident is certainly the most striking example of the increasing hardness in his personality, there are other signs that point in the same direction. His sharpened partisanship and vindictiveness went hand-in-hand with his *völkisch* activity and his ideological devotion to the extreme Right. He had reached the peak of alienation from the day-to-day world around him, not merely because he rejected current conditions and was preparing to work to change them, but because his whole mentality was now attuned to ruthless struggle on behalf of a cause. Mariele Rauschmayer was right; he had acquired the characteristics of a fanatic.

It was this combination of personal and ideological problems coupled with his unrealistic hopes for a prestigious post in agriculture which made it difficult for him to find his place in 1924. His state of mind ruled out an inferior position from which he would have to work his way up. A position at the top might have offered compensations to offset the losses that would have been entailed in giving up his role as an ideological combatant; but with his training and experience he could not attain such a position.* Dedication of his life and professional hopes to the cause seemed to offer the best way out of his dilemma.

In late June a chance to follow this road beckoned. Gregor Strasser, a leader of the *Nationalsozialistische Freiheitsbewegung* and its *Gauleiter* for Lower Bavaria, needed someone to act as his secretary and general assistant. Heinrich seized the opportunity and applied for the job without delay. As soon as he was accepted (in early July), he left Munich to assume his duties in Landshut where Strasser maintained his office. He seems to have known that he was embarking on an important new road and to have realized that he was turning his back on much that had gone before. When he left, he did not inform even his closest friends where he was going. It was not until early November that Lu and Kaethe discovered that he was gone. His new job also marked

---

*See above, pp. 139-140.

a sharp break with the wishes of his parents who had wanted him to go to work but looked with foreboding on his decision to prolong what they considered political romanticism. When people inquired what had happened to Heinrich, they gave vague and evasive replies. The move to Landshut also widened the gap between Heinrich and his brothers, who remained within the Himmler family orbit and the accepted political and social norms.[79]

Heinrich could bear these sharp breaks and the parental disapproval for the same reasons that, perched above Strasser's drugstore in Landshut, he could find satisfaction in his secretarial duties. He had found a role which embodied his hopes and ideas, which gave him a vehicle through which he could apply his talents in a fight without compromise. As he said in a letter to Robert Kistler, who was still trying to help him find a farming job, he had become a "heroic martyr":

> The organizational work, which I run by myself [*sic*] pleases me very much and the thing would be beautiful, if one could work for victory or the war of liberation in the near future. But for us *Völkische* it is a toil of self-sacrifice which in the near future will not bring visible fruit. . . . [We work] with the awareness that the fruit of this labor will come in later years, and that perhaps our labor is, for the moment, at a lost post. However, we few do this hard work undeterred, out of boundless love for the German homeland. . . . It is a selfless service to a great idea and a great cause.[80]

After a long search and the anguish of jettisoning many of his dearest beliefs and closest human associations, he had found his place at last.

Chapter X

The Party Worker

In early 1924 Heinrich assumed his new duties in Landshut. During the five years that had passed since he left this city to begin his first, ill-fated *Praktikum* in Oberhaunstadt life in the sleepy little community on the Isar had gone on much as before. A number of the Himmlers' friends and relatives, notably the Zahler family and Falk Zipperer's parents, still resided there. Heinrich had remained in contact with many Landshut people over the years and easily resumed relations with them. Thus, even as he embarked on a new career, he was surrounded by people who could provide much of the warmth and support of home.

Comforting echoes of an earlier day could only play a supporting role, however, for he had come to Landshut to begin a career in party work. The *Nationalsozialistische Freiheitsbewegung* (*NSFB*) with which he had cast his lot provided an excellent outlet for his pent-up energies. It was a loosely organized group, held together by the memory of Nazi strength and the hope of making political capital out of the divisions and mutual recriminations which followed the *Putsch* attempt of 1923. In Strasser and Ludendorff it had leadership of a fair quality; its paramount need was for competent staff and administrative workers to consolidate its position. Wherever Heinrich looked he found much to be done, and he set to work without delay.

His primary responsibility was to serve as Strasser's deputy as *Gauleiter* for Lower Bavaria. Beyond that he was required to organize the business side of his chief's activity as party leader at the national level. Strasser spent much of his time traveling about Germany giving speeches, encouraging local leaders, and mediating disputes. Heinrich had to make the administrative machine in Strasser's home base as efficient as possible and at the same time take care of the details of his peripatetic life. He handled the routine correspondence, maintained the files, and took care of scheduling and transportation.

Although secretarial duties remained the core of his responsibility, he was soon involved in party activities on a broad front. He assisted in the preparation of the *Gau* newspaper, *Der Kurier für Niederbayern*, and worked diligently at selling subscriptions. He also traveled through northern Bavaria working with local party leaders to make the administrative system more uniform and efficient. Sometimes he went by train, but normally he used a recently acquired motorcycle to shuttle from one little village to another. Everywhere he went he carried the same message: the need to strive for party growth and unity. When the *Reichstag* was dissolved in late October 1924, the task of aiding in an election campaign was added to his other duties. His scheduling activities became more important as he arranged campaign appearances and tried to galvanize the party faithful and their leaders for an all-out effort. Whenever possible he participated directly in the campaign, making speeches in the smaller towns and villages.[1]

The campaign of October-December 1924 was a disaster for the *NSFB* whose representation in the *Reichstag* was reduced from thirty-two to fourteen. Strasser managed to win a seat, which lightened some of the gloom in Landshut, and Heinrich could draw some satisfaction from the political experience he had gained. But the voters' decision on December 7 could only mean that the party as a whole had failed to create a permanent political organization out of the potentially favorable circumstances of 1923-24. The rightist political mood of the electorate had begun to turn, and the *NSFB* had failed to unify the numerous *völkisch* splinter groups. Unity had never been one of the hallmarks of the *völkisch* cause, but during 1924 factionalism had become more pronounced than ever. The legal ban imposed by the state governments on those groups which had participated in the *Putsch* of November 1923 led to the formation of countless sports clubs and patriotic societies as front organizations. Since the central offices of the *NSDAP, Oberland,* and *Reichskriegsflagge* had been suppressed and the names of the new formations varied from state to state and region to region, authority tended to be local, and the leaders who emerged were extremely jealous of their prerogatives. To make matters worse, Hitler, imprisoned in the old fortress of Landsberg for his part in the November *Putsch,* refused to commit himself to any faction or political program.

The *NSFB* made a heroic effort to solve the problem, but the factionalism was too strong. Much of Heinrich's time and effort in 1924 was spent on an attempt to mollify the various cliques and special-interest groups, but once it was clear that no election plums were to be secured by unity, the last barrier to *völkisch* anarchy was swept away.[2] After the December 7 elections the *NSFB* could do little but wait and hope for the emergence of an issue or an individual to serve as a rallying point for the various groups. Such was the situation when on December 12, 1924, Adolf Hitler was released from prison.

Hitler was the only major leader who had increased his prestige in the aftermath of the *Putsch.* He had seized the opportunity provided by his trial and imprisonment to establish himself as the martyred *völkisch* hero. His stance of aloofness during the factional fights of 1924 exempted him from most of the bitterness and recrimination involved. And he could claim that he was not responsible for the election strategy which had ended in the defeat of December 7. From every point of view, if he could solve the problem of factionalism and come up with a strategy for the future, Hitler was in a very favorable position.

For two months (December 1924-February 1925) Hitler bided his time and prepared the groundwork. Prolonged preparations were necessary, for he had decided on two basic changes: abandonment of the *Putsch* strategy and rejection of any coalition between the *NSDAP* and other groups. He was convinced that the only chance of success lay in a unified and independent party which was prepared to accept a long struggle in its drive to develop a mass following. In the long run this strategy would give greater weight to political organizers in the movement than to those who toyed with independent paramilitary activity. It would also demand a leader with charismatic qualities who would be able to form a cohesive organization and sustain his followers during dark days.

In the short run Hitler could not confine himself to former *NSDAP* members but had to salvage all the manpower he could from the various warring factions, including all those who had been involved in the *Deutscher Kampfbund* in 1923 or had broken with the government due to the events of 8-9 November. In early February his cautious maneuvering achieved a major victory when Gregor Strasser and the other leaders of the *NSFB* agreed to dissolve their organization. On February 27, 1925, at a mass meeting held in Munich Hitler announced the refounding of the *NSDAP.* He stressed that only the new Nazi party offered the *völkisch* cause a road to salvation and that only through his person could the necessary unity be achieved. The climax of the meeting came when he called upon the leaders of the various factions to bury their animosities and take their place in the Nazi fold. Although some of the men in question had previously made their peace with Hitler, they were now called upon publicly to embrace their old opponents and pledge a new beginning. This ritual placed Hitler in a commanding position over those, such as Strasser, who agreed to cooperate. In the months that followed *der Führer* made it clear that his goal of unity and subordination could not be lightly disregarded. Backsliders were brought to heel, and groups and leaders who refused to submit were warned that they could expect war to the knife.

The paramilitary groups that had previously been associated with Hitler posed an especially ticklish problem. Although the ban on the *NSDAP* had been lifted in most states, the earlier paramilitary formations of the party and its former allies were still outlawed nearly everywhere. During 1924 cover organizations had been formed, for example, the *Frontbann* for *SA* members and the *Alt-Reichsflagge* for the former *Reichskriegsflagge.* When the *NSDAP* was refounded the paramilitary commanders wanted to maintain their existing formations in a quasi-autonomous position. They pointed out that it was illegal to reconstitute the old groups in the larger states and that new formations might sacrifice the organizational efficiency already attained. Here again, however, Hitler would accept nothing short of absolute subordination to the party and himself. Many paramilitary cover organizations were dissolved. Leaders who refused to submit were cut adrift. Among the latter was Ernst Röhm who on May 1, 1925, resigned his position in the *Frontbann* (he had lost his *Reichstag* seat in the December 1924 election), severed his connection with Hitler, and soon left Germany to serve as a military adviser to the Bolivian army.[3]

Only eighteen months earlier Heinrich had been Röhm's man. Yet Röhm's departure had no effect on him. By May 1925 Röhm had nothing to offer except abandonment of the cause, and Heinrich was too deeply committed to give it up for old times' sake. In addition, during the previous year young Himmler's attention and involvement had shifted from paramilitary to administrative and political activity. His love of soldiering was not dead, but it had been fitted into a political and party context. To the degree that Gregor Strasser represented an emphasis on political organization, Heinrich was his man in 1925, not Röhm's.

Since Strasser had played a crucial role in the establishment of Hitler's new *NSDAP,* it was only natural that an easy transition should be arranged for former members of the *NSFB.* In most areas the organizations which Strasser had created, including the *Gaue* and *Ortsgruppen,* were merely relabeled and emerged as integral parts of the *NSDAP.* The *Völkischer Beobachter* casually reported on May 12, 1925, that Strasser's whole organization in Lower Bavaria had crossed over to the *NSDAP* and that the party functionaries, including *Gau* deputy leader Heinrich Himmler, would retain their former posts.[4] Thus through a casual and routine change of party names the young Himmler became a local Nazi party official.

Much of Heinrich's time as a provincial *NSDAP* official was spent on the same tasks that he had performed before. He was basically a secretary, and it was the administrative side of the *NSDAP*'s activities in Lower Bavaria that concerned him most directly. He was still busy with the circulation problems of the *Kurier für Niederbayern* which continued under the same name. The propaganda activities in the *Gau* and Strasser's agitational work throughout Germany occupied more and more of his time. He also made increasingly frequent public appearances and often spoke at local Nazi rallies in the *Gau.* Especially during the election campaigns, however, he went further afield and appeared at party meetings and campaign rallies in many parts of Germany.[5]

Most of Heinrich's speeches focused on the condition of the German peasants and the need for radical measures to assist them. He stressed the important role the peasants must play in German recovery; for only if they gained their rightful place would Germany again become strong and triumphant. And only through the *NSDAP,* he argued, was there a chance for agricultural reform. In denouncing the enemies of the peasants and Germany, Himmler went down the list of Nazi villains: the Jews, the French, the Communists, and the republic. His major stress, however, was on the economic and social woes of the existing system. His ideological orthodoxy appears in the title of one of his speeches, "What Does Adolf Hitler Want? "–a title which was used by many Nazi speakers and showed up again and again in the *Völkischer Beobachter* in the section on party news. But his emphasis on the social and peasant side also appears in his repertoire of speeches; two of his favorite themes were "National or International Socialism? " and "The Destruction of the German Peasantry."[6]

The only Himmler speech surviving from this period begins with the assertion that the republic represents "the spirit of money" and Jewish exploitation. It goes on to paint a picture of economic woe, complete with grasping middlemen and usurious moneylenders. Heinrich's answer to the peasants' problem was the victory of the *NSDAP* and the establishment of "national socialism," by which he meant the use of the state's power to beat down the evil tendencies of money and allow the old-fashioned life of the peasantry to continue.[7] The danger of money capital was an old Nazi theme; Heinrich merely pumped new life into it by relating it to the group in German society which was then most liable to injury in the fluctuations of financial capitalism.

Heinrich also edged forward in the direction of linking the party's racial message to the idealization of the peasantry. Some of his reading and writing during this period may have been influenced by the *Artamanen Bund,* a utopian group which expounded the doctrine of "blood and soil" and argued that only through the revitalization of peasant communities could racial and national strength revive.[8] This line of thinking clearly pointed toward the racial and peasant community notions which were to play so important a role in the mystical ethos of the *SS* during the years of Nazi power. It was of grave import for the future. In this period, however, the primary emphasis of Heinrich's public agitation for the party was not on utopian peasant communities but on economic and social grievances.

The reason for this emphasis is not far to seek. Once again Heinrich was conditioned by the political environment in which he found himself. In the course of 1925-26 Gregor Strasser and his associates were involved in an attempt to organize those groups in the *NSDAP* that wanted to emphasize the social revolutionary features in the Nazi program. Strasser and his friends wished to exploit the social-economic discontent within Germany by offering a platform which denounced the evils of capitalism and expounded the virtues of a fuzzy theory of social cooperation which might best be described as that of the corporate state. Gregor Strasser, his brother Otto, the young Paul Joseph Goebbels, and a group of northern *Gauleiter* worked together within the *NSDAP* to give organizational structure to these ideas. Opinion among historians today is deeply divided on the question of what Strasser and his friends were after in 1925-26. It seems most likely, however, that their object was to move Hitler away from his heavy reliance on the Munich anti-Semites with their upper-class orientation; they wanted the party to proclaim a message of social revolution with only a spice of anti-Semitism.[9] In any event the organizational and ideological squabbles between the Strasser group and the rest of the party dragged on throughout late 1925 and early 1926 until finally in February 1926 Hitler asserted his leadership and rejected all changes in the party program.

Heinrich played no leading role in these developments; he merely served his immediate superior and took care of assigned tasks. But the incessant meetings and maneuvering gave him an opportunity to become familiar with Goebbels and Strasser's other leading allies. Goebbels was impressed by Himmler's abilities and described him as "a good guy and very intelligent."[10] Himmler was allowed to attend some of the organizational meetings with Strasser but was not invited to the showdown meeting with Hitler in Bamberg in February 1926.[11]

The major effect of the whole affair on Heinrich was the influence it exerted on the style and content of his public statements. From Strasser and his friends he learned to focus the attention of his listeners on the social and economic grievances of the peasantry. On occasion he employed the same kind of radical economic arguments as Strasser. In the course of his speech on October 13, 1926, Himmler described the rise of economic power in the following terms: "Capitalism made itself master of the machine and with it enslaved the people. As a result, there was a longing for freedom by the people, and this will to freedom expressed itself in the class struggle of the workers."[12] This kind of homespun Marxist phraseology came directly from Strasser, who used it to underscore his social-economic radicalism. After Hitler decided against him, the Marxian phrases gradually disappeared from Strasser's speeches, and Heinrich's Marxian gloss soon vanished too. But his emphasis on the social and economic problems of the peasantry remained.

The mystical features of the blood and soil doctrine which in the hands of the *Artamanen Bund* pointed toward utopian communities, seldom intruded into Heinrich's public statements, a fact that greatly enhanced his value as a party worker. Hitler continuously fought against the mystical and occult tendencies among his followers, for his primary goal was the seizure of power, and for this he needed, not quacks and mystics, but an efficient political machine. Certain spiritualist tendencies had to be tolerated—Hitler's own ideas often had mystical overtones—but party members with such leanings had to keep their ideas subordinated to political considerations if they were to enjoy any future in the party. Heinrich's development in 1925-26 of a public political position based on bread-and-butter issues thus helped him to fit more easily into Hitler's political machine.

If Heinrich's future as a party worker depended on his overcoming his mystical bent, his dreams of military glory were an even graver threat to his career. Throughout 1925-26 Hitler fought a running battle with those who sought to establish autonomous paramilitary formations or hoped to use the party's units for a *Putsch* or a military adventure. A rising man in Hitler's system had to withstand the temptation to play soldier except when political considerations made this necessary. In 1924, while the *NSDAP* was outlawed, Heinrich had joined the *Alt-Reichsflagge* and been active in the *völkisch* veterans' group, the *Deutschvölkischer Offiziersbund* (*DVOB*). In this group he remained active during 1925 and early 1926, even though Hitler was gradually sharpening the lines of demarcation between the *NSDAP* and all other *völkisch* organizations. Part of Heinrich's desire to remain in the *DVOB* probably arose from the fact that it had close relations with the *Reichswehr* and its members periodically received indoctrination and training by regular army officers, as they did in January 1926. As late as February 1926 Himmler continued to serve in the *DVOB* and even recruited members among his friends. By June 1926, however, Hitler forbade *NSDAP* members to participate in such groups, and Heinrich quickly submitted to his *Führer* and resigned. The last reference to the *DVOB* in his private papers is an angry letter, dated June 18, 1926, from a *DVOB* official accusing him of intriguing against the local *DVOB* chapter as part of a Nazi plot to destroy the organization.[13]

Although Hitler drew a sharp dividing line between the party and outside paramilitary groups, he was less successful in eliminating the confusion which surrounded the party's own units. When the *NSDAP* was reestablished in 1925, the *SA* was still banned in most German states. In order to keep his political machine completely autonomous, Hitler was forced to establish a new Nazi paramilitary group. Building on the *Stosstrupp* (protective guards unit) which had been a small party formation prior to the *Putsch,* Hitler authorized the formation of the *Schutzstaffel* (*SS*), whose major function was to serve as a reliable paramilitary unit of the party in states where the *SA* was still outlawed. In Bavaria, where the *SA* was legalized in the course of 1925, the *SS* had to find functions which would minimize friction with the larger and better established Brown Shirts. This led on the one hand to an emphasis on the elitist role of the *SS* as a special honor guard in the tradition of the *Stosstrupp* and on the other to the assumption by the *SS* of a series of petty duties which other organizations refused to perform. Thus the *SS* was given the special assignment of selling subscriptions to the *Völkischer Beobachter,* received the exclusive right to sell shirts to the *SA,* and finally, in October 1926, took over the job of selling *SA* caps as well.[14]

The significance of Heinrich's role in the *SS* at this time should be evaluated in the light of this situation. He joined the *SA* and the *SS* in 1925 and soon became the chief of the *SS* in *Gau Niederbayern.*[15] However, his position was the direct result of the party's effort to keep the paramilitary organizations in the hands of regular party officials and brought little glory with it. Most of the activities he supervised in the *SS* paralleled the routine administrative duties he performed as deputy leader of the *Gau.* Only rarely did the activities of the *SS* at this time give any hint of its future fame and power; for most of the time its members served as newspaper salesmen and purveyors of uniforms. The party leadership was never able completely to subdue the tendency of these units to play soldiers but on the whole the *SA* and *SS* were given political rather than military assignments.[16] Like an old fire horse, Heinrich was always lured by a whiff of military smoke (in 1926 he was engaged in a clandestine effort to locate weapons left over from World War I), but he managed to adapt himself to the limited paramilitary role demanded by the party and learned to curb his enthusiasm.

By the middle of 1926 the young Himmler had overcome the most important personal obstacles to a successful party career. He had steered clear of factionalism, had learned to control his mystical inclinations, and had become part of the machinery by which the paramilitary groups were subordinated to party discipline. In his unobtrusive and humdrum way he had also revealed abilities that marked him out as an unusually competent provincial administrator. Through Strasser and through his own social and paramilitary activities he had made many personal contacts throughout Germany which enabled him to get things done. He possessed an ingrained bureaucratic bias which made it easy for him to establish precise procedures and maintain an efficient set of records. Since many of his fellow provincial officials were military or ideological enthusiasts with little taste or ability for administration, Heinrich's talents shone brightly. As Hitler and the party struggled to establish administrative order and centralized control, the relative efficiency of *Gau Niederbayern* could not but enhance Heinrich's reputation in Munich. Even more important was his early training as a courtier. From infancy he had been taught that it was vital to accommodate important people and work his way up through their favor. One of the most serious problems he had faced between 1919 and 1923 was his inability to make this approach work in the more fluid situation under the Weimar Republic. Once committed to the *NSDAP,* however, he found in the hierarchical structure of the party a perfect milieu for the operation of his administrative ability and courtier mentality.

The only serious challenge to his career lay in the dismal prospects of the party itself. In 1925-26, the *NSDAP* was the smallest political party in Germany, and Hitler's policies were severing connections with numerous groups which had previously cooperated with it. The Weimar Republic appeared stronger and more stable during this period than at any time since its inception, and the chances of recovering German power and prestige through a policy of reconciliation seemed promising. To the vast majority of Germans, Hitler and the *NSDAP* looked like a band of cranks. Despite his success in adjusting to the requirements of the *NSDAP,* Heinrich cannot have totally blinded himself to the fact that he was attached to a microscopic party which was short of funds and, by normal standards, had few prospects. The price of his attachment to this cause had been the sacrifice of many of the friendships of his student years and the evaporation of most of the closeness which he had enjoyed with relatives and family friends.[17] Even his parents made it clear that they not only disapproved of his party work but looked on him as the proverbial lost son. An occasional happy Christmas vacation at home cannot have concealed the fact that in their eyes he was a failure.[18]

He seems to have accepted this situation, which would have been unbearable a few years earlier, as a necessary concomitant of his commitment to the Nazi cause. Neither completely rejecting his parents nor trying to cling to them, he was satisfied to leave the relationship in a state of polite reserve and gain his emotional satisfaction from his party work.

The doubts which crept in about his personal future and that of the cause must have been reinforced by the wretchedly low wages he received. The exact figure cannot be determined, but his salary did not exceed 150 marks a month. Scattered through his papers are signs that he was having great difficulty making ends meet. He borrowed money frequently (sometimes as much as 50 marks at a time) and had to suffer the indignity of being dunned for repayment.[19] Of the sixty books which he read during his two years in Landshut, at least two-thirds were loaned by friends or fellow party workers.[20] After his three-year struggle to get along on little money at the *Technische Hochschule* it must have been doubly difficult for him to resign himself to the prospect of permanent poverty.

From time to time he was caught by the old desire to push the party work away and obtain a solid position as a farm administrator. He even toyed again with the notion of emigrating to Turkey. But his tentative approaches led invariably to the same result: he was not qualified for an important post in Germany, and the prospects in Turkey seemed risky and insufficiently remunerative.[21] In the end he always pulled back, remained at his party post, and tried to quiet his doubts by immersing himself in the role of a Nazi expert on agriculture. As he said in a letter to a writer on farm subjects which he wrote on April 22, 1926, "I am myself a farmer [*Bauer*] even though I don't have a farm."[22]

His faith in the movement and his own commitment had to be sustained by the emotional satisfaction he derived from toiling at a lonely post. To overcome his doubts he scoured the polemical *völkisch* literature for supportive arguments and attempted to discover *völkisch* morals in everything he read. The basic pattern of his reading remained the same: numerous works on *völkisch* and patriotic themes were interspersed with books on religion, spiritualism, and sex. An occasional adventure story appeared in the list as well as a few works of classical German literature. The only new themes were in three books on espionage and police work and four titles on communism and the USSR.

What awakened his interest in crime and spying is not clear. He was horrified by a large volume on human torture, noting that it is a "frightening book about the beast in man which manifests itself in every century and in every state."[23] Yet he was curious about espionage and police control and was eager to learn about them. On Walter Nicolai's *Geheime Mächte* (The secret powers) he comments, "Very interesting. One can really learn something."[24] His curiosity did not take him very far, however, and he was unable to divorce his inquiry from his desire to discover *völkisch* lessons. In summarizing his opinion of Popoff's *Tscheka,* he writes that "the word Jew is not once mentioned in connection with the Cheka, which is almost completely Jewish, nor is it mentioned in relation to the earlier Tsarist Ochrana. A bad book."[25] His pretentious fanaticism led to the odd equation of secret-police work with Jews; at this time he did not relish the image of the secret-police power that he was subsequently to wield through the *SS* and the Gestapo.

Heinrich's comments on communism and the USSR also reveal his tendency to find anti-Semitic and *völkisch* lessons whenever possible. In early 1926, at the time when Strasser's effort to emphasize social-economic radicalism in the *NSDAP* was reaching its climax, Heinrich read three books on the USSR. Significantly, two of the three were borrowed from Strasser. Heinrich tried hard to be open-minded; on one book, he notes that the author's "attitude to Bolshevism is not instinctively hostile";[26] after reading another he grants grudgingly that "one must concede, even though there is a demonic element, a performance and an achievement."[27] He was simply unable, however, to keep his anti-Semitic views out of the way, dismissing one book as "friendly regarding the Jewish question" and characterizing another as "gripping, rich in ideas, Jewish."[28] The third work, an anti-Bolshevik polemic by a Russian refugee, swept away all his effort to be objective. An "account of the cruel terror of the Jewish Bolsheviks in Kiev," he writes and adds, "The Jews got control over the common people and that broke up everything."[29] The fact that the author did not mention Jews in the book (though a postscript by Alfred Rosenberg did) proved no barrier to the equation of Jews, Bolsheviks, and evil.

Heinrich's anti-Semitic fantasies became ever wilder, and his desire to believe had at all costs to be satisfied. A few doubts crept in when he read a pamphlet that branded William II a Jew, but ultimately he swallowed it. "One has the conviction that there is a meaningful *granum salis* in the claim of Wilhelm II's Jewish blood," he wrote and added that "the claim of the Jewish blood of the English is interesting."[30] The first claim consisted of the assertion that Queen Victoria's husband, the Prince Consort, was half Jewish, the second, of the statement that the Scots were one of the lost tribes of Israel because they did not eat pork. When the author of another pamphlet asserted that he was victimized by a Jewish plot to harass him by soft whistling whenever he entered a streetcar, the maximum objectivity that Heinrich can muster is: "Description of the Jewish system of moral torment. It is possible that a certain amount of paranoia may be involved. However, there is no question the system exists and is used by the Jews."[31]

Occasionally there are signs of his old academic caution, but they are in reference to trivial matters only or to assertions that created problems for his beliefs. Whenever a work threatens to raise questions which would overtax his biases, he simply ignores the problem. After a hard struggle with the "Grand Inquisitor" chapter in Dostoievsky's *Brothers Karamazov* he merely notes, "Talk between the Grand Inquisitor and Jesus Christ."[32] His ability to dodge an issue is paralleled by his willingness to be cast in the role of the solitary believer. Commenting on one of the characters in Werner Jansen's *Das Buch der Leidenschaft,* he writes: "Dietrich of Bern must have been an actual person, otherwise he would not have penetrated so deeply into the heart of the people. Therefore I feel that he belonged to these Germanic people, even though I may be completely alone in that belief today."[33] Similarly, when commenting on Jansen's *Das Buch Liebe* he stresses his adherence to his beliefs no matter what appearance there may be to the contrary: "The glorious song to the Nordic woman. It is the ideal picture about which we Germans dreamed in our youth and are ready to die for as men. One believes it all the time even though one is continuously being disillusioned."[34]

At every point he was resolved to hold to his party faith and persevere in the political struggle. By 1926 his employment prospects, strained family relations, and psychological makeup required that he fight on as one of the party faithful, hoping that his talents would be recognized and that his loyalty to the *NSDAP* would ultimately be rewarded. In this sense he was cornered. But within that corner the needs and demands of the party matched his own talents and devotion. It was merely a question of time until an opportunity would present itself that would allow him to move from his provincial post to a place in the central organization of the *NSDAP*.

Finally in September 1926, as part of a general reshuffling of party offices, the call came. Probably as compensation for his defeat on the party program, Gregor Strasser was given the post of Reich propaganda leader for the party. Himmler was made his deputy. Since propaganda operations had to be conducted in the party's central headquarters in Munich and Strasser traveled too much to exercise effective supervision, Heinrich was ordered to move to Munich on September 12 and take over the administration of the propaganda office. Nominally he was Strasser's deputy, but actually the day-to-day operations of the office were in his hands. Neither Strasser nor Himmler gave up their positions in *Gau Niederbayern,* they simply moved the *Gau* office to Munich so that Heinrich could handle the administrative side of both positions simultaneously.[35]

For a short period Himmler continued in his anomalous position as a provincial official and an officer of party headquarters. He even assumed the position of deputy leader for *Gau Oberbayern* as well.[36] But the logic of the move to Munich gradually asserted itself. He had turned his back on Landshut and the provinces. He was no longer Strasser's man, but a member of party headquarters with an opportunity to make a career for himself. He had no flair for propaganda, but he could now make full use of his talents as a bureaucrat and a courtier under the watchful eye of Hitler and the other party leaders. All the pieces of his life had fallen into place, for he was perfectly equipped to thrive in the bizarre world of professional Nazism. It was only necessary that in future years he act like the man he was in order to reap all the glory and power that Hitler's party could bestow.

Chapter XI

Portents of the Third Reich

Heinrich Himmler's career as a professional Nazi was the product of a gradual personal development which was neither irrational nor demonic. Challenged by the revolutionary changes which had begun to convulse traditional social institutions by the time of World War I, he responded by attempting to adapt the old values and patterns to the new conditions. As the changes became more rapid and erratic, however, he was unable to develop ideals and modes of conduct which would preserve the traditions he had already absorbed and still allow him to function effectively in the world in which he lived. Rather than throw off the ingrained codes of his childhood, he sought answers in activities and theories that alienated him more and more from the world around him. The military dreams and *völkisch* dogmas that supported him through the trials of late adolescence and early adulthood made impossible any reconciliation with existing society.

The rigidity, however, which barred the door to easy adjustment at the same time preserved the skills and behavior patterns which the old system prized. Once he had found the strength to make open avowal of his alienation from postwar society and to seek out a framework which fitted his values and personal needs, he was able to put these talents to work. His strengths and skills could be galvanized only in a setting which satisfied him ideologically. Of necessity such an environment had to be on the fringes of the social order and therefore desperately in need of the kind of contribution he could make. Thus Nazism provided the solution to his problems, while he in turn proved a valuable asset to it.

Granted the reasonableness of his commitment to Nazism, what were the signs, if any, in Himmler's early development that the commitment would be directed toward an organization such as the *SS*? (He was appointed deputy leader in 1927 and *Reichsführer SS* in 1929.)[1] Obviously, his enthusiasm for the military and his fruitless efforts to become a professional soldier pointed in this direction. The depth of his ideological devotion also foreshadowed the fanaticism which he later implanted in the *SS*. His class-conscious family background may have played some part in heightening his receptivity to elitist doctrines; certainly the period he spent as a member of the small band of professional Nazis fostered his differentiation from the common herd. As early as 1924 he envisioned a future dominated by an elite band of the racially pure. Commenting on Tacitus, *Germania* in September of that year he wrote: "How morally pure and elevated our forefathers were. So shall we be again, or at least some of us will."[2] After finishing Franz Haiser's *Freimaurer und Gegenmauerer im Kampf um die Welt Herrschaft* (Freemasons and anti-Freemasons in a fight for world domination) in March 1925 he exclaimed, "We must become a Kshatriya caste!"*[3]

His period of service under Röhm in the *Reichsflagge* and *Reichskriegsflagge* may also have helped to shape the ideas he used in the *SS.* In November 1929, while his former chief was still in Bolivia, Heinrich wrote him, "Many *SS* leaders have felt the effect of the training I received from you."[4] In a second letter of the same period he told Röhm, "When the organization [the *SS*] is at its peak you'll have great joy when I give you a complete report including pictures of this organization which is a successor of the *Reichskriegsflagge.*"[5] One must be cautious about accepting these remarks at face value, because in 1929 Heinrich was trying to get Röhm to raise money for the *SS,* and a touch of flattery may have been involved. However, there is probably a kernel of truth in his assertion that the style of the *Reichskriegsflagge* was carried over into the *SS.*

Yet none of these hints and foreshadowings get to the root of what perplexes us about Heinrich Himmler and the later *SS.* What disturbs us so profoundly is not the organization of the *SS* nor Himmler's ultimate position as Reich police chief, but the torture of millions of human beings and the extermination of millions more. No direct answer to these questions is to be found in Himmler's childhood and youth; the twentieth century cannot escape from its monstrosities by uncovering a mark of Cain or a Mephistophelean pact with the devil. Nazi ruthlessness and mass-extermination policies were the result of an intertwining of social forces and personal idiosyncracies. Like other cataclysms of our age, they defy simple explanation and seem to have evolved over

*An ancient Aryan warrior caste which has been carried over into modern India.

long periods of time. There is no doubt, however, that when the time came Heinrich Himmler accepted the role of remote-control torturer and mass murderer and carried out these tasks with organizations that he had helped to form.

Again, all the influences that inclined Himmler toward elitism and toward devotion to the Nazi party and its ideology may have contributed to his ultimate willingness to carry out torture and mass murder. Even in 1924 his extreme partisanship bore the marks of fanaticism, and his ability to carry out a protracted campaign of harassment and vilification against his prospective sister-in-law indicates that, once aroused, he recognized no limits. A more direct connection between his early ideas and his later activities is to be found in his concept of *Treue* or loyalty. Praise of company or party loyalty is common in organizations, but *völkisch* writers and speakers in the early 1920s elevated it to the paramount position in their value system. Loyalty became the bedrock of the *völkisch* faith. Heinrich went even further and made the vague notion of *Treue* synonymous with the upholding of all his likes and dislikes. *Treue* came to mean consistency with his beliefs on sexual behavior and political activity, regardless of the social consequences or the opinions of others. Gradually *Treue* came to be focused on the absolute necessity of carrying out the wishes of the party and its *Führer,* Adolf Hitler. The slogan of the *SS, Meine Ehre heisst Treue,* marked the institutionalization of this concept inside the Nazi system. But if the heart of one's value system is party *Treue,* then what actions are to be regarded as proof of one's virtue? Certainly not the actions performed in obedience to orders of the kind that most men are willing to obey. Only by the willing execution of orders and the assumption of responsibilities that others find immoral or distasteful can one truly demonstrate the highest commitment to *Treue.* The youthful devotion to *Treue* as solving the problems of conflicting values ultimately placed Himmler in a position where he could rationalize as a demonstration of virtue his assumption of responsibility for evil.

The idea of *Treue* would not have had the murderous consequences it did if Himmler had been in a position to exercise his judgment in detachment from his party commitment. Any opportunity to look at the situation from another point of view would have given him some means of grappling with the moral and social implications of his actions. But for him no such opportunity was possible. For Heinrich Himmler was not an adult convert to Nazism; it was through his commitment to the party and its ideology that he became an adult. It was his role as a professional party worker which allowed him to overcome his problems of identity and become a man. An adult Heinrich Himmler separate from the party and its ideology never existed. Himmler *was* Nazism. Short of death he could draw no line between the party and himself.

> Die alten Burschen leben noch,
> Noch lebt die alte Treue,
> Noch lebt die alte Treue.*

*Refrain of "O alte Burschenherrlichkeit," a German fraternity song of the mid-nineteenth century.

Appendix

Heinrich Himmler's Book List, 1919-26

The following listing of Heinrich Himmler's reading during this period of his life is taken from the future *Reichsführer*'s own annotated Book List, now preserved among the Himmler Documents in the *Bundesarchiv* at Koblenz. (Copies are available at the Hoover Institution, Stanford University.)

Approximately two hundred of the items listed were found in libraries in the United States. Of the rest, five (numbers 122, 168, 226(b), 232, and 233) defied every effort to trace them. Except for these five and a handful of works by such well-known writers as Goethe and Ibsen, bibliographical data have been supplied. Wherever it has proved possible to determine which edition of a publication Himmler actually read, the data given are for this edition. If the exact edition could not be determined, the data given are for the edition published nearest to the date at which he read the book.

1. Kügelgen, Wilhelm V. *Jugenderinnerungen eines alten Mannes.* Leipzig, 1919.
2. Ossian (James Macpherson?). *Fingal.*
3. Ossian (James Macpherson?). *Temora.*
4. Schmidt, Maximilian. *Naturalistische Volkserzählungen. (Gesammelte Werke).* Leipzig, 1908.
5. Schmidt, Maximilian. *Der Bubenrichter von Mittenwald. (Gesammelte Werke).* Leipzig, 1908.
6. Schmidt, Maximilian. *Humor. Lustige Geschichten. (Gesammelte Werke).* Leipzig, 1908.
7. Nabor, Felix (Karl Allmendinger). *Furchtlos und Treu!* Regensburg, 1913.
8. Aurbacher, Ludwig. *Ein Volksbüchlein.*
9. Blumröder, Gustav (Antonius Anthus). *Geist und Welt bei Tische, humoristische Vorlesungen über Esskunst.* 2 vols. Berlin, 1852.
10. Mann, Thomas. *Königliche Hoheit.*
11. Goethe, Johann Wolfgang von. *Faust (II).*
12. Verne, Jules. *Die Reise nach dem Mittelpunkt der Erde.*
13. Verne, Jules. *Die Reise durch die Sonnenwelt.*
14. Verne, Jules. *Von der Erde zum Mond.*
15. Verne, Jules. *20,000 Meilen unter dem Meer; Die geheimnisvolle Insel; Die Kinder des Kapitän Grant; Reise um die Erde in 80 Tagen; Michael Strogoff.*
16. Verne, Jules. *Fünf Skizzen* ("Eine Idee des Dr. Ox," etc.).
17. Verne, Jules. *Der Chancellor; Tagebuch des Passagier; I. R. Kazollern; Martin Paz.*
18. Wildermuth, Ottilie. *Frauenleben II. (Aus dem Frauenleben).* Stuttgart, 1891-94.
19. *Pro-Palästina Schriften,* I-VIII. Berlin, 1918.

20. Verne, Jules. *Die Schwimmende Stadt.*
21. Brey, Henriette. *Mein Bruder bist Du!* Berlin, 1918.
22. Nabor, Felix (Karl Allmendinger). *Mysterium crucis. Roman aus der Zeit Neros.* Regensburg, 1912.
23. Wichtl, Friedrich. *Weltfreimauerei, Weltrevolution, Weltrepublik. Eine Untersuchung über Ursprung und Endziele des Weltkrieges.* Munich, 1920.
24. Schrott-Fiechtl, Hans. *Sonnseitige Menschen.* Freiburg i.B., 1920.
25. Verne, Jules. *Schwarzindien.*
26. Mylius, Otfrid (Hermann Friedrich Wilhelm Karl Müller). *Geheimnisse der Bastille.* Stuttgart, 1864.
27. Crawford, F. Marion. *Mr. Isaacs, eine Erzählung heutigen Indien.*
28. Meyer, Maximilian Wilhelm. *Die Entstehung der Erde.* Berlin, 1888.
29. Federer, Heinrich. *Der Fürchtemacher.* Freiburg i.B., 1919.
30. Grillparzer, Franz. *Das goldene Vlies.*
31. Christ, Lena. *Lausdirndlgeschichten.* Munich, 1913.
32. Rodenbach, Georges. *Das tote Brügge.* Leipzig, 1910.
33. Tavaststjerna, Carl A. *Das Geheimnis des finnischen Meerbusens.* Leipzig, 1914.
34. Stieler, Karl. *Ein Winteridyll.*
35. Conscience, Heinrich. *Flamisches Stillleben in drei kleinen Erzählungen.*
36. Daiber, Albert Ludwig. *Elf Jahre Freimaurer!* Stuttgart, 1920.
37. Smidt, Heinrich. *Seeschlachten und Abenteuer.* Berlin, 1902.
38. Biedenkapp, Georg. *Aus Deutschlands Urzeit.* Berlin, 1904.
39. Finckh, Ludwig. *Der Rosen Doktor.* Stuttgart, 1914.
40. Dehmel, Richard. *Blinde Liebe.* Berlin, 1912.
41. Gogol, Nikolai. *Der Mantel.*
42. Ibsen, Henrik. *Nora, oder das Puppenhaus.*
43. Wilde, Oskar. *Der Priester und der Mess(!)nerknabe.* Hannover, 1919.
44. Flex, Walter. *Vom grossen Abendmahl, Verse und Gedanken aus dem Feld.* Munich, 1918.
45. Böhme, Margarete (Margarete Schlüter). *Tagebuch einer Verlorenen.* Berlin, 1917.
46. Binding, Rudolf G. *Der Opfergang.*
47. Dinter, Arthur. *Die Sünde wider das Blut.* Leipzig, 1918.
48. Sienkiewicz, Heinrich. *Die Kreuzritter.*
49. Suttner, Bertha von. *Die Waffen nieder!* Berlin, 1917.
50. Wegener, Hans. *Wir jungen Männer.* Königstein (Taunus), 1912.
51. Spielhagen, Friedrich. *Ultimo.* Leipzig, 1883.
52. Sienkiewicz, Heinrich. *Ihm lasst uns folgen.*
53. Heidenstam, Verner von. *Kampf und Tod Karls des Zwölften.* Munich, 1917.
54. Prehn von Dewitz, H. *Die Französische Revolution.* Stuttgart, 1919.
55. Bierbaum, Otto Julius. *Prinz Kuckuck. Leben, Taten, Meinungen und Höllenfahrt eines Wohllüstlings.* Munich, 1908.
56. Hartmann, Friedrich K. L. *Vor Arras. Kriegsgedichte.* Munich, 1916.
57. Haupt, D. R. *Die Deutsche Insel. Ein Gedenkbuch kriegsgefangener Offiziere.* Munich, 1920.
58. Meyer, Christian. *Zur Erhebung Deutschlands bis 1814.* Munich, 1915.
59. Mayrhofer, Johannes. *Spanien. Reisebilder.* Freiburg i.B., 1921.
60. Ibsen, Henrik. *Die Stützen der Gesellschaft.*
61. Howald, Johannes. *Goethe und Schiller. Eine Monographie aus der Geschichte der deutschen Literatur.* Constance, 1903.
62. Handel-Mazzetti, Enrika von. *Die Arme Margaret.* Kempten, 1910.
63. Ibsen, Henrik. *Die Komödie der Liebe.*
64. Senestrey, Theodor. *Lieder eines fahrenden Schülers.* Munich, 1913.
65. Ibsen, Henrik. *Brand.*
66. Achleitner, Arthur. *Bayern wie es war und ist.* Stuttgart, 1900.

67. Stratz, Rudolf. *Das Licht vom Osten.* Berlin, 1919.
68. Probst, Hans. *Rothenburger Geschichten.* Nürnberg, 1919.
69. Ganter, Peter. *Flucht in der Offentlichkeit! Ein Nachwort zum Fall: "Doppelte Moral."* Munich, 1909.
70. Bolanden, Conrad von (Joseph E. K. Bischoff). *Der Teufel in der Schule.* Munich, 1908.
71. Bolanden, Conrad von (Joseph E. K. Bischoff). *Die Sünde wider den Heiligen Geist.* Munich, 1908.
72. Günther, Agnes. *Die Hielige und ihr Narr.* Stuttgart, 1919.
73. Wirth, Albrecht. *Das Deutschtum der Erde.* Berlin, 1920.
74. Stieler, Karl. *Ein Winteridyll;* Mörike, Eduard. *Der alte Turmhahn.*
75. Schierbaum, Heinrich. *Reden der Nationalversammlung zu Frankfurt am Main.* Leipzig, 1914.
76. Heer, Jacob Christoph. *Der König der Bernina.*
77. Bolanden, Conrad von (Joseph E. K. Bischoff). *Wider Kaiser und Reich.* Mainz, 1886.
78. Bolanden, Conrad von (Joseph E. K. Bischoff). *Wider Kaiser und Reich, II.* Mainz, 1886.
79. Ibsen, Henrik. *Die Kronprätendenten.*
80. Dumas, Alexander. *Der Graf von Monte Christo.*
81. Mützelburg, Adolf. *Der Herr der Welt.* Stuttgart, 1918.
82. Dumas, Alexander [*sic*], and Adolf Mützelburg. *Graf von Monte Christo.* 3 Teil; *Die Millionenbraut.* Stuttgart, 1918.
83. Baldi, Alexander. *Ausgewählte Abhandlungen und Reden,* II. Bamberg, 1908.
84. Schopenhauer, Arthur. *Uber Lesen und Bücher.*
85. (a) Gotthelf, Jeremias (Albert Bitzius). *Wie Uli, der Knecht, glücklich wird.* Leipzig, 1919.
85. (b) Gotthelf, Jeremias (Albert Bitzius). *Uli der Pächter.* Braunschweig, 1921.
86. Fidler, Matthias. *Die Toten Leben.* Leipzig, 1909.
87. Kerschensteiner, Georg. *Deutschlands Recht.* Munich, 1919.
88. Authenrieth, Otto. Die drei kommenden Kriege. Naumburg an der Saale, 1921.
89. Patin, Wilhelm August. *Das bayerische Religionsedikt vom 20 Mai 1818 und seine Grundlagen.* Inaugural Dissertation. Erlangen, 1918.
90. Dahn, Felix (Julius Sophus). *Ein Kampf um Rom.* Leipzig, 1919.
91. Schiller, Friedrich. *Gedichte.*
92. Zahn, Ernst. *Die Frauen von Tanno.* Stuttgart, 1911.
93. Vogt, Martin. *Dschiu-Dschitsu. Der Japaner.* Munich, 1909.
94. Weule, Karl. *Vom Kerbstock zum Alphabet.* Stuttgart, 1921.
95. Damrich, Johann. *Die altschwäbische Malerei.* Leipzig, 1913.
96. Pauls, Eilhard Erich. *Jan Jites Wanderbuch.* Leipzig, 1916.

97 to 105. [These entries are missing.]

106. Meister, Wilhelm. *Judas Schuldbuch.* Munich, 1919.
107. Chamberlain, Houston Stewart. *Rasse und Nation.* Munich, 1920.
108. Tafel, Paul. *Parlementarismus und Volksvertretung.* Munich, 1922.
109. Heer, Jacob Christoph. *Heinrichs Romfahrt.*
110. Burte, Hermann. *Wiltfeber, der ewige Deutsche.* Leipzig, 1912.
111. Farkas, Paul. *Die Hand des unsichtbaren Iman.* Munich, 1921.
112. Kahlenberg, Hans von (Helene Kessler) . *Eva Sehring.* Berlin, 1901.
113. Heer, Jacob Christoph. *Laubgewind.*
114. Lettow-Vorbeck, Paul von. *Heia Safari.* Leipzig, 1920.
115. Blüher, Hans. *Die Roller der Erotik in der männlichen Gesellschaft.* Jena, 1917.
116. Bauer, Hermann. *Die Sizilianische Vesper.* Munich, 1921.
117. Dunzinger, Albert. *K.B. 11 Infanterie-Regiment von der Tann.* Munich, 1921.

118. *Deutschlands Neubewaffung und Freiheitskampf.* Naumburg a.d. Saale, 1922.
119. *Krieg und Sieg. Nach Berichten der Zeitgenossen. Die Winterschlacht in Masuren.* Berlin, 1915.
120. Rothes, Walter. *Anton van Dyck.* Munich, 1918.
121. Dauthendey, Max. *Der Garten ohne Jahreszeiten.* Munich, 1914.
122. Brukner, Bruno. *Lohn und Preisbildung* (? ?).
123. Zola, Emile. *Mutter Erde.*
124. Schenk, Otto. *Mit falschem Kurs unter englischen Kommando.* Berlin, 1918.
125. *Der Gespensterkrieg.* Stuttgart, 1915.
126. *Erinnerungen des Kronprinz Wilhelm.*
127. Kurz, Peter; ed. *Moltke Aufzeichnungen. Briefe. Schriften. Reden.* Ebenhausen, 1922.
128. Voss, Richard. *Zwei Menschen.* Stuttgart, 1920.
129. Schiller, Friedrich. *Die Räuber.*
130. Meyr, Melchior. *Bauerngeschichten aus dem Ries. (Erzählungen aus dem Ries).* Munich, 1906.
131. Stratz, Rudolf. *König und Kärrner.* Berlin, 1914.
132. Reichel, Joachim von. *Balkanerlebnisse eines deutschen Geheimkuriers.* Berlin, 1917.
133. Eichacker, Reinhold. *Hass Antwort deutscher Dichter auf Versailles.* Munich, 1921.
134. Zola, Emile. *Nana.*
135. Thoma, Ludwig. *Der Postsekretär im Himmel.*
136. Schlicht, Friedrich von (Wolf Graf von Baudissin). *Die Tochter des Kommandeurs.* Berlin, 1908.
137. Authenrieth, Otto. *Bismarck II.* Munich, 1921.
138. Wolff, Ludwig. *Der Sohn des Hannibal.* Vienna and Berlin, 1914.
139. Bartsch, Rudolf Hans. *Der Letzte Student.* Berlin, 1913.
140. Kellermann, Bernhard. *Yester und Li.* Leipzig, 1904.
141. Ewald, Theodor. *Die Stiefel-Kathrine.* Berlin, 1920.
142. Steuert, Ludwig. *Die Königliche Bayr. Akademie Weihenstephen und ihre Vorgeschichte.* Berlin, 1905.
143. Frenssen, Gustav. *Jörn Uhl.*
144. Jensen, Wilhelm. *Hunnenblut.* [In *Chiemgau Novellen,* see number 163.]
145. Grube, August Wilhelm. *Naturbilder.* Stuttgart, 1911-12.
146. Gobineau, Arthur Comte de. *Die Renaissance.*
147. Beck, Otto. *Das Herrscherhaus Hohenzollern. Etymologie des Namens Hohenzollern.* Mainz, 1916.
148. Du Prel, Karl. *Der Spiritismus.* Leipzig, 1922.
149. Eyth, Max. *Der Kampf um die Cheopspyramide.* Heidelberg, 1920.
150. Haushofer, Max. *Planetenfeur.* Stuttgart, 1899.
151. Haushofer, Max. *Geschichten zwischen diesseits und jenseits.* Leipzig, 1910.
152. Ludendorff, Erich. *Meine Kriegserinnerungen 1914-1918.*
153. Bavaricus. *Die Seewelt Oberbayerns.* Munich, 1922.
154. Thoma, Ludwig. *Pistole oder Sabel.*
155. *Escherichhefte. Von Eisner bis Eglhofer.* Munich, 1922.
156. Vogel, Walther. *Die Befreiung Siebenbürgens und die Schlachten bei Targu Jiu und am Argesch.* Oldenburg, 1918.
157. Hillern, Wilhelmine von. *Am Kreuz. Ein Passionsroman aus Oberberammergau.* Stuttgart, 1920.
158. Zschokke, Heinrich. *Hans Dampf in allen Gassen.* Leipzig, 1920.
159. Bismarck, Otto von. [No title listed.]
160. Sperl, August. *Burschen heraus.* Munich, 1914.
161. Wilhelm II. *Ereignisse und Gestalten 1878-1918.*
162. Bjornson, Björnjerne. *Mary.*
163. Jensen, Wilhelm. *Chiemgau Novellen.* Weimar, 1897.

164. Zell, Theodor (Leopold Bauke). *Ist das Tier unvernünftig?* Stuttgart, 1912.
165. Jansen, Werner. *Das Buch Treue.* Hamburg, 1916.
166. Rothes, Walter. *Rembrandt.* Munich, 1922.
167. Eppes, Kittisch. *Noch a Beitraagk zu Israels Verkehr und Geist.* Speyer, 1823.
168. Schneider, Alfons (? ?). *Arras und Somme.* Munich, ?.
169. Mager, Carl. *Hans Cardon, der Student von Ingolstadt.* Donauwörth, 1923.
170. Bartsch, Rudolf Hans. *Frau Utta und der Jaeger.* Leipzig, 1915.
171. Fritsch, Theodor. *Handbuch der Judenfrage.* Hamburg, 1919.
172. Doering, Oskar. *Das Tagebuch des König Ludwig II.* Munich, 1918.
173. Böhmer, Heinrich. *Die Jesuiten.* Leipzig, 1913.
174. Rothes, Walter. *Drei Meister deutschen Gemütes.* Munich, 1920.
175. Zurbonsen, Friedrich. *Das Zweite Gesicht.* Cologne, 1909.
176. Fritsch, Theodor. *Der falsche Gott.* Leipzig, 1920.
177. Tirpitz, Alfred von. *Erinnerungen.* Leipzig, 1919.
178. Rosen, Erwin (Erwin Carlé). *Der deutsche Lausbub in Amerika.* Stuttgart, 1921.
179. Homer. *Die Odyssee.* Edited by Hermann von Schelling. Leipzig, 1911.
180. *Das Nibelungenlied.*
181. Renan, Joseph Ernest. *Das Leben Jesu.* Leipzig, 1919.
182. Meyer, Conrad Ferdinand. *Angela Borgia.* Leipzig, 1921.
183. Birt, Theodor. *Von Hass und Liebe.* Leipzig, 1919.
184. Florian, Jean Pierre. "Le bon fils," *Théâtre complet.* Leipzig, 1854.
185. Haller, Johannes. *Die Aera Bülow.* Stuttgart, 1922.
186. *Der entlarvte Präsident des Weltkrieges.* Munich, 1922.
187. Kletke, G. M. *Militärisches Dichter Album.* Berlin, 1853.
188. Maurer, Wolfgang. *Historische Unterhaltungen aus der bayerischen Geschichte.* Passau, 1822.
189. Koerber, Adolf Viktor von. *Adolf Hitler. Sein Leben und seine Reden.* Munich, 1923.
190. Klopstock, Friedrich Gottlieb. *Samtliche Werke.* Leipzig, 1810.
191. Häckel, Ernst. *Die Welträtsel.* Leipzig, 1919.
192. Nettelbeck, Joachim. *Bürger zu Colberg.* Leipzig, 1920.
193. Schlichtegroll, Carl Felix von (K. F. Stauffer). *Ein Sadist im Priesterrock.* Leipzig, 1904.
194. Merzenich, Friedel. *Strandkorb 57.* Berlin, 1921.
195. Busch, Paula. *Einer vom Zirkus.* Berlin, 1921.
196. Blei, Franz. *Das Lustwäldchen.* Munich, 1907.
197. Thoma, Ludwig. *Die Dachserin. Geschichten aus dem Nachlass.*
198. Koerber, Adolf Viktor von. *Bestien im Lande.* Munich, 1923.
199. Johannes, Martin Otto (Johannes Rädlein). *Adel verpflichtet.* Leipzig, 1920.
200. Kühn, Erich. *Rasse?* Munich, 1921.
201. Stilgebauer, Eduard. *Das Liebesnest. Die Lügner des Lebens.* Berlin, 1908.
202. Günther, Hans. *Ritter, Tod und Teufel.* Munich, 1920.
203. Goeringer, Irma (Irma Schurter-Goeringer). *Schlingpfanzen.* Munich, 1908.
204. Westphal, Fr. *Als Kolonist im Brasilianischen Urwald.* Minden i. Westphalen, 1924.
205. Chamberlain, Houston Stewart. *Richard Wagner.* Leipzig, 1907.
206. Reventlow, Graf Ernst zu. *Indien, seine Bedeutung für Grossbritannien, Deutschland, und die Zukunft.* Berlin, 1917.
207. Miller, Alfred. *Ultramontanes Schuldbuch.* Breslau, 1922.
208. Eckart, Dietrich. *Der Bolschewismus von Moses bis Lenin.* Munich, 1925.
209. Dostojewski, Fëdor M. *Memoiren aus einem Totenhaus.*
210. *Richard Wagner an Mathilde Wesendock. Tagebuchblätter und Briefe 1853-1871.* Berlin, 1904.
211. Dominik, Hans. *Die Macht der Drei.* Leipzig, 1922.

212. Kronacher, Carl. *Allgemeine Tierzucht, ein Lehr- und Handbuch für Studierende und Züchter.* Berlin, 1916.
213. Ossendowski, Ferdinand. *Tiere, Menschen, Götter.* Frankfurt a.M., 1925.
214. Fendrich, Anton. *Mehr Sonne.* Stuttgart, 1924.
215. Carlyle, Thomas. *Schiller.*
216. *Eine unbewusste Blutschande. Der Untergang Deutschlands. Naturgesetze über die Rassenlehre.* Grossenhain i. Sachsen, 1921.
217. Jansen, Werner. *Das Buch der Leidenschaft.* Braunschweig, 1920.
218. Tacitus, P. Cornelius. *Germania.*
219. Thompson, Ernest Seton. *Prärietiere und ihre Schicksale.*
220. Jansen, Werner. *Das Buch Liebe. Gudrun.* Braunschweig, 1918.
221. Osten-Sacken, Baron Gotthard von der. *In der Gewalt dunkler Mächte.* Munich, 1924.
222. Hoffmann, Richard. *Stark wie der Leu, gläubig und treu.* Munich, 1917. [Heinrich Himmler's copy of this book is in the Library of Congress, Washington, D.C.]
223. Hesse, Hermann. *Demian, die Geschichte von Emil Sinclairs Jugend.*
224. Olmet, Luis Anton del. *Der Sieg Deutschlands.* Munich, 1916.
225. Thompson, Ernest Seton. *Bingo und andere Tiergeschichte.*
226. (a) Gobineau, Arthur Comte de. *Gamber-Alis Geschichte aus den asiatischen Novellen.*
226. (b) Marschall, Fritz *Escorian* (?). *Innige Lieder und sinnige Gedanken aus dem Tagebuch des Kl. bayr. Oberltnts. Fritz Marschall.*
227. Hesse, Hermann. *Siddhartha.*
228. *Semi-Imperator.* Munich, 1919.
229. Widdumhoff, K. von. *Die entdeckten, schwarzen Henker des deutschen Volkes.* Weissenburg i. Bayern, 1924.
230. Lassberg, Dietrich Freiherr von. *Mein Kriegstagebuch aus dem deutsch-franz. Kriege 1870-1871.* Munich and Berlin, 1906.
231. Werfel, Franz. *Verdi, Roman der Oper.*
232. Bruger, Ferdinand. *Heimliche Garten.* Magdeburg, ?.
233. *Liller-Kriegszeitung. Eine Auslese aus Nummer 1-40.* Berlin, Leipzig, Wien,? [Numbers 1-40 of this German army paper are available in the Library of the University of California, Berkeley.]
234. Dostojewski, Fëdor M. *Der Grossinquisitor. Eine Phantasie.*
235. Haiser, Franz. *Freimaurer und Gegenmaurer im Kampf um die Weltherrschaft.* Munich, 1924.
236. Novalis. *Gesammelte Werke.*
237. Paulk, Emil Gustav (Paul Kemski). *Das Buch des Mannes. Eine psychokratische Unterweisüng.* Wiesbaden, 1917.
238. Paulk, Emil Gustav (Paul Kemski). *Die Manneslehre. Eine erotokratische Unterweisüng.* Wiesbaden, 1918.
239. Voss, Richard. *Der Heilige Hass.* Berlin, 1915.
240. Wencker, F., ed. *Im Solde Frankreichs. Schicksale und Abenteur, Irrfahrten und Leiden deutscher Fremendenlegionäre.* Minden i. Westfalen, 1925.
241. Frenssen, Gustav. *Die Sandgräfin.*
242. Schwarz, Hermann. *Über Gottesvorstellungen grosser Denker.* Munich, 1921.
243. Seeliger, Ewald Gerhard. *Peter Voss der Millionendieb.* Berlin, 1913.
244. Franke, Helmut. *Der Staat im Staate.* Magdeburg, 1924.
245. Prokopios. *Gothenkrieg.*
246. Jürgens, Heinrich. *Pendelpraxis und Pendelmagie.* Pfullingen, 1925.
247. Popoff, Georg. *Tscheka, der Staat im Staate.* Frankfurt a.M., 1925.
248. Arentino, Pietro. *Kurtisanen–Gespräche.* Leipzig, 1922.
249. Storm, Theodor. *Von Jenseits des Meeres.* Berlin, 1926.
250. Popert, Hermann. *Hellmut Harringa.* Dresden, 1918.

251. Schmidt, Richard. *Liebe und Ehe im alten und modernen Indien.* Berlin, 1904.
252. Thomsen, Andreas. *Der Völker Vergehen und Werden.* Leipzig, 1925.
253. Monar, Karl Ludwig, and Alwin Böhme. *In 4 Wochen 15 Jahre jünger!* Berlin, 1925.
254. Nicolai, Walter. *Geheimen Mächte, Internationale Spionage und ihre Bekämpfung im Weltkrieg und heute.* Berlin, 1923.
255. Falb, Alfred. *Luther und die Juden.* Munich, 1921.
256. Franke, Helmut. *Der Staat im Staate.* Magdeburg, 1924. [The same as item 244.]
257. Langen, F. E. *Das jüdische Geheimgesetz.* Munich, 1919.
258. Heise, Karl. *Okkultes Logentum.* Leipzig, 1921.
259. Freytag, Gustav. *Aus der Römerzeit. (Bilder aus der deutschen Vergangenheit.)*
260. Bauer, Max. *Das Land der Roten Zaren.* Munich, 1925.
261. Blum, Oskar. *Russische Köpfe.* Berlin, 1923.
262. Haug-Haough, Katharina. *Hinter den Kulissen des Bolschewismus. Erlebnisse einer Russin.* Leipzig, 1925.
263. Schleich, Carl Ludwig. *Besonnte Vergangenheit. Lebenserinnerungen von 1859-1919.* Berlin, 1921.
264. Gerling, Reinhold. *Hypnotische Unterrichtbriefe.* Oranienburg, 1921.
265. Reuter, Wilhelm. *Muttererde–Vaterländische Gedichte eines Bauern.* Wetzlar, 1925.
266. Hugo, Viktor. *Das Jahr der Guillotin.*
267. Ruge, Arnold. *Todsünde.* Leipzig, 1926.
268. Allmers, Nils. *Die Herzogin von Choiseul-Praslin.* Berlin, 1921.
269. (a) Schlier, Paula. *Petras Aufzeichnungen.* Innsbruck, 1926.
269. (b) Helbing, Franz, and Max Bauer. *Die Tortur.* Berlin, 1926.
270. Casanova, Giovanni Jacopo. *Memoiren.*

Notes

Abbreviations used in these notes:

HH–Heinrich Himmler.
GH–Gebhard Himmler.
HD–Himmler Documents. Copies at Hoover Institution, Stanford University.
HHD–Heinrich Himmler's Diaries 1914-24. Originals at Hoover Institution, Stanford University.
RFSS–*Reichsführer SS.* Micro-Copy T-175 in National Archives, Washington, D.C.
HHBL–Heinrich Himmler's Book List. Part of the Himmler Documents collection (see HD above).
HHCR–Heinrich Himmler's Correspondence Record. Part of the Himmler Documents collection (see HD above).
HHBCR–Heinrich Himmler's Business Correspondence Record. Part of the Himmler Documents collection (see HD above).

Introduction

1. Konrad Heiden, *Der Fuehrer,* pp. 305-7.

2. Otto Strasser and Michael Stern, *Flight from Terror,* pp. 20-21; Otto Strasser, *Hitler and I,* pp. 35-36.

3. Douglas Reed, *Nemesis?,* pp. 59 and 71-72; *idem, The Prisoner of Ottawa,* pp. 41, 52-53, and 61.

4. Willi Frischauer, *Himmler.* [Hereafter cited as Frischauer.]

5. Werner T. Angress and Bradley F. Smith, "Diaries of Heinrich Himmler's Early Years," *Journal of Modern History,* Vol. 31, September 1959.

6. Two recent volumes on Himmler and the *SS* fail to present convincing pictures of Himmler's development largely because they ignore many of the Himmler documents now available, especially those difficult to decipher and collate: Roger Manvell and Heinrich Fraenkel, *Heinrich Himmler;* Heinz Höhne, *Der Orden unter dem Totenkopf.*

7. Heinrich's comment on item 144 in his Book List (Wilhelm Jensen, *Hunnenblut*) specifically refers to a diary. The comment is dated January 23, 1923. Himmler Documents [hereafter referred to as HD], Roll 18A, Hoover Institution, Stanford.

Chapter I

1. Summary Document in *Ahnentafel* Research, Micro Copy T-175, *Reichsführer SS* [hereafter referred to as *RFSS*], National Archives, Washington, D.C., Roll 142, Frame 2670488.

2. *Ibid.*; Frischauer, p. 15.

3. Summary Document, *RFSS,* Roll 142, Frame 2670488; *RFSS,* Roll 99, Frame 2619639. The course of Johann Himmler's life offers numerous parallels with the life of Hitler's father.

4. *RFSS,* Roll 99, Frame 2619639.

5. *Ibid.,* Roll 142, Frame 2670488.

6. *Amtliches Verzeichnis Ludwig Max. Universität zu München, 1884/1885.*

7. Gebhard Himmler's transition from philosophy to philology is revealed by comparing *Amtliches Verzeichnis Ludwig Max. Universität ze München 1884/1885* with *Festschrift zu Vierhundert-Jahr-Feier des Wilhelms Gymnasium 1559-1959,* p. 242.

8. *Hof und Staatshandbuch des Königreich Bayern 1894,* pp. 117 and 407. For later contacts with the princess see p. 47.

9. *Festschrift zu Vierhundert-Jahr-Feier des Wilhelms Gymnasium 1559-1959,* p. 242; *Blätter für das Gymnasial Schulwesen,* Vol. 33, No. 5 and 6, May-June, 1897, p. 528.

10. *RFSS,* Roll 99, Frame 2619639; Frischauer, p. 17.

11. Heinz Höhne, *Der Orden unter dem Totenkopf,* p. 35, lists the address as Hildegardstrasse 2. A card addressed to the Himmlers and dated 29.8.1900 bears the address given in the text, HD, Roll 98, Folder 1.

12. Records of Gebhard Himmler, HD, Roll 98, Folder 1.

Chapter II

1. Gebhard Himmler [hereafter referred to as GH] to Prince Heinrich, 30.8 and 20.12.1903, and 1906, HD, Roll 99, Folder 9.

2. *Ibid.,* 21.6.1900.

3. *Ibid.,* 8.10.1900.

4. Roger Manvell and Heinrich Fraenkel, *Heinrich Himmler* [hereafter cited as Manvell and Fraenkel], p. 254; Prince Heinrich to GH, 16.7.1901, HD, Roll 99, Folder 9.

5. Records of GH, HD, Roll 98, Folder 1; Prince Heinrich to GH, 26.2.1902, HD, Roll 99, Folder 9.

6. *Blätter für das Gymnasial Schulwesen,* Vol. 38, No. 9-10, Sept-Oct, 1902, p. 665; Heinrich Himmler's Correspondence Record [hereafter cited as HHCR] (family Schmid), HD, Roll 98, Folder 6; telegram Dr. Quenstedt to GH, 1903, HD, Roll 99, Folder 9.

7. *Veröffentlichen des Kaiserlichen Gesundheitsamtes,* Vol. 27, No. 18, May 6, 1903; Dr. M. Schmid to GH, 15.7.1903, HD, Roll 99, Folder 9; Prince Heinrich to GH, HD, Roll 99, Folder 9.

8. GH to Prince Heinrich, 30.8.1903 and 1906, HD, Roll 99, Folder 9.

9. *Ibid.,* 30.8.1903.

10. *Ibid.,* 20.12.1903.

11. *Blätter für das Gymnasial Schulwesen,* Vol. 40, No. 9-10, Sept-Oct, 1904, p. 684.

12. George Hallgarten's recollection that the Himmlers lived on the Liebigstrasse during the period when he knew Heinrich is incorrect. George W. F. Hallgarten, "Mein Mitschüler Heinrich Himmler," *Germania Judaica,* 1960/61, No. 2 [hereafter cited as Hallgarten], p. 4. The Himmlers lived on the Amalienstrasse from 1903 to 1913 when they left Munich. See, for example, *Adressbuch für München und Umgebung* 1910 and two letters from 1912 and 1913 addressed to Heinrich at the Amalienstrasse address, *RFSS,* Roll 99, Frames 2619909-10 and 2620176-77.

13. Records of GH, HD, Roll 98, Folder 1.

14. *Ibid.*

15. *Ibid.*

16. *Ibid.*

17. *Ibid.*

18. Heinrich Himmler [hereafter referred to as HH] Diary, 13.7.1910, HD, Roll 18A, Folder 11.

19. *Ibid.,* 14.7, 28.7, 31.7, and 8.8.1910.

20. *Ibid.,* 22.7 and 10.8.1910.

21. *Ibid.,* 15.7.1910.

22. *Ibid.,* 5.8.1910.

23. *Ibid.,* 1.8.1910.

24. *Ibid.,* 20.7 and 7.8.1910. A number of cards and letters in the Himmler papers have the stamps removed. The earliest one seems to date from 1911, *RFSS,* Roll 99, Frame 2619830.

25. Hallgarten, p. 4 and p. 6, *note.*

26. *Ibid.,* p. 6

27. *Ibid.,* pp. 4-5.

28. HH Diary, 23.7 and 8.8.1911, HD, Roll 18A, Folder 11; Prof. Huolezeck to HH, 21.8.1911 (?), *RFSS,* Roll 99, Frame 2619830. That the individuals in question were *Wilhelms Gymnasium* teachers is shown by the following sources: Hallgarten, p. 4; *Münchener Jahrbuch,* 1912, p. 374; *idem,* 1914, p. 370.

29. HH Diary, 8.8.1911, HD, Roll 18A, Folder 11.

30. *Ibid.,* 21.7 to 23.8.1913.

31. Announcement concerning Wilhelm A. Patin, HD, Roll 99, Folder 9. The Patins' relation to the Himmlers is described in HD, Roll 98, Folder 7. For Patin's position at court see *Hof und Staatshandbuch des Königreich Bayern,* 1908, p. 126; *idem,* 1914, pp. 102-3 and 113; and *Münchener Jahrbuch,* 1918, p. 279. GH was employed in the court circle fourteen years before Wilhelm Patin.

32. HH Diary, 20.8.1911, HD, Roll 18A, Folder 11.

33. *Ibid.,* 18.8.1911.

34. Hallgarten, p. 5 and p. 6, *note.* Hallgarten bases his case for Heinrich's envy of nobles on alleged incidents with pages from the *Maximilianeum* who joined the *Wilhelms Gymnasium* students in their fourth year. Heinrich did not attend the *Wilhelms Gynmasium* that year (1913) for he was in Landshut.

35. *Ibid.,* p. 6 *note.*

36. HH Diary, 24.8.1912, HD, Roll 18A, Folder 11; Uncle Hennenberger to HH, Sept. 1913, *RFSS,* Roll 99, Frame 2619835.

37. HH Diary, *passim,* HD, Roll 18A, Folder 11.

38. *Ibid.,* 26.7 and 15.8.1912.

39. *Ibid.,* 17.7.1912.

40. *Ibid.,* 28.8.1911.

41. *Ibid.,* 14.8.1913. It should be noted that the precise recording of the activities of important people which showed up in the diary in 1910 had been extended to everyone by 1913.

42. Karl Oskar von Sodon to GH (Jr.), 13.9.1913, *RFSS,* Roll 99, Frames 2620094-02.

43. *Ibid.,* 17.10.1913, *RFSS,* Roll 99, 2620100-02; Falk Zipperer to HH and Hallgarten to HH, *RFSS,* Roll 99, Frames 2619838-39 and 2620256-57; HHCR (Karl Schäzler and Willi Michel [?], HD, Roll 98, Folder 6.

44. Karl Oskar von Sodon to GH (Jr.), 17.10 and 24.12.1913, and 12.5.1914, *RFSS,* Roll 99, Frames 2620100-02, 2620106-07, and 2620110-13.

45. Falk Zipperer to HH, 12.9.1913 and 16.3.1914, *RFSS,* Roll 99, Frames 2620217-18, 2620256-57; *Hof und Staatshandbuch des Königreich Bayern,* 1912, p. 227; *Münchener Jahrbuch,* 1918, p. 315.

46. HH Diary, 15.7.1914, HD, Roll 18A, Folder 11.

47. *Ibid.,* 16.7, 18.7, and 19.7.1914.

48. *Ibid.,* 23.7.1914.

49. *Ibid.,* 21.7 and 28.7.1914.

50. *Ibid.,* 29.7.1914.

51. *Ibid.,* 29-31.7.1914.

52. *Ibid.,* 1-6.8.1914.

Chapter III

1. Heinrich Himmler's Diaries [hereafter cited as HHD], Hoover Institution, Stanford University, 23.8.1914.

2. *Ibid.*, 28.8.1914.

3. *Ibid.*, 26.8.1914.

4. *Ibid.*, 28.8.1914.

5. *Ibid.*, 29.7.1915.

6. *Ibid.*, 4.9.1914.

7. R. Hornburger to HH (no date), *RFSS*, Roll 99, Frames 2619902-03.

8. HHD, 3.9.1914.

9. Heinrich Himmler's Newspaper Collection, *RFSS*, Roll 99, Frame 2620533.

10. HHD, 27 and 30.8.1914, and 6.9.1914.

11. *Ibid.*, 27.8.1914.

12. *Ibid.*, 28.7.1915.

13. *Ibid.*, 28.8.1914; Falk Zipperer to HH, 18.8.1915, *RFSS*, Roll 99, Frames 2620220-21.

14. HHD, 29.8.1914.

15. *Ibid.*, 1.5.1916.

16. *Ibid.*, 16.2 and 19.9.1915, and 1.5.1916.

17. *Ibid.*, 27.9.1914.

18. *Ibid.*, 4.2, 31.7, and 25.9.1915.

19. *Ibid.*, 28.4.1914, 14.2.1915, and 1.1.1916. On the way to their summer home in 1915 the family stopped at Tittmoning. Although "tired and hungry" they could not go to a restaurant for as Heinrich noted there were only "peasant cafes" open. *Ibid.*, 28.7.1915.

20. *Ibid.*, 2.2 and 7.2.1915.

21. *Turnverein Landshut* card, 6.2.1917, HD, Roll 98, Folder 1; HHD, 1-2.5.1916.

22. HHCR (especially "*Grossmutter*"), HD, Roll 98, Folders 5 and 6; HHD, 3.9.1914, 2.8.1915, and 7.5.1916.

23. HHD, 3.2 and 17.9.1915, and 14.5.1916; Falk Zipperer to HH, 18.8.1915, *RFSS*, Roll 99, Frames 2620220-21.

24. HHD, 7.8 and 26.9.1915, and 1.1.1916.

25. *Ibid.*, 22.2.1915.

26. *Ibid.*, 23.9 and 29-30.9.1914, and 26.9.1915.

27. *Ibid.*, 24.9.1914.

28. *Ibid.*, 28.7.1915.

29. *Ibid.*, 4.8.1915.

30. HH Newspaper Collection, HD, Roll 98, Folder 6.

31. HHD, 1-2.5.1916; HHCR (Luisa Hager, Folder 5), HD, Roll 98, Folders 5 and 6.

32. HHD, 2.1.1916; Sodon to GH, 22.8.1916, *RFSS*, Roll 99, Frames 260120-21. The exact date of Gebhard's enlistment does not appear in the documents. He was with the family in May 1916 and in the service by the fall.

33. HHD, 3.5.1916.

34. Konrad Krafft von Dellmensingen, ed., *Das Bayernbuch vom Weltkriege 1914-1918*, p. 184.

35. Dicknether to GH, 9.11.1916, HD, Roll 99, Folder 9.

Chapter IV

1. *Das Königliche Bayerische 16 Infanterie-Regiment Grossherzog Ferdinand von Toskana in Weltkrieg 1914-1918,* provides an account of the major actions of Gebhard's regiment. For Falk's enlistment see GH Class Book, January 1919, HD, Roll 17A.

2. Hofmarschall von Prinzessin Arnulf to GH, 4.6.1917, and GH to Hofmarschall, 7.6.1917, HD, Roll 98, Folder 1.

3. Hofmarschall to GH, 11.6.1917, HD, Roll 98, Folder 1. The princess also sent other mementoes. Princess Arnulf to GH, 23.6.1917, HD, Roll 99, Folder 9.

4. GH to Hofmarschall, 14.6.1917, HD, Roll 98, Folder 2.

5. *Fragebogen 1 Ersatzbataillon, 1 Inf. Regts.,* 23.6.1917, HD, Roll 98, Folder 2.

6. Falk Zipperer to HH, 2.8.1917, *RFSS,* Roll 99, Frames 260225-26; HHCR shows clearly that he was in Bad Tolz for the summer, HD, Roll 98, Folders 5 and 6.

7. Records of GH; Eduard Lacher to GH, 6.10.1917, Shorthand *Fragebogen* notes, HD, Roll 98, Folder 2.

8. Magistrat der K.B. Kreishauptstadt Landshut to GH, 6.10.1917, HD, Roll 98, Folder 1.

9. GH Class Book, January 1919, HD, Roll 17A.

10. Shorthand note of GH addressed to the Education Ministry, 18.4.1918, HD, Roll 98, Folder 2; HHCR, HD, Roll 98, Folders 5 and 6.

11. British General Staff, *Handbook of the Germany Army in War,* p. 23. Dr. Alfred Vagts kindly provided the author with general information on the training program of German officers.

12. HH to his parents (and Ernst Himmler), 4.1.1918 and 6.1.1918, HD, Roll 98, Folder 2. Postmarks on the envelopes show that all letters from Regensburg marked 1917 were dated incorrectly by Heinrich and should have read 1918. Many of Heinrich's letters in 1918 were written in shorthand. The main reason for using shorthand was conservation of time and paper. Rarely did he use it for privacy or secrecy.

13. Records of GH; HH to his parents, 24.1, 26.1, and 29.1.1918, HD, Roll 98, Folder 2.

14. HH to his parents 3.1, 10.1, and 12.1.1918, HD, Roll 98, Folder 2. On the letter of 3.1.1918 his mother checked off the items as she readied the shipment.

15. *Ibid.,* 21.1.1918.

16. *Ibid.,* 3.1, 7.1, 9.1, and 17.1.1918.

17. *Ibid.,* 8.1, 15.1, and 21.1.1918; note by "Zahler," 9.2.1918, HD, Roll 98, Folder 2. There was a Lt. Hans Zahler in the 11th Regiment, but the contact through Frau Himmler suggests that this was Ludwig Zahler. *Bayerns Goldenes Ehrenbuch.* For the Zahler family's relation to the Himmlers, see HD, Roll 98, Folders 6 and 7. For Ludwig Zahler's position in the 11th Infantry Regiment see below, page 59.

18. HH to his parents, 12.2, 13.2, 18.2, and 19.2.1918, HD, Roll 98, Folder 2.

19. *Ibid.,* 12.2, 28.2, and 13.3.1918.

20. *Ibid.,* 8.1 and 28.1.1918.

21. HH to his mother, 23.3.1918, HD, Roll 98, Folder 2.

22. HH to his parents, 7.5.1918, HD, Roll 98, Folder 2.

23. GH to Frau Himmler, 2.2.1918, HD, Roll 98, Folder 2. Aside from direct references in his letters, his trips home show up clearly in the addresses used in his correspondence. HHCR, HD, Roll 98, Folders 5 and 6.

24. A list of items sent to Heinrich dated 14.5.1918 is in HD, Roll 98, Folder 1. For his apologies see HH to his parents, 11.3.1918, HD, Roll 98, Folder 2. The

Zola reference is in HH to his mother, 1.3.1918, HD, Roll 98, Folder 2. The first reference to Zola in his Book List was in May 1922. Heinrich Himmler's Book List [hereafter cited as HHBL], item 123, HD, Roll 18A.

25. HH to his parents, 13.3, 28.2, 4.4, 7.4, and 16.4.1918, HD, Roll 98, Folder 2.

26. *Ibid.,* 26.2, 23.3, 24.5, and 5.6.1918, HD, Roll 98, Folder 2.

27. *Ibid.,* 10.4 and 26.4, and 28.5.1918; HH Expenditure Record, HD, Roll 98, Folder 6; draft of letter from GH to Bavarian Education Ministry, 18.4.1918, HD, Roll 98, Folder 2; *Münchener Jahrbuch,* 1918, p. 192.

28. HH to his parents, 6.5, 7.5, 15.5, and 22.5.1918, and HH to 11th *Bayerische Inf. Regt.,* 17.6.1919, HD, Roll 98, Folder 2.

29. HH to his parents, 17.6, 20.6, 23.6, and 25.6 1918, HD, Roll 98, Folder 2.

30. *Ibid.,* 5.8 and 2.7.1918.

31. *Ibid.,* 14.7 and 23.7.1918.

32. *Ibid.,* 17.6, 20.6, 21.6, 4.7, 9.7, and 11.7.1918.

33. *Ibid.,* 4.8 and 13.8.1918.

34. *Ibid.,* 26.8.1918; GH to HH, 4.9.1918, HD, Roll 98, Folder 2.

35. Eugen (?) to HH, 1.9.1918, HD, Roll 98, Folder 2.

36. HH to his parents, 17.9 and 22.9.1918, HD, Roll 98, Folder 2.

37. *Ibid.,* 16.10, 17.10, and 23.10.1918.

38. *Ibid.,* 16.10.1918. Many of those close to the Himmlers also showed signs of pessimism. Falk Zipperer to HH, 1.11.1918, *RFSS,* Roll 99, Frames 260258-63; Princess Arnulf to GH, 5.11.1918, HD, Roll 99, Folder 9.

39. Heinrich's letter to his parents, 29.9.1919, indicates that Gebhard had received some honor. HD Roll 98, Folder 2. Gebhard received the Iron Cross First Class in 1921 for wartime bravery. *Das Königliche Bayerische 16 Infanterie-Regiment Grossherzog Ferdinand von Toskana in Weltkrieg 1914-1918.* Gebhard was also promoted to Fähnrich during the war. "Wiener Abend" program, 25.1.1920, *RFSS,* Roll 99, Frame 2620441.

40. HH to his parents, 23.10.1918, HD, Roll 98, Folder 2.

41. Fritz Hahler (?) to HH, 16.11.1918, *RFSS,* Roll 99, Frames 2620136-37; HH to his parents, 4.12.1918, HD, Roll 98, Folder 2.

42. HH to his parents, 30.11, 6.12, 11.12, and 17.12.1918, HD, Roll 98, Folder 2.

43. *Ibid.,* 29.11 and 30.11.1918. Apparently Frau Himmler could not read shorthand.

44. *Ibid.,* 30.11 and 10.12.1918.

45. *Ibid.,* 4.12, 5.12, and 17.12.1918; Richard Spindler to HH, 7.12.1918, *RFSS,* Roll 99, Frames 2620138-39.

46. HH to 11th *Bayerische Inf. Regt.,* 17.6.1919, HD, Roll 98, Folder 2.

Chapter V

1. GH Class Book, January 1919, HD, Roll 17A; *Bayerisches Jahrbuch,* pp. 183-184.

2. GH Class Book, January 1919, HD, Roll 17A. Both Heinrich and his father had trouble spelling the name Meier, using Meyer and Meier interchangeably.

3. *Ibid.* Since the Class Book is written in shorthand it is unlikely that he had to follow a prescribed form.

4. *RFSS,* Roll 99, Frames 2620350-51. A number of other poems by Falk are included on this microfilm roll.

5. HD, Roll 98, Folder 1.

6. HHCR (Luisa Hager), HD, Roll 98, Folder 5. The picture of a young girl, dated 18.3.1919 and tucked into a pocket of Heinrich's diary number 4 may be Luisa Hager. *Idem* (Ludwig Zahler), HD, Roll 98, Folder 6.

7. HHBL, items 15 and 28, HD, Roll 18A. Manvell and Fraenkel's statement (p. 255, *note* 3) that the book list "strangely enough" includes no comments is simply an error. The vast majority of the entries include comments though they are usually in Gabelsberger shorthand.

8. For conditions in Bavaria during this period, see Allan Mitchell, *Revolution in Bavaria, 1918-1919,* and Karl Schwend, *Bayern zwischen Monarchie und Diktatur.*

9. Sodon to HH, 23.12 and 30.12.1918, and 9.1.1919, *RFSS,* Roll 99, Frames 2620124-27. A shorthand entry in Heinrich's Business Correspondence Record [hereafter cited as HHBCR] dated 9.1.1919 also indicates that he was recruiting for the *BVP.*

10. Adalbert Holzapfel to HH, 19.4.1919, *RFSS,* Roll 99, Frame 2619824.

11. Ernst Röhm, *Die Geschichte eines Hochverräters,* p. 87. The two books written by Otto Strasser, as well as the two inspired by Strasser and written by Douglas Reed have the dates and relationships of Himmler's life prior to 1925 badly garbled. Otto Strasser and Michael Stern, *Flight from Terror,* pp. 20-21; Otto Strasser, *Hitler and I,* pp. 35-36; Douglas Reed, *Nemesis?,* pp. 59 and 71-72; *idem, The Prisoner of Ottawa,* pp. 41, 52-53, and 61.

12. Statement by *Gymnasialrektorat,* 26.4.1919, HD, Roll 98, Folder 1. A combination of negative factors makes it probable that Heinrich did not participate in the march on Munich. He was enrolled in the *Sonderklasse* and thus immediately under his father's control. All the letters in his correspondence record for this time were mailed from Landshut and he did not record any letters to or from his parents. Finally, although during later years he often exaggerated his role in World War I, there is no evidence that he claimed to have participated in the Munich march. If he had been there, he would not have been reticent about it.

13. *Ausweis* written by HH for the commander of *Ergänzungskompagnie Oberland,* 13.7.1919, HD, Roll 98, Folder 1. Heinrich Himmler's *SS* Records which the author studied at the Berlin Document Center (they have not been filmed) listed four *Freikorps* affiliations: *Landshut, Oberland, Alarm Batl. München, Reichskriegsflagge.* The dates listed were "1919 to 9.11.1923." The only two units that could apply to 1919 were *Landshut* and *Oberland.* Von Epp's account of his unpleasant relations with *Oberland* appears in General Records Collection, T-84, Roll 10, Frames 9924-26, National Archives, Washington, D.C.

14. HHCR (Nachtigalls), HD, Roll 98, Folder 6; HH to the 11th *Bayr. Inf. Regt.,* 17.6.1919, HD, Roll 98, Folder 2.

15. HHCR (Schinkl [?] and Rud), HD, Roll 98, Folder 6; HH Newspaper Collection, *RFSS,* Roll 99, Frame 2620550.

16. See footnote 19, chapter 3 .

17. Gebhard was studying at the *Technische Hochschule* at this time. Sodon to GH, 16.2.1919, *RFSS,* Roll 99, Frame 2620123. There are a number of hints of

Ernst's scientific interest; see, for example, HHD, 22-23.12.1919.

18. Karl Otto to GH, 29.12.1919, HD, Roll 98, Folder 2; HHCR (Rud, L. Zahler, W. Patin, Thilde H., B. Kiene, Zahler family), HD, Roll 98, Folder 6; *Münchener Jahrbuch,* p. 341.

19. HH to his parents, 1.8, 3.8, and 10.8.1919, HD, Roll 98, Folder 2. Apparently Joseph Strasser was not related to Gregor and Otto Strasser.

20. *Ibid.,* 3.8.1919.

21. *Ibid.,* 3.8; 10.8.1919.

22. *Ibid.,* 10.8.1919.

23. *Ibid.,* 1.8, 10.8, and 24.8.1919.

24. *Ibid.,* 10.8.1919 (two letters on this day).

25. *Ibid.,* 15.8.1919.

26. HHD, 2.9, 4.9, and 25.9.1919; HH to his parents, 9.9.1919, HD, Roll 98, Folder 2; Ludwig Zahler to HH, 10.9.1919, *RFSS,* Roll 99, Frames 2619959-60.

27. HHD, 7.9, 14.9, 18.9, 21.9, and 23.9.1919; HH to his mother, 9.9 and 20.9.1919, HD, Roll 98, Folder 2.

28. HHD, 15.9, 23.9, and 24.9.1919; Dr. Quenstedt to GH, 24.9.1919, HD, Roll 99, Folder 9.

29. Falk Zipperer to HH, 4.9.1919, *RFSS,* Roll 99, Frame 2620324.

30. HHBL, HD, Roll 18A.

31. *Ibid.,* items 9, 10, and 18.

32. *Ibid.,* item 23.

33. *Ibid.,* items 6, 7, and 9.

34. *Ibid.,* item 8.

35. *Ibid.,* item 21.

36. *Ibid.,* items 12, 13, 14, 16, 17, 20, 25, and 37. The last book, which was begun in October 1919, was not completed until January 1920.

37. *Ibid.,* item 29.

38. *Ibid.,* items 2 and 3.

39. *Ibid.,* item 24.

40. *Ibid.,* item 23.

41. *Ibid.,* item 19.

Chapter VI

[NOTE: In this chapter as well as in chapter VIII I have attempted to quote examples other than those which have already appeared in print. For other material on this period see Werner T. Angress and Bradley F. Smith, "Diaries of Heinrich Himmler's Early Years," *Journal of Modern History*, Vol. 31, No. 3 (September 1959), pp. 206-224.]

1. Dr. Quenstedt to GH, 18.10.1919, HD, Roll 99, Folder 9; HHD, 18.10.1919.
2. HHD, 18-28.10.1919. His study plan, receipts and registration slips are in HD, Roll 98, Folder 1.
3. His changes of address show up in the university and *TH* records, HD, Roll 98, Folder 1. For the Loritz family see *Adressbuch für München u. Umgebung*, 1910.
4. 14th Alarm Company registration, 4.11.1919, *RFSS*, Roll 99, Frame 2620429. Heinrich's rank appears on a 14th Alarm Company *Ausweis*, 6 Feb. 1920, *RFSS*, Roll 99, Frame 2620436. Heinrich's membership in this unit may be the origin of the story that he was once a member of *Freikorps Lautenbacher*. In the reorganization after the occupation of Munich in the summer of 1919 *Freikorps Lautenbacher* became the 20th Alarm Company of the *Schützenbrigade* 21. Robert G. L. Waite, *Vanguard of Nazism*, p. 88, *note* 86; F. W. Oertzen, *Die Deutsche Freikorps 1918-23* (Munich, 1936), p. 342.
5. *RKTV* membership. 10.11.1919, HD, Roll 98, Folder 1, HHD, 17-18.11.1919.
6. HHD, 28.10, 5.11, and 8.12.1919.
7. *Ibid.*, 28.10, 5.11, and 8.12.1919.
8. *Ibid.*, 9.11, 17.11, 8.12, 10.12, and 21.12.1919.
9. *Ibid.*, 7.11 and 13.11.1919; Ludwig Zahler to HH, 14.4.1920, *RFSS*, Roll 99, Frames 2619971-74; Kaethe to HH, 16.4.1920, *RFSS*, Roll 99, Frames 2619873-76.
10. HHD, 27.12.1919.
11. *Ibid.*, 21.1.1919.
12. HHBL, item 53, HD, Roll 18A.
13. HHD, 24.1 and 27.1.1920; Ludwig Zahler to HH, 7.3.1920, *RFSS*, Roll 99, Frames 2619961-62.
14. HHD, 14.11.1919 and 1.1.1920.
15. *Ibid.*, 17.11.1919; HHBL, item 46, HD, Roll 18A.
16. HHD, 7.12, 18.12, and 24.12.1919; HH to his parents, 13.11.1919, HD, Roll 98, Folder 2.
17. HH to his parents, 13.11.1919 and 18.1;3.3.1920, HD, Roll 98, Folder 2; HHD, 18.12.1919.
18. HHD, 25.11 and 28.11.1919.
19. *Ibid.*, 19.1 and 23.1.1920.
20. *Ibid.*, 19.11.1919; Heinrich Himmler's Weekly Schedule, spring 1920, *RFSS*, Roll 99, Frame 2620469; Georg Heer, *Geschichte der Deutschen Burschenschaft*, p. 269; Max Haushofer, *Die Ludwig Maximilian Universität*, p. 72.
21. HHD, 28.1.1920 and *passim;* Calendar, February 1920, *RFSS*, Roll 99, Frame 2620464; Manvell and Fraenkel, p. 8.
22. HHD, 22.11.1919; HH to GH, 8.4.1936, *RFSS*, Roll 99, Frame 2620585; HH letter, 10.4.1936, HD, Roll 98, Folder 1.
23. HHD, 4.11, 8.11, and 16.11.1919, and 4-8.1 and 10.1.1920.
24. *Ibid.*, 26.11.1919 and 13.1.1920. On the *AGV* see Georg Leidinger, *Geschichte des Akadem. Gesang Vereins München, 1881-1911*. On his finances, see HHD, 12.1.1920, and *Technische Hochschule* receipts, HD, Roll 98, Folder 1.

On the *AAK* see HH Calendars for April and May 1920, *RFSS,* Roll 99, Frames 2620456-57, and the records of the course, *RFSS,* Roll 99, Frame 2620411-15. The operation of the *AAK* is explained in *Münchener Jahrbuch,* p. 187.

25. HHD, 2.11, 24.11, and 1925, 18.12.1919, and 28.1.1920.

26. HHD, 24.11.1919.

27. HHBL, item 39, HD, Roll 18A.

28. *Ibid.,* item 45.

29. *Ibid.,* item 50.

30. HHBL, item 43.

31. HHD, 15.12 and 26.12.1919.

32. Heinrich to his parents, 20.3.1920, HD, Roll 98, Folder 2.

33. HHD, 31.12.1919.

34. *Ibid.,* 7.11, 9.11, and 27.12.1919.

35. HHBL, items 44 and 52, HD, Roll 18A.

36. *Ibid.,* items 59 and 61 (Johannes Mayerhofer, *Spanien. Reisebilder* and Johannes Howald, *Goethe und Schiller eine Monographie aus der Geschichte der deutschen Literatur*).

37. HHD, 31.12.1919. A heavily marked newspaper clipping on the *BVP* and separatism, from early 1920 is in his newspaper collection, *RFSS,* Roll 99, Frames 2620498-99.

38. HHBL, item 60, HD, Roll 18A.

39. HH Newspaper Collection, *RFSS,* Roll 99, Frames 2620474-555; HHD, 4.11.1919.

40. HHD, 14.11.1919.

41. HHBL, item 48, HD, Roll 18A.

42. HH to his parents, 3.3.1920, HD, Roll 98, Folder 2.

43. HH, GH and Ludwig Zahler to the Himmlers, 24.3.1920, HD, Roll 98, Folder 2.

44. HHD, 17.1.1920; HH to his parents, 18.1.20, HD, Roll 98, Folder 2. He also collected material on Arco in his newspaper collection, *RFSS,* Roll 99, Frames 2620493, 2620518-530.

45. HHBL, item 49, HD, Roll 18A.

46. *Ibid.,* item 36.

47. *Ibid.,* item 51.

48. HHD, 15.12.1919.

49. Ludwig Zahler to HH, 1.9.1920, *RFSS,* Roll 99, Frames 2619991-92.

50. HHBL, item 106 (begun 25.12.1921, completed 5.1.1923), HD, Roll 18A. An additional anti-Semitic sign appears in the material on the *AAK.* On the back of an *AAK* announcement, Heinrich wrote *"Verjudung,"* but it is impossible to determine when this was written, *RFSS,* Roll 99, Frames 2620412-3.

51. HHBL, item 47, HD, Roll 18A.

52. HHD, 11.11 and 13-17.11.1919.

53. *Ibid.,* 8.12.1919.

54. HH to his parents, 3.3.1920, HD, Roll 98, Folder 2. Material on Heinrich's transfer to the *Einwohnerwehr* appears in the following sources: *Empfangs-Schein* and insurance forms, HD, Roll 98, Folder 1; special orders and transfer procedure, *RFSS,* Roll 99, Frames 2620417 and 2620446. General material on *Schützengesellschaft Freiweg* is in HD, Roll 98, Folder 1. Lu mentions *Freiweg* in a letter to Heinrich in June 1921 which suggests that Heinrich joined before he left Munich in August 1920. Ludwig Zahler to HH, 9.6.1921, *RFSS,* Roll 99, Frames 2619921-22.

55. HHD, 14.11 and 28.11.1919.

56. HH to his parents, 3.3.1920, HD, Roll 98, Folder 2.

57. HH to Examination Commission of the Agricultural Section of the *Technische Hochschule,* 27.1.1920, *RFSS,* Roll 99, Frames 2620418-19. His class schedules and registration forms are in HD, Roll 98, Folder 1.

58. HHCR (thank you letter to A. Rehrl), 16.5.1920, HD, Roll 98, Folder 6; Letter from A. Rehrl to GH, 1.6.1920, HD, Roll 98, Folder 1.

Chapter VII

1. HH Calendar, August 1920, *RFSS,* Roll 99, Frame 2620452; Manvell and Fraenkel, p. 255, *note* 9. His Touring Club membership for 1922 suggests the machine was an Opel, HD, Roll 98, Folder 1.

2. HH to his parents, 9.9.1920, HD, Roll 98, Folder 2; Ludwig Zahler to HH, 20.9.1920; Kaethe Loritz to HH, 21.9.1920, *RFSS,* Roll 99, Frames 2619987-90, 2619883-85.

3. HH to his parents, 15.9.1920, HD, Roll 98, Folder 2.

4. *Ibid.,* 19.9 and 4.10.1920; Ludwig Zahler to HH, 20.9.1920; Kaethe Loritz to HH, 21.9.1920, *RFSS,* Roll 99, Frames 2619987-90, 2619883-85.

5. Alois Rehrl to GH, 1.6.1920, HD, Roll 98, Folder 1; HH to his parents, 19.9 and 10.10.1920, HD, Roll 98, Folder 2.

6. HH to his parents, 4.10.1920, HD, Roll 98, Folder 2.

7. *Ibid.,* 15.9 and 4.10.1920.

8. *Ibid.,* 25.10, 3.12, and 14.12.1920, HD, Roll 98, Folder 2; HHD, 9.6.1922.

9. HH to his parents, 9.10, 10.10, 25.10, and 18.11.1920, and 23.1.1921, HD, Roll 98, Folder 2; Calendar, October 1920, *RFSS,* Roll 99, Frame 2620463. Heinrich was particularly fond of Stieler's *Ein Winteridyll,* which he read in 1919 and again in 1921. HHBL, items 34 and 74, HD, Roll 18A.

10. HH to his parents, 8.5 and 2.6.1921, HD, Roll 98, Folder 2.

11. *Ibid.,* 14.5.1921; HHBL, items 85a and 85b, HD, Roll 18A.

12. HH to his parents, 26.9 and 11.11.1920, and 6.2, 12.2, and 14.5.1921, HD, Roll 98, Folder 2; HH Calendar, *RFSS,* Roll 99, Frame 2620462; Mariele and Ludwig Zahler, and Kaethe Loritz to HH, 22.12 and 30.12.1920, *RFSS,* Roll 99, Frames 2619849-53, 2619858-59.

13. HH to his parents, 14-15.5.1921, HD, Roll 98, Folder 2.

14. *Ibid.,* 19.9, 26.9, and 14.12.1920, and 25.3 and 29.3.1921.

15. HHBL, item 62 (Enrika von Handel-Mazzetti, *Die Arme Margaret*), HD, Roll 18A.

16. *Ibid.,* item 78.

17. HH to his parents, 15.9, 19.9, 4.10, and 4.11.1920, HD, Roll 98, Folder 2; Kaethe Loritz to HH, 15.10.1920; and Ludwig Zahler to HH, 18.10.1920, *RFSS,* Roll 99, Frames 2619886-87, 2619997-98.

18. HH to his parents, 25.10 and 28.11.1920, and 18.1, 6.2, 7.3, and 20.4.1921, HD, Roll 98, Folder 2; *Alpenverein* card, HD, Roll 98, Folder 1; HHBCR, Deutsche Touring Klub, 13.1.1921, HD, Roll 98, Folder 6.

19. HH to his parents, 7.3 and 11.4.1921, HD, Roll 98, Folder 2.

20. HH to his parents, 23.1, 12.2, 25.3, 14.6, and 29.6.1921, HD, Roll 99, Folder 2.

21. Most of the letters in *RFSS,* Roll 99, include the date and time of receipt.

22. HH to Ernst Himmler, 14.11.1920; HH to his parents, 25.3 and 14.6.1921, HD, Roll 98, Folder 2.

23. HH to his parents, 8.5.1921, HD, Roll 98, Folder 2.

24. HH to his parents, 29.3, 8.5, and 24.6.1921.

25. *Ibid.,* 25.10 and 18.11.1920, and 18.2.1921.

26. *Ibid.,* 10.10.1920.

27. *Ibid.,* 25.3, 14.5, and 2.6.1921.

28. *Ibid.,* 14.5.1921.

29. *Ibid.,* 15.9.1920; Ludwig Zahler to HH, 22.11.1920, and 21.3.1921, *RFSS,* Roll 99, Frames 2619999-02 and 2619949-50.

30. Ludwig Zahler to HH, 26.1.1921, *RFSS,* Roll 99, Frames 2619953-54; HH to his parents, 26.1.1921, HD, Roll 98, Folder 2; *Das Königliche Bayerische 16 Infanterie Regiment.*

31. Ludwig Zahler to HH, 22.11.1920 and 21.2.1921; Kaethe Loritz to HH, 7.12.1920, *RFSS,* Roll 99, Frames 2619999-02, 2619925-26, and 2619888-91.

32. Ludwig Zahler to HH, 18.10.1920; Kaethe Loritz to HH, 26.1.1921, *RFSS,* Roll 99, Frames 2619997-98 and 2619892-95; HHBCR (Maja Keipp, 29.1 and 2.2.1921), HD, Roll 98, Folder 2; HH to his parents, 10.10.1920, HD, Roll 98, Folder 2.

33. HH to his parents, 18.2.1921, HD, Roll 98, Folder 2.

34. *Ibid.,* 3.2.1920 and 18.2.1921.

35. *Ibid.,* 3.12.1921.

36. HH Budget Record, 10.7.1921, HD, Roll 98, Folder 2.

37. HH to his parents, 15.9.1920, HD, Roll 98, Folder 2; Ludwig Zahler to HH, 27.9.1920, *RFSS,* Roll 99, Frames 2619993-94.

38. HH to his parents, 11.11.1920, HD, Roll 98, Folder 2.

39. *Ibid.,* HH to his parents, 7.3.1921.

40. *Ibid.*

41. *Ibid.,* 25.10 and 11.11.1920; HH Shooting Record, 3-5.12.1920, *RFSS,* Roll 99, Frame 2620429; Ludwig Zahler to HH, 22.11.1920 and 9.6.1921, *RFSS,* Roll 99, Frames 2619921-22 and 2619999-02; *Freiweg* Announcement, 6.11.1920, *RFSS,* Roll 99, Frame 2620428.

42. Ludwig Zahler to HH, 10.12.1920, and 6.7, 10.3, and 4.7.1921, *RFSS,* Roll 99, Frames 2619955-58, 2619860-63, 2619923-24. Heinrich's applications were addressed to a man named Obermeier (or Obermeyer) who apparently was the same man who signed the *Freiweg* announcements, *RFSS,* Roll 99, Frame 2620428. The officer in charge of the 2nd *Einwohnerwehr Bezirk* (Heinrich was in the 5th *Bezirk*) was Captain Paul Obermeyer. See Rudolf Kanzler, *Bayerns Kampf gegen den Bolschewismus,* p. 151.

43. Ludwig Zahler to HH, 4.7.1921, *RFSS,* Roll 99, Frames 2619923-24.

44. HHBL, item 89, W. A. Patin, *Das Bayerische Religionsedikt vom 20 Mai 1818 und seine Grundlagen* (the author was Heinrich's cousin), and item 72, Agnes Günther, *Die Heilige und ihr Narr,* HD, Roll 18A.

45. *Ibid.,* item 71, Bolanden, *Die Sünde wider den Heiligen Geist.* This work does not contain clear references to Freemasons. Heinrich seems to have equated freethinkers and Freemasons, an interchange of labels that was not uncommon among conservatives.

46. *Ibid.,* items 75, Heinrich Schierbaum, *Reden der Nationalversammlung zu Frankfurt a. Main,* and 78, Bolanden, *Wider Kaiser und Reich: Historische Erzählungen.*

47. *Ibid.,* items 28 and 91.

48. *Ibid.,* item 86.

49. *Ibid.,* item 84; HH Collection of Quotations, HD, Roll 98, Folder 2.

50. HHBL, item 84, HD, Roll 18A.

51. *Ibid.,* item 65.

52. *Ibid.,* item 79.

53. HHBCR, Paelmann, 23.5, 30.5, and 18.7.1921, HD, Roll 98, Folder 6; HH notes, *RFSS,* Roll 99, Frame 2619901.

54. HH Collection of Quotations, HD, Roll 98, Folder 2.

55. HH to his parents, 4.11.1920 and 7.3.1921, HD, Roll 98, Folder 2; *Technische Hochschule* notification 3.6.1921, HD, Roll 98, Folder 1.

56. HH to his parents, 25.10, 14.11, and 18.11.1920, HD, Roll 98, Folder 2.

57. Statement of Herr Rehrl, 31.8.1921, and statement of *Vereinigte Fabriken Landwirtschaftlicher Maschinen,* HD, Roll 98, Folder 1; HH to his parents, 11.4.1921, HD, Roll 98, Folder 2.

Chapter VIII

[NOTE: In this chapter, as in chapter VI, I have attempted to quote examples other than those which have already appeared in print. For additional material on this period, see Angress and Smith, "Diaries of Heinrich Himmler's Early Years."]

1. HHBCR, Frau Wolff, 8.10.1921, HD, Roll 98, Folder 6. For his address see membership cards of *Kriegsteilnehmer Verband,* HD, Roll 98, Folder 1. HHD, 14.11 and 2.12.1921; HH to his mother, 1.11.1921, HD, Roll 98, Folder 2.

2. HH to his parents, 2.12.1921 and 28.2.1922, HD, Roll 98, Folder 2; Ludwig Zahler to HH, 10.12.1920 and 11.8.1921, *RFSS,* Roll 99, Frames 2619955-58 and 2619864-66; HHD, 17.11.1921, and 3.6. and 6.6.1922.

3. HH to his parents, 1.11.1921, HD, Roll 98, Folder 2; HHD, 5.11, 18.11, 27.11, and 30.11.1921, and 23.3.1922.

4. HHD, 4.11 and 9.11.1921, and 20.2.1922; HH to his parents, 20.2.1922, HD, Roll 98, Folder 2.

5. HHD, 8.11, 9.11, and 11.11.1921, and 17.2, 18.2, 27.2, 28.2, and 10.6.1922; memberships: *Alpenverein, D. Touring Klub, D. Gesellschaft für Zucktungskunde, D. Landwirtsgesellschaft,* HD, Roll 98, Folder 1.

6. HHD, 8.11 and 18.11.1921, and 13.2, 22.2, 26.2, 17.6, and 18.6.1922.

7. *Ibid.,* 26.11.1921, and 15.1 and 22.1.1922.

8. *Ibid.,* 4.7.1922 is a good example.

9. *Ibid.,* 11.2, 23.2, and 28.6.1922.

10. *Ibid.,* 11.11.1921, and 22.2 and 24.2.1922.

11. *Ibid.,* 3.6 and 22.6.1922.

12. *Ibid.,* 22.6.1922.

13. *Ibid.,* 19.11.1921 and 28.5.1922. He was not always critical of Prussians, see *ibid.,* 9.2.1922.

14. *Ibid.,* 19.11, 23.11, and 6.12.1921, and 13.1, 11.2, 17.2, 6.3, 10.6, and 14.6.1922.

15. *Ibid.,* 6.12.1921, and 27.2 and 27.5.1922.

16. *Ibid.,* 6.6.1922.

17. *Ibid.,* 26.5.1922.

18. *Ibid.,* 26.2 and 6.6.1922.

19. *Ibid.,* 17.2, 27.2, and 28.2.1922.

20. *Ibid.,* 6.12.1921, and 11.2 and 10.6.1922.

21. *Ibid.,* 19.11.1921, and 6.6 and 21.6.1922.

22. *Ibid.,* 3.1, 15.1, and 19.6.1922.

23. *Ibid.,* 4.3.1922; HHBL, item 115, HD, Roll 18A.

24. HHD, 7.6, 13.6, and 3.7.1922.

25. *Ibid.,* 7.11.1921 and 28.1.1922; HH to his parents, 3.3.1922, HD, Roll 98, Folder 2; Family S. to HH, 10.11.1921, *RFSS,* Roll 99, Frames 2620180-81.

26. HH to his parents, 3.3 and 10.3.1922, HD, Roll 98, Folder 2.

27. HHD, 28.2.1922.

28. *Ibid.,* 10.11, 24.11, and 7.12.1921; and 16.1, 17.1, 18.1, and 22.1.1922.

29. *Ibid.,* 18.11, and 4.12.1921, and 4.2 and 22.2.1922.

30. *Ibid.,* 13.11.1921.

31. *Ibid.,* 13.2.1922.

32. *Ibid.,* 22.6.1922.

33. *Ibid.,* 6.11.1921; HHBL, item 113, HD, Roll 18A.

34. HHD, 4.11 and 16.11.1921.

35. *Ibid.,* 7.12.1921 and 30.5.1922.

36. HH to his parents, 20.2.1922, HD, Roll 98, Folder 2; HHD, 6.3.1922.

37. HHD, 20-21.1.1922; HH to his parents, 20-21.1.1922, HD, Roll 98, Folder 2.

38. HHD, 9.2, 23.2, 27.2, and 2.7.1922; HH to his parents, 10.2 and 24.7.1922, HD, Roll 98, Folder 2; HH Education Records, HD, Roll 98, Folder 1. At the time of his *Hauptprufung* Himmler stopped writing his diary.

39. HHD, 8.12.1921, and 29.5, 30.5, 5.6, and 26.6.1922; *Münchener Jahrbuch,* 1925, p. 350; HH to his mother, 9.5.1922, HD, Roll 98, Folder 2.

40. HH to his parents, 9.12.1921 and 1.2.1922, HD, Roll 98, Folder 2; HHD, 4.11.1921.

41. HHD, 13-14.11.1921, and 3.2, 21.2, 9.6, and 2.7.1922; HHBCR, 23.5 and 9.6.1922, HD, Roll 98, Folder 6; HH to his parents, 28.7.1922, HD, Roll 98, Folder 2.

42. HHD, 30.6.1922.

43. *Ibid.,* 20.11 and 30.12.1921, and 15.1.1922. HHBL, items 106-31, HD, Roll 18A.

44. HHBL, item 116, HD, Roll 18A.

45. HHD, 28.1.1922; Hanna Kastl to HH, 28.1.1922, HD, Roll 98, Folder 2.

46. HHBL, item 106, HD, Roll 18A.

47. *Ibid.,* item 107.

48. This is a reference to the editor, Karl Rosner. HHBL, item 126, HD, Roll 18A.

49. HHD, 12.1, 4.2, 4.3, and 15.6.1922.

50. *Ibid.,* 12.1.1922.

51. *Ibid.,* 22.6.1922.

52. *Ibid.,* 3.7.1922.

53. For his interest in the Orient and sex see especially HHBL, item 121 (Max Dauthendey, *Der Garten ohne Jahreszeiten),* HD, Roll 18A. For an example of the special stereotype portrayal of Jewish girls, see Spielhagen, *Ultimo,* HHBL, item 51.

54. HHD, 3.7.1922.

55. HHBL, item 110, HD, Roll 18A.

56. HHD, 3.6.1922.

57. The quotation is dated 6.6.1922, but the first entry is 26.5.1922, because he was ten days behind in writing his diaries.

58. The text used on the last page of *Judas Schuldbuch* may be compared with the original, Emanuel Geibels, *Werke,* pp. 357-358.

59. HHD, 12.2.1922.

60. *Ibid.,* 24.6.1922.

61. *Ibid.,* 26.6.1922.

62. *Ibid.,* 2.7.1922.

63. *Ibid.,* 28.6.1922.

64. *Ibid.,* 15.6, 5.7, and 6.7.1922.

65. *Ibid.,* 17.2 and 18.3.1922.

66. *Ibid.,* 14.6 and 29.6.1922.

67. *Ibid.,* 5.7.1922.

68. *Ibid.,* 26.1.1922.

69. *Ibid.,* 9.11.1921 and 28.6.1922.

70. *Ibid.,* 26.2.1922.

71. *Ibid.,* 30.11.1921, and 28.1 and 9.6.1922; HH to his parents, 2.12.1921, HD, Roll 98, Folder 2.

72. HHD, 20.2.1922.

73. *Ibid.,* 9.11 and 23.11.1921, and 25.1.1922.

74. Prof. Huolezeck to HH, 15.8.1922, *RFSS,* Roll 99, Frame 2619831; HHBCR (a letter sent to Schleissheim 22.8.1922), HD, Roll 98, Folder 6.

75. Prof. Huolezeck to HH, 15.8.1922.

Chapter IX

1. *Zeugnis* of *Stickstoff-Land-G.m.b.H.,* 30.8.1923, HD, Roll 98, Folder 1.

2. Frau Himmler to HH, 7.11.1922; employee insurance card of HH, 5.9.1922, HD, Roll 98, Folder 1.

3. HHBCR, 21.11.1922, HD, Roll 98, Folder 6; GH to Ludwig Zahler, 14.3.1923, *RFSS,* Roll 99, Frames 2620190-92.

4. The best documented treatment of these developments is to be found in Ernst Deuerlein, ed., *Der Hitler-Putsch.* General von Epp's papers provide additional information, *General Records Collection,* T-84, Roll 10, National Archives, Washington, D.C.

5. One of the munitions plants was planned for Schleissheim, General von Epp's Notes, *General Records Collection,* T-84, Roll 10, Frames 10044-56.

6. *Ibid.,* Frames 9954-9962.

7. *Offizierverbände, Unpolitische Vereine* and *Wirtschaftliche Verbände.* A detailed survey of the paramilitary groups involved in the May Day encounter appears in Deuerlein, *Der Hitler Putsch,* pp. 58-60.

8. *Oberland, Reichsflagge, Bund Unterland, Organization Lenz.*

9. Ernst Röhm, *Die Geschichte eines Hochverräters,* pp. 206-221; Heinrich Himmler's *SS* Records, Berlin Document Center, and Micro-Copy T-580, Roll 37, Ordner 238II.

10. Röhm, *Die Geschichte eines Hochverräters,* pp. 200-222. The registration records of the *Reichkriegsflagge* are in *Hauptarchiv der NSDAP,* Roll 83, Folder 1683, Hoover Institution, Stanford University.

11. Heinrich Himmler's *SS* Records. Prof. Harold Gordon of the University of Massachusetts kindly provided the author with information on *Kompanie Werner.*

12. Heinrich Himmler's *SS* Records.

13. Ernst Deuerlein, *Der Hitler-Putsch,* p. 499; HHD, 15.2.1924.

14. A description of HH on November 9, 1923, appears in a letter of Mariele Rauschmayer, 18.11.1923, HD, Roll 98, Folder 1. The letter was not sent to Heinrich until seven months after the *Putsch.* Mariele Rauschmayer to HH, 13.6.1924, *RFSS,* Roll 99, Frames 2620050-53.

15. Fehler and others to HH, 4.12.1923, HD, Roll 98, Folder 1; statement by Heinrich Gärtner and letter HH to Gärtner, 25.1.1924, *Hauptarchiv der NSDAP,* Roll 52, Folder 1222; HHCR (Gärtner), HD, Roll 98, Folder 6.

16. HH to Heinrich Gärtner, 25.1.1924, *Hauptarchiv der NSDAP,* Roll 52, Folder 1222.

17. HHD, 15.2.1924.

18. *Ibid.,* 12.2, 21.2, 23.2, and 24.2.1924.

19. *Ibid.,* 12.2.1924.

20. Program of the *Gedächtnisfeier* of the *DVOB,* 26.5.1924, HD, Roll 98, Folder 1.

21. HHCR (Mazbar Bey), HD, Roll 98, Folder 6; Mazbar to HH, 18.9.1923, *RFSS,* Roll 99, Frames 2620005-08.

22. HH to Heinrich Gärtner, 28.12.1923 and 25.1.1924, *Hauptarchiv der NSDAP,* Roll 52, Folder 1222.

23. HHD, 12.2.1924; HHBCR, HD, Roll 98, Folder 6.

24. HHD, 12.2.1924. He may even have inquired about farming prospects in Korea. See HHBCR, 21.11.1923, HD, Roll 98, Folder 6.

25. Mazbar to HH, 10.4.1924, *RFSS,* Roll 99, Frames 2620015-18.

26. Robert Kistler to HH, 17.6.1924, HD, Roll 98, Folder 1. For his earlier association with Kistler, see p. 56.

27. HHD, 24.2.1924.

28. A typical letter of the period is one dated 19.7.1923, *RFSS,* Roll 99, Frames 2619868-71. Heinrich used the bank where Lu worked and the *Fasching Apotheke* as clandestine mail drops. Heinrich Gärtner's statement and Heinrich

Himmler to Heinrich Gärtner, 7.1.1924. *Haptarchiv der NSDAP,* Roll 52, Folder 1222. Himmler's diary fragments for February 1924 include numerous visits to these businesses.

29. HHD, 13.2.1924.

30. [Mariele Rauschmayer to HH, 2.8.1924, *RFSS,* Roll 99, Frames 2620054-61.

31. HHBL, item 180, HD, Roll 18A.

32. *Ibid.*, item 190.

33. *Ibid.*, item 192.

34. *Ibid.*, item 187 (G. M. Kletke, *Militärisches Dichter Album*).

35. *Ibid.*, item 192.

36. *Ibid.*, item 170 (Rudolf Hans Bartsch, *Frau Utta und der Jaeger*).

37. *Ibid.*, item 143.

38. *Ibid.*, item 165.

39. *Ibid.*, item 199.

40. *Ibid.*, item 202.

41. *Ibid.*, item 162.

42. *Ibid.*, item 133 (Reinhold Eichacker, *Hass Antwort deutscher Dichter auf Versailles*).

43. *Ibid.*, item 138 (Ludwig Wolff, *Der Sohn des Hannibal.*)

44. *Ibid.*, item 171. He read this book just before, during, and after the *Putsch* (September 25-November 21, 1923).

45. *Ibid.*, item 167 (*Eppes Kittisch*).

46. *Ibid.*, item 201.

47. *Ibid.*, item 200.

48. HHD, 12.2 and 20.2.1924.

49. HHBL, item 193, HD, Roll 18A.

50. *Ibid.*, item 196.

51. *Ibid.*, items 149 and 150 (Max Eyth, *Der Kampf um die Cheopspyramide,* and Max Haushofer, *Planetenfeuer, ein Zukunftsroman*).

52. *Ibid.*, item 161.

53. *Ibid.*, item 141.

54. *Ibid.*, item 137 (Otto Authenrieth, *Bismarck II, der Roman der deutschen Zunkunft*).

55. *Ibid.*, item 177.

56. *Ibid.*, item 152.

57. *Ibid.*, items 185, 193, and 198 (Johannes Haller, *Die Aera Bülow,* Carl Felix Schlichtegroll, *Ein Sadist im Priesterrock,* and Adolf Viktor von Koerber, *Bestien im Lande*).

58. *Ibid.*, items 157 and 174 (Wilhelmine von Hillern, *Am Kreuz–Ein Passionsroman,* and Walter Rothes, *Drei Meister deutschen Gemütes*).

59. *Ibid.*, item 173.

60. *Ibid.*, item 181.

61. *Ibid.*, item 191.

62. *Ibid.*, item 151 (Max Haushofer, *Geschichten zwischen diesseits und jenseits*).

63. *Ibid.*, item 148.

64. HHD, 20.2.1924.

65. HHBL, item 207, HD, Roll 18A.

66. *Ibid.*, items 189 and 208.

67. *Ibid.*, item 189.

68. *Ibid.*, items 146 and 205.

69. *Ibid.*, item 205.

70. HHD, 24.2.1924.

71. GH to Ludwig Zahler, 14.3.1923, *RFSS,* Roll 99, Frames 2620190-92.

72. HH to Paula S., 18.4.1923, HD, Roll 98, Folder 1.

73. Paula S. to HH, 6.7.1923, *RFSS,* Roll 99, Frames 2620195-96 and 2620199-200.

74. HHD, 11-15.2.1924.

75. *Ibid.,* 18-19.2.1924.

76. Herr S. to GH, and Paula S. to GH, 4.3.1924, *RFSS,* Roll 99, Frames 2620204-06.

77. HH to Herr Rössner, 12.3.1924, HD, Roll 98, Folder 1.

78. Max Blüml to HH, 12.3.1924, HD, Roll 98, Folder 1; Herr Rössner to HH, 18.3.1924, *RFSS,* Roll 99, Frame 2620210; note by HH, *RFSS,* Roll 99, Frame 2620208; GH and HH to Hugo Höfl, 22-23.5.1924, *RFSS,* Roll 99, Frames 2619755-59.

79. Ludwig Zahler to HH, 16.7.1924, *RFSS,* Roll 99, Frame 2619948.

80. HH to Robert Kistler, 22.8.1924, HD, Roll 98, Folder 1.

Chapter X

1. E. Wäckerly to HH, 1.9.1924, *RFSS,* Roll 99, Frame 2620238. The locations noted in his book list provide indications of his main movements: HHBL, HD, Roll 18A.

2. HH to the *Elfervereinigung,* 13.12.1924, HD, Roll 98, Folder 1.

3. *Völkischer Beobachter,* 1.5.1925, p. 3.

4. *Ibid.,* 12.5.1925, p. 3.

5. HHBL, 1925-26, HD, Roll 18A.

6. HH to Albert Wierheim, 10.9.1926, HD, Roll 98, Folder 1; *Völkischer Beobachter,* 1925-26, *passim.*

7. "Nationaler oder Internationaler Sozialismus," 12.10.1926, HD, Roll 98, Folder 1.

8. Himmler's comments on a racist pamphlet he read in late 1924 stressed the benefits of race-conscious breeding. HHBL, item 216 (*Eine unbewusste Blutschande. Der Untergang Deutschlands*), HD, Roll 18A. Three drafts on *völkisch* farm and peasant policies in Himmler's papers show signs of *Artamanen* influence. They obviously date from late 1924 or early 1925 (Manvell and Fraenkel [p. 256] erroneously date them much earlier), but they are typed and unsigned which makes a firm conclusion on authorship impossible. HD, Roll 98, Folder 1. For the *Artamanen,* see George L. Mosse, *The Crisis of German Ideology,* pp. 116-20.

9. Joseph L. Nyomarkay, *Charisma and Factionalism in the Nazi Party,* pp. 71-89; Dietrich Orlow, "The Conversion of Myths into Political Power: The Case of the Nazi Party, 1925-1926," *American Historical Review,* Vol. 72, No. 3, April 1967, pp. 906-24; Reinhard Kühnl, "Zur Programmatik der nationalsozialistischen Linken: Das Strasser-Program von 1925-1926," *Vierteljahrshefte für Zeitgeschichte,* Vol. 14, No. 3, July 1966, pp. 317-33.

10. Helmut Heiber, ed., *Das Tagebuch von Joseph Goebbels 1925-1926,* p. 72.

11. Himmler's pocket calendar which showed he was present at Hanover, but not at the Bamberg meeting was apparently not microfilmed by the Hoover Institution although it was originally in Folder 11 of the Berlin Document Center material. An inquiry to the *Bundesarchiv* has failed to establish its present whereabouts. See also HH to P. Goebbels, 7.2.1926, Micro-Copy T-580, Roll 37.

12. "Nationaler oder Internationaler Sozialismus," 12.10.1926, HD, Roll 98, Folder 1.

13. Material on Himmler and the *DVOB,* beginning 19.5.1924, is in HD, Roll 98, Folder 1.

14. *Völkischer Beobachter,* 13-14.6.1926 and 7.10.1926, pp. 3-4.

15. Heinrich Himmler's *SS* Records, Berlin Document Center.

16. HH to E. Wäckerly, 5.1.1926, *RFSS,* Frames 2620251-52.

17. A bland card on his name day was the only echo of his close friendship with Kaethe and Lu. Ludwig and Kaethe Zahler to HH, 14.7.1925, *RFSS,* Roll 99, Frames 2619854-55.

18. Ludwig and Kaethe Zahler to HH, 16.7.1924, *RFSS,* Roll 99, Frame 2619948; Mariane Nuss to HH, 8.9.1926, HD, Roll 98, Folder 1.

19. Falk Zipperer to HH, 13.8 and 7.9.1925, *RFSS,* Roll 99, Frames 2620374 and 2620377; HH to Herr Roschatt, 17.7.1926, *RFSS,* Roll 99, Frames 2620089-90.

20. HHBL, HD, Roll 18A.

21. *Reichsbund Akad. gebild. Landwirte* to HH, 5.11.1924, *RFSS,* Roll 99, Frame 2620068; HHBCR, 21.2.1925, HD, Roll 98, Folder 6; Mazbar to HH, March 1925, *RFSS,* Roll 99, Frames 2620019-20.

22. HH to Wilhelm Reuter, 22.4.1926, HD, Roll 98, Folder 1.

23. HHBL, item 269 (b) (Franz Helbing and Max Bauer, *Die Tortur*), HD, Roll 18A. A German transcription of a portion of Himmler's Book List (1925-1934) is included in the captured German material at the Library of Congress. The last phrase on this entry is transcribed therein as *"Juden feindlich"* but should read *"Juden freundlich."* Transcript in German of HH Notebook, Captured German Material Container 418, Library of Congress, Washington, D.C.

24. HHBL, item 254, HD, Roll 18A.

25. *Ibid.*, item 247.

26. *Ibid.*, item 260 (Max Bauer, *Das Land der Roten Zaren*).

27. *Ibid.*, item 261 (Oskar Blum, *Russische Köpfe*).

28. *Ibid.*, items 260 and 261.

29. *Ibid.*, item 262 (Katharina Haug-Haough, *Hinter den Kulissen des Bolschewismus*).

30. *Ibid.*, item 228 (*Semi-Imperator*).

31. *Ibid.*, item 221 (Gotthard von der Osten-Sacken, *In der Gewalt dunkler Mächte*).

32. *Ibid.*, item 234.

33. *Ibid.*, item 217.

34. *Ibid.*, item 220.

35. HH to Albert Wierheim, 10.9.1926, HD, Roll 98, Folder 1.

36. *Das Deutsche Führerlexikon, 1934-1935,* p. 196.

Chapter XI

1. Heinrich Himmler's *SS* Records.
2. HHBL, item 218, HD, Roll 18A.
3. *Ibid.,* item 235.
4. HH to Ernst Röhm, 4.11.1929, *RFSS,* Roll 199, Frame 2739870.
5. *Ibid.* (n/d), *RFSS,* Roll 199, Frame 2739868.

Bibliography

Unpublished Materials

A. Stanford. Hoover Institution, Stanford University:

Heinrich Himmler Diaries 1914-24. (Referred to in the notes as HHD.)
Himmler Documents (original documents formerly in the Berlin Document Center, now in the *Bundesarchiv*, Koblenz), Rolls 98, 99, 17A, 18A. (Referred to in the notes as HD.)
Hauptarchiv der NSDAP (original documents formerly in the Berlin Document Center, now in the *Bundesarchiv*, Koblenz), Rolls 52 and 83.
International Military Tribunal. Case No. 1, U. S. vs. Dr. Brandt et al., Dr. Gebhardt's testimony.

B. Washington, D.C. National Archives (original documents formerly in Arlington, Va., now in the *Bundesarchiv*, Koblenz):

Micro Copy T-84, General Records Collection, Roll 10.
Micro Copy T-175, *Reichsführer SS*, Rolls 99, 142 and 199. (Referred to in the notes as *RFSS*.)
Micro Copy T-580, Roll 37, Ordner 238II.

C. Berlin. Berlin Document Center:

Heinrich Himmler's *SS* Records (no identifying numbers).

D. Washington, D.C. Library of Congress:

Typed transcript in German of Heinrich Himmler's Notebook (a portion of the Book List), Captured German Material, Container 418.

Works on Himmler and Nazism

A. Books

Aronson, Shlomo. *Heydrich und die Anfänge des SD und der Gestapo (1931-1935)*. Berlin, 1967. Inaugural Dissertation der Philosophischen Fakultät der Freien Universität Berlin.
Deuerlein, Ernst, ed. *Der Hitler-Putsch Bayerische Dokumente zum 8/9 November 1923*. Stuttgart, 1962.
Das Deutsche Führerlexikon 1934/1935. Berlin, 1934.
Frischauer, Willi. *Himmler: The Evil Genius of the Third Reich*. London, 1953.
Heiber, Helmut, ed. *Reichsführer!* Stuttgart, 1968.
———, ed. *Das Tagebuch von Joseph Goebbels 1925/1926*. Stuttgart, n/d.
Heiden, Konrad. *Der Führer*. Translated by Ralph Manheim. Boston, 1944.
Höhne, Heinz. *Der Orden unter dem Totenkopf. Die Geschichte der SS*. Gütersloh, 1967.
Manvell, Roger, and Heinrich Fraenkel. *Heinrich Himmler*. London, 1965.
Mosse, George L. *The Crisis of German Ideology*. New York, 1964.
Nyomarkay, Joseph L. *Charisma and Factionalism in the Nazi Party*. Minneapolis, 1967.
Reed, Douglas. *Nemesis?* London, 1940.

———. *The Prisoner of Ottawa: Otto Strasser.* London, 1953.
Reitlinger, Gerald. *The SS: Alibi of a Nation, 1922-1945.* New York, 1957.
Röhm, Ernst. *Die Geschichte eines Hochverräters.* 8th ed. Munich, 1934.
Strasser, Otto, and Michael Stern. *Flight from Terror.* New York, 1943.
Strasser, Otto. *Hitler and I.* Translated by Gwenda David and Eric Mosbacher. Boston, 1940.
Volz, Hans. *Daten der Geschichte der NSDAP.* 5th ed. Berlin, Leipzig, 1935.

B. Articles:

Angress, Werner T., and Bradley F. Smith. "Diaries of Heinrich Himmler's Early Years." *Journal of Modern History,* Vol. 31 (September, 1959).
Franz, George. "Munich: Birthplace and Center of the National Socialist German Workers' Party." *Journal of Modern History,* Vol. 24 (1957), pp. 319-334.
Hallgarten, George W. F. "Mein Mitschüler Heinrich Himmler." *Germania Judaica,* 1960/61, No. 2, pp. 4-7.
Kühnl, Reinhard. "Zur Programmatik der nationalsozialistischen Linken: Das Strasser-Program von 1925/1926." *Vierteljahrshefte für Zeitgeschichte,* Vol. 14, No. 3 (July 1966), pp. 317-33.
Nyomarkay, Joseph L. "Factionalism in the NSDAP 1925-1926: The Myth and Reality of the Northern Faction." *Political Science Quarterly,* Vol. 80, No. 1 (March 1965), pp. 22-47.
Orlow, Dietrich. "The Conversion of Myths into Political Power: The Case of the Nazi Party, 1925-1926." *American Historical Review,* Vol. 72, No. 3 (April 1967), pp. 906-24.
———. "The Organizational History and Structure of the NSDAP, 1919-1923." *Journal of Modern History,* Vol. 37, No. 2 (June 1965), pp. 208-226.
Phelps, Reginald H. "Before Hitler Came: Thule Society and Germanen Orden." *Journal of Modern History,* Vol. 35, No. 3 (September 1963), pp. 245-62.
Sauer, Wolfgang. "National Socialism: Totalitarianism or Fascism?" *American Historical Review,* Vol. 73, No. 2 (December 1967), pp. 404-424.
Waldenfels, Otto, Freiherr von. "Legendenbildung um Hitler. Die königlichbayerischen Edelknaben und die SS." *Zeitschrift für bayerische Landesgeschichte,* No. 26, 1963, pp. 400-407.

C. Newspapers:

Völkischer Beobachter, Munich, 1925-26, 1928.

General Works

A. Books:

Armeson, Robert B. *Total Warfare and Compulsory Labor.* The Hague, 1964.
Carsten, F. L. *The Rise of Fascism.* Berkeley and Los Angeles, 1967.
Erger, Johannes. *Der Kapp-Lüttwitz-Putsch. Ein Beitrag zur deutschen Innenpolitik, 1919/1920.* Düsseldorf, 1967.
Eyck, Erich. *Geschichte der Weimarer Republik.* 2nd ed., 2 vols. Zurich-Stuttgart, 1957.
Halperin, S. William. *Germany Tried Democracy.* New York, 1946.
Kanzler, Rudolf. *Bayerns Kampf gegen den Bolschewismus.* Munich, 1931.

Klemperer, Klemens von. *Germany's New Conservatism: Its History and Dilemma in the Twentieth Century.* Princeton, N.J., 1968.
Mitchell, Allan. *Revolution in Bavaria 1918-1919. The Eisner Regime and the Soviet Republic.* Princeton, N.J., 1965.
Schwend, Karl. *Bayern zwischen Monarchie und Diktatur: Beitrag zur bayerischen Frage in der Zeit von 1918 bis 1933.* Munich, 1954.
Waite, Robert G. L. *Vanguard of Nazism.* Cambridge, Mass., 1952.

Reference Works

Adressbuch für München und Umgebung. Munich, 1910.
Amtliches Verzeichnis Ludwig Max. Universität zu München, 1884/1885. Munich, 1890.
Bayerisches Jahrbuch. Munich, 1919.
Bayerns Goldenes Ehrenbuch. Munich, 1928.
Blätter für das Gymnasial Schulwesen, Vol. 33, No. 5/6 (May/June 1897); Vol. 38, No. 9/10 (September/October 1902); Vol. 40, No. 9/10 (September/October 1904).
British General Staff. *Handbook of the German Army in War.* London (?), April 1918.
Dellmensingen, Konrad Krafft von, ed. *Das Bayernbuch vom Weltkriege 1914–1918.* Stuttgart, 1930.
Dennhardt, Alfred, and Ernst H. Himmler. *Leitfaden der Rundfunkenstörung.* Berlin, 1935.
Festschrift zu Vierhundert-Jahr-Feier des Wilhelms Gymnasium 1559-1959. Munich, 1959.
Geibels, Emanuel. *Werke.* 4 vols. in 1. Leipzig, 1915.
Haushofer, Max. *Die Ludwig Maximilian Universität.* Munich, 1890.
Heer, Georg. *Geschichte der Deutschen Burschenschaft.* Vol. 4. Heidelberg, 1939.
Hof und Staatshandbuch des Königreich Bayern. Munich, 1894, 1908, 1912, 1913, 1914.
Das Königliche Bayerische 16 Infanterie-Regiment Grossherzog Ferdinand von Toskana in Weltkrieg, 1914-1918. Munich, 1931.
Leidinger, Georg. *Geschichte des Akademischer Gesang Vereins München, 1881-1911.* Munich, 1911.
Münchener Jahrbuch. Munich, 1912, 1914, 1918, 1920, and 1925.
Munich Telephone Book, 1932.
Veröffentlichen des Kaiserlichen Gesundheitsamtes, Vol. 27, No. 18 (May 6, 1903).
Webster, Nesta H. *Secret Societies and Subversive Movements.* Hawthorne, Calif., 1964.

Index